From Emmanuel
to the Somme

From Emmanuel
to the Somme

The War Writings of
A.E. Tomlinson
1892-1968

Edited and introduced by
Michael Copp

The Lutterworth Press
Cambridge

For Barbara

The Lutterworth Press
PO Box 60
Cambridge
CB1 2NT

British Library Cataloguing in Publication Data:
A catalogue record for this book is available from the British Library

ISBN 0 7188 2963 8

First published by The Lutterworth Press 1997

Printed in Great Britain by
St Edmundsbury Press

Contents

Introduction

Cambridge and the War

The Cambridge War Memorial, or, to be more precise, the memorial TO THE MEN OF CAMBRIDGESHIRE AND THE ISLE OF ELY AND THE BOROUGH AND UNIVERSITY OF CAMBRIDGE WHO SERVED IN THE GREAT WAR 1914-1919, as the inscription on the plinth reads, is awkwardly placed for the passer-by to examine. It stands on a small traffic island, in the middle of the busy intersection of Hills Road and Station Road. The commissioned sculptor, Robert Tait McKenzie, called his work 'The Homecoming' (Inglis 583-605). He has depicted a young soldier, returning from the War. He is bareheaded, carrying his own helmet and a rose in his right hand, and has a German helmet as a souvenir, slung on his back; in his left hand he holds his rifle, which rests on his shoulder; there is a laurel wreath dangling from the rifle. He is an exceptionally beautiful young man. Although his features cannot be said to be an identifiable likeness of a particular individual, nevertheless, one cannot help but call to mind those photographic portraits of Rupert Brooke by Sherrill Schell. This means that it is not easy to see him as a convincing representative of the youth of the first three elements referred to on the plinth's inscription. He is, quite clearly, a student, returning from the War, striding eagerly once more (or for the first time) towards his college. He is the archetypal public-school/university young man of his time. If his stride, '2 ins. longer than normal to give a feeling of elation' (Boorman 130-131), is aimed at the heart of the town, his gaze, as he turns his head over his shoulder, is directed towards the station where he has just arrived, and so must extend, in his mind's eye, right back to the horrors of the trenches and of No Man's Land which he has left behind for good, not to mention those comrades who did not come back.

Many such young men would enter one of the Cambridge colleges in 1919, thus replenishing the student population which had suffered such grievous depredations as a result of the War. To get some idea of the scale of these losses, one only has to scrutinise the lists of the War dead displayed on each college's War memorial. In all, 2162 Cambridge men were killed, and 2902 wounded. These figures combined represent approximately one third of all the Cambridge men who served. The effect that the War had on lowering the total student population of Cambridge becomes clear from the following figures for undergraduates in residence (figures as quoted in the *Cambridge*

Magazine of 26 January 1918):

Jan.   1914   3181
        1915   1227
        1916   665
        1917   425
Jan.   1918   408

The ratio of men to women in January 1918 was very close to that existing in Cambridge in the 1990s, since Newnham and Girton together gave a total of more than 350 students.

For those left in Cambridge the atmosphere of the University was significantly altered, so much so that Florence Edgar Hobson could write wistfully in her poem, 'Cambridge in War Time' *(Cambridge Magazine, 27 May 1916):*

How changed, how sad, how pitiful to view,
Thine aspect now, beneath War's baneful spell! . . .

Our footsteps wander o'er forsaken lawns,
Our lowered voices wake no answering tones,
With wisdom, truth and beauty in suspense,
As if enchanted stand thy stately stones. . . .

Cambridge! Thou art a city of the dead,
The very reason of thy being fled. . . .

The *Cambridge Magazine* for 16 October 1915 states that by this date 470 Cambridge men had been killed, of whom 150 were undergraduates when they enlisted. And for Emmanuel College the reduction brought about by the War can be readily appreciated when one considers the following numbers of undergraduates in residence:

Before the War   225
October 1914   157
October 1915   58
October 1916   30

Undergraduates were not the only ones who left their college to play their part in the War. The *Emmanuel College Magazine War Edition* of August 1915 lists nine College servants and employees absent on service. The article notes that there was a magnanimous guarantee that neither the servants nor their dependants should 'suffer financially on this account, and that their places are kept open for them on their return.' Details regarding these College servants are given as follows:

A.W. Smith (Tutors' and Bursar's clerk), was acting as Quartermaster (with the rank of Lieutenant) to the 3rd/lst Cambs. (T.F.).

P. Fisher (Second Porter at the Front Gate), was serving as a private in the R.A.M.C. at the 1st Eastern General Hospital.

W.H. Thompson (Hostel servant, and also scorer for the College cricket XI), was engaged on patrol duty on the East Coast with the National Reserve.

F. Bloy (Junior Porter at the Front Gate), was a private in the A.S.C.

L. Easton (Bicycle Boy) and W. Wright (Buttery Boy), were serving as privates in the 1st Cambs. Regt. (T.F.).

H. Wright (Pastrycook), was acting as cook on board HMS Sapphire.

T. Merryweather (Apprentice), was serving as a private in the A.S.C.

H. Johnson (Porter), was serving as a private in the R.A.M.C.

Tomlinson at Cambridge

Albert Ernest Tomlinson (1892-1968), the son of Fred Tomlinson, a Middlesbrough accountant, came up to Cambridge from Middlesbrough High School in 1912. On arriving in Cambridge Tomlinson would have made his way from the station, turning right at the junction where the War Memorial now stands, before reaching the entrance to Emmanuel College, some 3/4 mile away. He read Modern Languages, and completed seven terms at Emmanuel, taking his B.A. in 1916.

While a student at Cambridge Tomlinson clearly had aspirations to be a writer. He was in touch with both C.K. Ogden (the founder of the *Cambridge Magazine,* and inventor of Basic English) and Arthur Quiller Couch (Professor of English Literature, and man of letters who wrote under the pseudonym of 'Q'). In a note dated 31 January 1914 Professor Couch wrote: 'I have read your poems and should like to talk with you about them. A talk is ever so much better than writing. What do you say to Thursday next, 5 o'clock, in my room at the Divinity Schools?' One of three brief, undated notes from C.K. Ogden reads: 'I should certainly be glad to use your amusing 'Hall'. But (I) No university paper ever pays or ever has paid, alas! (2) I should like it not to be more than 1000 words. Could you call to my editorial Tea. (First door on left, top floor, Falcon Yard, Petty Cury), and you could settle the matter.' One of the other notes indicates an affectionate relationship between the two men: 'My *dear* man think of you getting biffed in!' (this being addressed to Tomlinson recuperating from his wounds in a London hospital in 1916).

Besides these contacts, Tomlinson was involved in one of the numerous, shortlived University literary magazines, *Mandragora.* Published by Galloway & Porter, it appeared twice only: in May Week 1913, and in May Week 1914. Tomlinson contributed two rather anodyne poems to the 1913 issue: 'Long, Long Ago', and 'The Barcarolle'. They are very different from the verse he was soon to produce, as the following brief extracts indicate:

> Life death our living feet for ever sprung,
> Rich as the gardened gloom of coral seas,
>
> from 'Long, Long Ago'
>
> Out of the starry dusk, expectant still,
> The first notes break, soft wavelets on the beach,
> Then passionate Hope cries out in louder speech;
>
> from 'The Barcarolle'

The 1913 issue also contained a poem, 'The Departure', by Harold Monro, the founder of the influential *Poetry Review* and of the 'The Poetry Bookshop', as well as 'Barnett and Harrison', a lighthearted piece by J.C. Squire, and two drawings by Henri Gaudier-Brzeska. For the 1914 issue Tomlinson coedited the magazine along with Geoffrey Pyke. Tomlinson contributed a poem on an industrial topic, 'Furnaces' (see Appendix D), and this issue also contained 'Pont', a Futurist poem by Marinetti, and 'Gust of Spring in London', another poem by Harold Monro.

Tomlinson was, apparently, a keen and aggressive footballer (see Letter L). He played for the College Ist XI, and among his papers is preserved a memento of a match played against Pembroke College, Oxford, on 6 November 1913. The souvenir match menu, apart from listing the courses for dinner, gives the two teams, and indicates that Tomlinson played at inside left.

One evening, in a room above a fish-shop in Petty Cury, Tomlinson heard Rupert Brooke lecture to the University literary society called the 'Heretics'. This irritating and unnerving experience prompted him to write a long and vitriolic article (unpublished) attacking Brooke for producing poetry which avoided tackling contemporary subject matter such as industrial Britain. As an ex-Grammar school boy from the North of England Tomlinson must have felt distinctly out of place surrounded as he was by Brooke's adoring audience, consisting mainly of students from the two women-only colleges, Girton and Newnham (see Appendix A). There also exists a very different account of this evening (Hassall 376-380).

Tomlinson in the Army

Tomlinson enlisted on 4 June 1915 in the 8th South Staffs Regiment (he had been a member of the University O.T.C. before receiving his commission). His first spell in France was from March 1916 to July 1916. He was wounded at Fricourt, on the Somme, and, after recuperating at the Hospital for Officers at 24 Park Street, London, spent the best part of a year working for the War Office in London. His second spell in France lasted from August 1917 to January 1918, when he was taken ill. When he recovered towards the end of the War he was sent out to India on 25 September 1918, and arrived there on 3 November. He was finally demobilised on 11 April 1919.

Tomlinson after the War

One of Tomlinson's earliest pieces to be published after the War was his poem, 'The Peace', in the *Cambridge Magazine* for 1 November 1919. This poem appeared again three years later in his collection of poems entitled *Candour*. Throughout the 1920s Tomlinson continued to seek to establish a niche for himself in the literary world. For example, the August 1924 issue of *The Adelphi*, the literary magazine edited by John Middleton Murry, contained Tomlinson's prose poem about industrial Middlesbrough, 'Twilight of the Works' (see Appendix D). Other contributors whose work was published in this issue included D.H. Lawrence, Edwin Muir and Iris Barry.

For reasons that are difficult to ascertain and pointless to speculate about, Tomlinson appears to have sunk slowly into obscurity as far as his literary ambitions and achievement were concerned. Only modest and occasional provincial success on a limited scale is apparent in the last two decades of his life. He does not seem to have been able to sustain or build on his youthful fire and promise, and his later, post-World War II writing (mostly poetry) is sadly impoverished and debilitated. In June 1948 the *Norwich Mercury* accepted one of his poems.

For having another of his poems, 'Lowestoft Quay', read on the BBC on 7 May 1949 Tomlinson received a fee of £3-3s. In 1950 he privately published a booklet (1000 copies, at a cost to Tomlinson of £10) of twenty poems called *Waveney Sonnets* (see Appendix E for two examples). It was mentioned by the *Times Literary Supplement* of 19 May 1950.

Three unpublished poems about Cambridge have survived. It seems probable they were written in the late 1950s or early 1960s (see Appendix E). Two ('Cambridge Memories', and 'King's Chapel') wallow unashamedly in nostalgia for a prelapsarian Cambridge. The third ('Cambridge') is a lament for change, and in it Tomlinson regrets the encroachment of some of the less appealing aspects of modern civilisation. In parts of this poem Tomlinson reveals a lightness of touch, and the gently satirical approach recalls some of his earlier, more successful writing in this manner.

In the 1950s and 1960s Tomlinson was living in Lowestoft and working as Acting Registrar of Births, Deaths and Marriages. He continued to write poetry, and in 1956 his poem, 'Suffolk Sky', won the Suffolk Poetry Society's top award, the Crabbe Memorial Cup. Another poem, 'Home Thoughts From the Isle of Wight', was published in the *East Anglian Magazine* in July 1963. The sad decline in Tomlinson's powers is evidenced by the final stanza:

Suffolk, Suffolk sea and sky,
Gracious space and clean sweet air,
Space to live and room to die
After tasting heaven there.

Finally, on 21 September 1969, that is, not long after Tomlinson's death, Paul Humphrey's BBC radio programme, 'Midland Poets', included a reading of 'Oulton Broads', from the *Waveney Sonnets*.

But it is Tomlinson's war writings that we should value and remember. Among the four main components of these writings, his Memoir, *Wound Stripe, But No V.C.*, and some of his war poems, stand out as probably his finest achievement. Some of the Memoir's early 'Close-ups' in particular ensure that this work stands comparison with the best of the published memoirs. The rest of his war writings supplement and reinforce the strengths of the Memoir and poetry in various ways: vivid descriptions, dramatic narrative, a sharp and accurate ear for the appropriate tone and idiom both of individuals and of social classes, trenchant comment, gentle satire, withering scorn, and a healthy scepticism, are scattered throughout his poems, letters and play. The fifth component, the propaganda material written for the War Office, adds an extraordinary, and possibly unique, dimension to Tomlinson's war writing. Here he is employed in writing 'for' the War; elsewhere he often writes passionately 'against' the War. And we should remember that he was holding both these apparently irreconcilable attitudes concurrently during the War. In addition Tomlinson's war writings can be regarded as the result of the coming together of, or even of the collision between, two contrasting worlds: the harsh, gritty realism of the industrial North of England and the soporific ivory-tower languor of pre-War Cambridge. It is difficult to think of anyone writing during and about the First World War who has attempted such a range. These diverse writings comprise a surprisingly rich and valuable addition to the literature of that War.

Michael Copp

Acknowledgements

I wish to express my gratitude to the Master and Fellows of Emmanuel College, Cambridge, for granting me access to the Tomlinson papers in the first instance, and subsequently for accepting my proposal to edit the papers in the form presented in this volume.

I must also thank a number of people at the College who have assisted me in various ways: Mrs. J.M. Morris (Assistant Archivist), Dr Stephen Oakley and Mr. Peter Spreadbury (Librarian), in particular, but also all the staff in the Library, and the members of the Library Committee.

Part I: The Memoir
Wound Stripe, But No V.C.

No Waving Plume, no tilted lance,
Just a shellhole out in France

CONTENTS

Introduction

Approximately half of Tomlinson's Memoir, 'Wound Stripe, but no V.C.' (i.e. the first four, and sixth 'Close-ups'), was written while Tomlinson was working for the War Office and living in London (July 1916-August 1917). This spell in London was preceded by his experiences on the Somme (March-July 1916; he was wounded on 11 July), and followed by his second tour of duty elsewhere on the Western Front (August 1917-January 1918, at the end of which he fell ill). Material for the fifth, seventh, eighth and ninth 'Close-ups' exists among Tomlinson's papers. These four were written immediately postwar, and cover some of the experiences of his second tour of duty, but they underwent substantial revision in the 1960s. At this time he also added material, such as the 'Preamble' and an occasional introductory paragraph for some sections, e.g. the 'Second Close-up: The Infantryman', and the 'Fourth Close-up: A Patrol'.

There is no evidence that Tomlinson sought to add his Memoir to the flood of memoirs and novels that were published between the years 1928 and 1932. Much later, in the mid 1960s, Tomlinson did submit the typescript of his Memoir to several publishers, but his attempts to place it were unsuccessful (their rejection slips and/or letters have been preserved among his papers). The mid 1960s were probably not the most opportune moment for publishing or republishing literature of the First World War. Had he lived longer Tomlinson might have been more successful in the late 1970s or early 1980s, a more auspicious period, when once more there was a revival in public and critical interest in the literary response to the Great War. During these years many 'forgotten' works were 'rediscovered', and a number of new ones received an airing.

In the 'First Close-up: Sunset' the noise of the guns and shells, the sky effects, the shadows cast by the setting sun, and the sounds uttered by dying men, are all powerfully conveyed by means of a consciously wrought style. At times the imagery reflects Tomlinson's northern industrial background: 'Low shafts of fire careered up the rails, scalding away their rusts like a smelter's hearth, till they shimmered and shone and steamed as though virgin-fresh and peeling from the mills.' This startling set piece represents Tomlinson's early prose writing at its most effective.

In the ' Second Close-up: The Infantryman' Tomlinson displays his ability to record with convincing authenticity the language of the front-line troops: the vocabulary, the speech rhythms, the good-natured banter, and the black humour.

In the 'Third Close-up: A Push' Tomlinson describes aspects of the action involving the 8th South Staffs around La Boisselle and Pozières in July 1916. The description of the death of a stretcher-bearer at the end of this section is one of Tomlinson's most poignant and affecting passages.

The 8th South Staffs spent April 1916 in the Armentières sector. The 'Fourth Close-up: A Patrol' recounts a night sortie made at this time by Tomlinson and two other men to reconnoitre the German wire.

The 'Fifth Close-up: A Trench Christmas' recounts a protracted journey up to the Front Line in a freezing, windowless train, the Christmas meal itself (everything tinned), and the experience of being forced to cower in a trench while being shelled. This section ends with the sudden and unexplained appearance in the trench of a tall high-ranking officer who exposes himself above the parapet with total disregard for personal safety, before disappearing just as mysteriously as he had materialised.

In the 'Sixth Close-up: We Gain an Objective' the 8th South Staffs were in the trenches near the village of Fricourt on the Somme from 2-11 July 1916. Tomlinson successfully conveys the chaos and muddle of an attack on the German stronghold of Mametz Wood on the night of 9 July 1916. Possibly no other small area of the War on the Western Front has received such intense literary attention, for, apart from Tomlinson's graphic narrative, there are Wyn Griffith's 'Up to Mametz', David Jones' 'In Parenthesis', Robert Graves' 'A Dead Boche', and Guy Chapman's 'Vain Glory', among many other literary treatments of aspects of the fighting at Mametz.

The next three 'Close-ups' (written or rewritten in the 1960s) are more loosely constructed than the first six, are more digressive and anecdotal, and are written in a much flatter, less consciously literary style.

The events described in the 'Seventh Close-up: Armentières' refer to April 1916 (see Letters I-IV).

In the 'Eighth Close-up: Second Time Out in the Tin-Hat Country' Tomlinson moves from Calais to Arras. He remembers an oddly inconclusive incident involving another officer and a nurse in a Calais restaurant, but most of this section deals with life in the forward trenches: periods of calm and boredom alternating with short bursts of obliterating violence and mind-numbing terror. The incident of the horrifically wounded soldier is the source of two of Tomlinson's most unforgettable poems: 'Manslaughter Morning' and 'Ghost of the Somme'.

The 'Ninth Close-up: Christmas at Cambrai' is set at the end of 1917 in a particularly isolated sector, where the 8th South Staffs were thinly strung out in a broken, undefined line of inadequately constructed trenches.

'The Last Close-up: Black Harvest' was written in the early 1960s. In this coda Tomlinson reflects on his war experiences from a perspective of fifty years. Among these random musings a couple of snapshot memories stand out: an incident involving German prisoners-of-war at a railway station, and the depressing experience of a postwar visit to a bureau for helping unemployed former officers to find jobs. The final sentence of Tomlinson's Memoir begins with deceptive portentousness, but ends on an appropriately bathetic note:

'Our God was the God of Battles, and His habitation MUD!'

PREAMBLE

When the Great War broke out in August, 1914, I was the very antithesis of a good soldier, and I don't know that I ever did make a really good soldier, although the metal of discipline had sunk pretty deep before the war finished. At its commencement, however, I was a pale young student at Cambridge, very interested in and very faithful to books which I, in part, mistook for life. I still do, thank the Lord!

My first step was to join the University Officers' Training Corps. A number of my friends had joined this years before the war and they were already on their way to the trenches, objects of wonder and admiration for us stay-at-homes – before I had learned how to clean a rifle. In spite of later experience in the front line, I never did learn how to clean or use a rifle properly, and I always considered them nearly as out-of-date as bows-and-arrows – quite mistakenly it is said.

I did not learn a great deal from that early training except that the kind of brains we had been taught to use for examinations were not the same kind we were (or were not?) supposed to use in the Army. I was somewhat under the Doctor for the first few months, and it was not until the following January that I made a triumphant recovery, putting on about three stone of flesh, and so qualifying for a second lieutenant's commission from His Majesty King George the Fifth, in the June of that year.

It was then that I became acutely aware of how many thousands of second loots there seemed to be in the British Army. Every training course and every camp I went to – Scarborough, Harrogate, Strensall, Cannock Chase – was positively lousy with them. We did a good deal of drilling together but we never seemed to have any men to drill ourselves. However, a very good time was had by all, especially at weekends. We were all young and every experience was fresh and new with plenty of that variety of duty and of scene, which is truthfully enough, the spice of life. Variety and youth – what a combination!

In between whiles I took a course at Otley, Yorks, and qualified as a battalion signaller– which was so much wasted effort because I was never detailed to do any actual signalling either at home or in Flanders. During these months I also learned that a "platoon is a small body of men entirely surrounded by officers" – that is, a platoon for home training purposes at any rate.

About this time I remember a very tall and rather elderly Major, also of temporary rank, saying to me: "They will make a soldier out of you, my lad, but they will never make one out of me". He was referring to the literary aspirations which were our ground of friendship, and which he refused to surrender to the more pressing needs of army discipline. Well, I suppose they did make some sort of soldier out of me because in March, 1916, after nine months as a second loot, I proceeded to join our service battalion in France.

When I first landed in France I can honestly say I didn't know the first thing about how to train or drill a platoon, but perhaps I had an inkling of how to lead one and set an example of sorts. This was as well because within a few days I marched up to the firing line and straight into my first war-time sunset – a very unusual sunset, as I shall now try to show.

The First Close-up
SUNSET IN CHAOS

In the trenches sunsets and other aesthetic luxuries were banned. The sun did not set. The night came, with all its horrors.

The 'night-rise' I have in my mind did not find us actually in the trenches, but on our way to relieve. All day long rumour had been tickling us under the arm-pits. The Boche intended to attack. Spies had been busy. He knew our plans for relief to the minute. Confirmation came about five o'clock when he began to bombard steadily, and he was still digging our ribs when we mustered for the line.

The sun was just setting, livid in an angry sky. Even in the tramp and scurry of departure men were agossip about the unusual splendour of the heavens. The whole West was in conflagration. Flames, gluttonous, uncontrollable, were devouring the clouds far and high. Equatorial crimsons, scarlets and carmines beat on our backs, forging wrathful channels to our very heart of hearts.

One man slackened in his step to murmur something about omens and lakes of blood. A considerate knee in the small of his pack cheered him immensely. That did not dispel, however, the unparalleled pageant of the horizon. The men were uneasy and muttered. They bunched and showed ugly; a little pile of willy-nilly rummage, dry-rot, inflammable, paraffined, packed about with coal, and in the hand of God – a burning taper.

The track to the trenches branched up to a disused railroad whose metals ran rustily ahead past farms in tatters, fences stoved-in, stagnant pools, fields untilled and weed-spread, direct to the flooded duck-boards. Behind us they ran plunk into the scathing sun. Low shafts of fire careered up the rails, scalding away their rusts like a smelter's hearth, till they shimmered and shone and steamed as though virgin-fresh and peeling from the mills.

The road had been badly crumped. Splintered sleepers and jagged struts of steel strewed the track knee-deep, or protruded perilously. There was much barking of shins and curses. There were shell-holes; some were pip-squeaks, while others – more volcanic – had to be forded. Several were just new, and their shelving sides were still patched with soot and sulphur, and twiddling fingers of smoke rose stinking like a nausea of November the Fifth.

The Bombardment was at its intensest. Mortars, minnenwerfers, howitzers and guns of every calibre and conceivable clangour bawled aves to the night. The remote bombing of the heavies was the slamming of the gates of Hell; then up above a strong, persistent purring, hardening to a shriek, a frenzy of howling and rending air, like a meteorite through space, and then . . . clods and stakes and very small dust clattering down upon us. The sun grinned in its scorchings, and prepared to go.

We ambled on in single file. Leaping shadows filled the interfiles, jigging and jogging grotesquely. It was as if the sun had grilled the most evil, blackest greases of self from every man, and flung them forward, writhing and lankily acrobatic beneath his neighbour's heels. Or, mayhap, the grand uproar of the guns had driven the coward in us to the floor, and whilst our disciplined selves marched upright, there he crawls on his belly in contorted exposure of our primest, ugliest natural impulses.

We followed the rails for a league or more, losing lightly from occasional shrapnel.

Eventually we reached a pavé road crossing the track, and there we halted to let the laggards close up before passing into the communication trench. The last slim arch of sun was within an ace of bankruptcy. It still held a royal flush, however. The sky about it was a bowl of tarnished bronze.

The platoons lined a low fosse across the road. We were well within range of whizz-bangs. The manner of whizz-bangs is this – a swish of skirt and a slitting fathom of linen, a dull explosive thud, no louder than a strong man's "damn", and two bucketsful of soil and rubble as high as a child's head. Simple, but we didn't like it. They were happening every few seconds, and didn't do our nerves any good. Less frequently a 'heavy' would croon through space on its way to Timbuctoo, mumbling, vibrating like the pistons of a high-powered auto accelerating on the steep.

At last the platoons reported present and correct. By then the sun had dived beyond dispute, leaving a few coppery burnishings of cloud to tell its funeral history. A breeze loitered towards us from the west. Night had come.

Straightaway Hell was unchained. The guns grew quicker, frantic, diabolical. The dusk was sifted through with hissing, racing metal, express with murder, choric with death. Men shivered and sweated, knelt for cover, grovelled before God. Some wallowed in the ditch, but might not escape.

With the roar of a train and the boom of the sea, death dug down to them, ripped them upwards, smacked them to earth, and buried their remnants five bags deep. There were sobs that were swansongs, howlings that were loppings of limbs, blubberings that meant eyeless for ever, hysteria, song, prophecy gone mad, and the last asthmatic rattlings of renegade breath. A sergeant with his arm and half his left side carved away, came to ask me if I had found his cap-badge.

The spit, spit, of machine-guns, drizzled on the pavé incessantly, unnoticed. From the front trenches flares were flung up. Their sapphire fulgence persisted like day, yet momentary too, throwing elastic, maniac shadows, like lightning of the Abyss. Human flesh showed blue and pallid like a man two hours drowned. Din and disaster hammered about, and derangement patted at the human mind. The cosmos was derailed, upheavalled, and her bowels still beating.

Steadily a fresh horror was born into the dark. First a dim whimper like the sobbing of a child in a far room, hardly heard save by the prescient mother; then vague metallic beatings like Kaffir tom-toms, coming and fading, very elusive; then the chill, godless certainty of a siren, one, two, three – a horde of hooters – howling louder, louder, louder, then soft again, softer – pleading, sighing, but threatening, yes, threatening throughout, then a thin, sweet smell of burned almonds – GAS. And the soughing of the sirens was like the passing of souls into limbo.

Afterwards, when the guns were wearied and a little miscalculated breeze from the sunset had sent the chlorine back to its begetters, there was a wonderful silence. It was as though sound could never have been at all, save in the moon. It was uncanny, ineffable, utter.

Such a silence will be again when the Earth is Ice.

The Second Close-up
THE INFANTRYMAN

I am glad I was an infantry soldier. The infantry was always well up amongst the dirt, duty, danger and decorations. He saw the war at a very close and intimate angle, and he didn't have to ask what it was all about because he knew first-hand. He didn't have to apologise for his existence either, even though he didn't enjoy one very long.

It is true that in the first place I enquired about a commission in the Royal Flying Corps, as it was then named, but was turned down largely on account of lack of technical knowledge and experience. They decided that I had guts enough for the infantry, however, which was a large compensation.

This chapter, then is in honour of a body of men of whom I learned a good deal during four years of war – the front-line infantryman, to whichever nation he may belong.

The infantryman was the grand protagonist of the Great War, he was the hardest driven, the most exposed, the jerriest-billeted, the shabbiest clad and the lowest paid – his role was one of supreme neglect. Our staff might be faulty, politicians meddlesome, our generals decrepit,

But the rank and file
Are Sans Pareil
And ever more shall be
The ill-paid Infantry.

The infantryman was master of the war; he knew it, and he made no bones about claiming it. His only reward was a simple, tacit, but sure, moral superiority above all other branches of the service. There was as much earnest as jest in his catchword, "Staffords do the work, R.E.'s get the money". Sheer desperation of redress had driven him to a most topsy-turvy philosophy, a kind of good-humoured glorification of his own miseries.

This happy-go-lucky, good-humoured logic was indeed his most pregnant quality. He seemed to win a smile from stony death itself. However vile the day, weary the fatigue, full the pack, or far the road, his jest and laughter never failed. Even when grumbling (and that was not seldom) he jeered at his own grumbles. An ordinary 'fatigue' provided more capital fun than the smartest of stage reviews. As the file of 'carriers' trudged the duck-boards, sandbags on high, clothes undistinguished from mother mud, faces set, every eye was alight with a myriad mirthful potentialities. Though every man was drenched thigh-deep, yet rough repartee and broad personalities passed unflagging up and down the line.

" 'Rest', ye call it", bawls one giant, who is balancing a sandbag on each shoulder. "*Some* rest, I don't think: six hours sleep on a *ceement* [sic] floor, six hours drill on a half-drained pond, six hours tumble down what's left of a railway, and six hours sandbags. The rest of the day you get to yourself. If that's rest, gi' me the firing line and a bit of peace!"

"Now then, Six Foot, always grousing. Do this for the duration, I could. Why, we haven't had any old iron over all the morning!", chirps in a thin lance corporal, whose married life is intimate to the whole company, as the depths of domestic disillusion.

"Oh, you've touched for it, you have, Slim Jim", retorts the giant. "This is a picture palace to you. Why, you daren't go home on pass for fear of the missis."

The whole platoon sniggers with joy; Slim Jim resorts to expert invective, and the fatigue carries on.

At the stickiest finish of the dustiest march the footslogger never failed for a joke. The company comes straggling into billets after twenty miles at a preposterous pace, in an impossible sun. At the head of the first platoon limps Six Foot bearing two packs, and a whole armoury of rifles. He looks more like an old bag-man than a reputable soldier. His section stagger behind him and not a one but yearns to sink and sleep in the traces. Six Foot knows well that it needs no more than one to fall out, and the whole section will fail him on the post. His back feels like a red-hot stove-pipe, his face is petrified with sweat and dust, his tongue swelled and pimpled like the back of a frog, but his eyes sparkle as he turns to shout the road-worn jest.

"Stick it, you lousy lot of skrimshanks, you're not a section of the Air Force, you blighters, you can't fall out when you like."

The feeble joke succeeds. Faces brighten, mouths relax, packs are hitched afresh, that awkward dry lump in the throat gulped down, and the section swings intact into its hay-spread billet.

The following was very popular in the platoons, and showed the infantryman ever ready to laugh his hardships away:

The father is interrogating his little boy

"What, my son, is a cavalryman?" "A soldier who rides a horse, father."

"And what is an artilleryman?" "A soldier who fires a gun, father."

"Then what is an infantryman, my son?"

The boy replies this time from life and not from the book.

"A soldier they hang things on, father."

That description was ever fresh and pleasing to those who went down the line in packs.

The humour of the infantryman did not spring from an imagination too dulled to grasp the real horrors of the war. In wartime jest was always a strain of grimness. It was the comic relief of tragedy – the grave-diggers of 'Hamlet' and the porter of 'Macbeth'. Naked truth would have been too intense. But for humour the war would have begotten not heroes but maniacs. Riddled bodies, shattered limbs, pouring blood, shells, shocks, screams and chlorinated lungs, cannot be faced stark and downright by any save lunatics. So the infantryman ballasted his mind with a splendid weight of laughter, but, even at its lightest, his mirth never lost its derivative grimness. For instance, a spare limb left lying outside a trench by an exuberant crump is not a nice sight, but it would provide a company with joke and jollity for a couple of days.

"Good-looking leg, that", says Bert, peering gingerly over the parapet.

"Seen better in Leicester Square", answers George.

"Them's shot silk, this is shot off. Look well in a show case with a Paris suspender round it, eh?"

"Wonder if he's got an advert in the 'Lost' column yet? Expect he feels silly without it."

"Orderly room for him tomorrow, losing by neglect; leg, one: Officers for the use of. The C.O.'ll make him smell hell."

"He's smelling some now – touched for blighty alright, whoever left that there."

"Wooden cross, or Charing Cross – don't matter much", says Bert, as he moves away, and soon he is heard in the next bay, singing, "The leg I left behind me".

There was a grimness too about the infantryman's perennial "Splendid". Whatever the peril, privation, calamity or success, that word never failed him. If Fritz exploded a mine under half a company, it was 'splendid'. If he was warned for patrol on a mid-January night, in a despicable drizzle and a Scotch mist, it was 'splendid'. Even when he had to sleep standing all night in three feet of arctic sludge, hourly expecting attack, it was 'splendid'. Attacks, bombardments, trench-snatching patrols, damp billets, and short rations, were all 'splendid'. The infantryman had made this word the grimmest in the English language. One calamity alone did it fail to counter: when the Q.M. disappointed him of his ration of rum – that was a misery muter than lockjaw.

His humour grimly transcended his other virtues, but he had a legion.

Practical altruism, endurance and valour, were all simple decencies to the infantry man. An assurance of duty fairly done was his, we hope.

Watch an infantry battalion, heads erect an extra inch, passing an A.S.C. convoy – hear the cross-jests, the good-humoured banter of 'Ally Sloper's Cavalry', and see the drivers' tingling cheeks. The balance rests with the footsloggers.

The infantryman was master of them all, and of the world besides.

The Third Close-up
A PUSH

Before dawn one Sunday we got the order – "Stand to". We were due for the line. There was a tremendous scuttle in the growing light to don full war-equipment, and for two hours we stood in little groups, gossiping tensely, waiting, taut and straining, for the admonitory whistle.

We knew we were due for a 'push'. We had never 'pushed' before, but soon the order "Fall in" ran along the line, and we were up and away. In the blue of the early daylight we must have looked like a four-breast troop of graveyard ghosts, clanking, glum but steady, over the crest to the tomb and ancestral death.

Through a long-neglected avenue of elms, past rose-smothered auberges, and cesspit-fronted farms, round the sharp corner by the pillaged church, and so out into the open, hedgeless, undulating plains.

The men began to cheer, and grew cordial with the warming of the day. Little chirps of whistling began to speckle the platoons with sound, proving infectious, spread from four to four, till the whole column was marching to shrill echoes of popular airs.

The road was heavy with dust, blocked with traffic of guns, and com-missariat, and ceaseless double strings of mules. Signs of civilian life and habit soon thinned away, and our path began to grow sinister with upriven tree, rubble-reduced cottage, ancient grass-healed trenches, rusted entanglements, and shell craters.

A dusty, sweating, capless squad of Boche prisoners, coming down from the fight, broke the monotony and cheered the men like morning rum.

Over the bleak, unhappy ridges we plodded into the desert land of La Boisselle, where ruin and desolation reigned as twin gaunt sisters of the God of Wars. Here we felt we were entering into our own, for here our brothers had been before, and many of them stayed for all time, though none to give us welcome.

This place has a name upon the map but very little to mark it in actuality. To call it the village of La Boisselle is the grimmest euphemism. A riven, fissured trunk, a bushel or so of chips and sawdust that was once a bolstering beam, flints, rubble, pumice and cement, the stone that was head of a corner, slates that are now sweepings, roofs that are wreckage, and a rude, gaping cellar or so, still defiant to the guns.

No other token of peace-time homes – nothing, indeed, but the anguished earth, ripped, torn, tormented into intolerable deformity, crumps, craters, sump-holes, strangled, congested trenches, grim with twisting wire and cans and garbage. The dreariest sight of all was the lines of long-laid, long-rotted sandbags, tattered, friable, bleached to the peculiar absolute whiteness of excavated skulls and human skeletons.

The place was a desert, but it denied us the desert's one compensation – peace. We marched in no Saharic silence, for here are always the guns. From the front, and again, away to the right, the boom of incessant artillery, the grinding furore of the guns.

We mounted a ridge, and the far side was one long picture of shell pits. Not an inch of land that wasn't a crump-mark. The slope might have been sprayed with shells, as if they were phosphates and fertilisers. Nor need any manurial analogy cease there. Every one of those holes, and every yard of ill-defined trenching, was sacred with decay. Flesh had cast its frailty upon that incline, and guns had throbbed and frowned in their strength, and the good ruby blood had made tunnels through the churned earth.

Everywhere the power of mechanics in our modern warring was most eloquently preached. Everywhere hosannas to the guns! By dire bombardment, by ceaseless cannonade, we had literally and brutally blasted our pathways to the Boche. Here, if anywhere, the meaning of 'artillery preparation' had been made manifest. Here, if anywhere, the man-made machine had mastered the man that made. So, triumph to the bombardiers!

On the chalk road that still twisted intact between the twin desolations of Pozières and La Boisselle the companies halted for deployment. "All officers to the C.O. at once", came the message. Then a matter of maps, commands in two words, watches synchronised, and in five minutes each platoon was plodding its separate track over the ridge to its allotted ditch in the front line.

That day and the days that followed are in my mind like a far, far-distant delirium. Shock on shock, doom on doom, choked our brains into bewilderment. Thought fled aghast to the ends of the earth; coherence and calculation followed it.

Time grew raving mad; matter and form topsied into turviness; and all things tangible span in tipsy debauch. A sprint down the bay, a crouch behind the traverse, a sprawl in the open, a hiss here, a whistle there, and roarings, riddlings and abundant hell everywhere.

One event alone gives you a smell of that hell.

In our first voyage 'over the top', the second morning after reaching the front line, I witnessed an action which was a very psalming of self-abnegation.

After a four-minute intensive bombardment like all the howls of hell, all the blizzards and tornadoes of earth, and all the high ravings of heaven, we scrambled over with bayonet, knobstick, bomb and revolver, and away for the Boche. We yelled like Yukon wolves, and chased like sled packs, whilst he fired a volley high and futile, hurled a last ineffective scattering of bombs, leaped his parados and bolted.

A machine-gun from the left sent whistling amongst my men death and manifold tortures. One platoon went to soil entire.

A second reached the trench, and the other drifted there in spatterings three, – four, – six at a time. Once in the levelled trench we crouched and watched. Behind came the stretcher-bearers casting their lives to duty. In five minutes they dotted the open like a small, cropping herd.

One man, huge and swift as a killer-bear, swept with his medicine-belt, stooping, dodging, sprinting to a shell-hole where a shape with half a head lay sobbing for release. The giant reached him as a bullet pinged, spurting on his own shoulder-blade. He tucked up and went over like a rabbit. An instant, and he was straight again, and at the stricken man's side, in ministration.

He continued there, exposed to straying death, ten minutes or more, till the trunk had earned its only possible allayment. As he stood up a crimson flake seemed to hover on his right jaw and then melt to a running streak. At the same time I noticed his puttee was ragged and clotted and red.

He took a swift survey of the land, and thirty seconds later was tending his second sufferer – a bomber, twisted, writhed, tormented, belly-down to the mud, one leg shattered, pulped, and grotesquely unvital as the limb of a child's rag doll.

After some time it has been staunched, and straightened, spliced and bound into a bolstered semblance of comfort, and the giant is upright and ready again for his task with casualty.

But, even as he turned to a scream from behind, I saw him straighten like a twitched rope, saw his features relax from tight agony to a wan, soft smile, saw him telescope, controlless, reluctant, to the tolerant mud.

A little pallid whisper grew to me across the intervening ground.

The Fourth Close-up
A PATROL

In the previous chapter I have described one of the infantryman's most hectic and unsavoury jobs, an attack in the face of stiff enemy opposition. He had many other jobs equally hectic while they lasted, if not quite so spectacular everyday, humdrum jobs which, however, might appear the wildest and most fantastic adventure to anyone seated in peace at a quiet fireside.

One of these – the patrolling of enemy barbed wire – was of daily, or rather, nightly, occurrence to battalions in the front line. None relished going on patrol, but your ordinary platoon officer was bound to 'click' for at least one such trip over the top during a spell in the front line. You might come back alive and whole, of course, and you might get medals out of it, but the prospect of leaving that nice, kind, sheltering bit of mud trench and wandering about in the pitch darkness of a bullet-swept No Man's Land was not quite so tempting as a walk around Leicester Square.

On the other hand, there were worse jobs – leading a raid on enemy trenches, for instance, when the prospects for the officer of coming back alive were practically minus. Also, a patrol allowed you a certain amount of personal discretion, and I have heard it said – in very low whispers – that there were patrols which never went any further than a few yards in front of our own wire, and there camped out temporarily until such time had elapsed as made a return home probable and plausible. A dead duck has no conscience!

The patrol I remember best was not one of these. It was in the Armentières sector, 1916. Between us and the enemy are three hundred yards of swampy land overgrown with tall grasses. Myself and the corporal and the tall bomber detailed for the patrol have been well prepared beforehand.

We have been shown – in daylight, of course – the zig-zag path through our wire, the course of the wide ditch which we are to follow up to the German line, and the point where their working-party is supposed to be operating each night.

Our particular night is dark with heavy clouds massed in the sky.

About eleven o'clock we three assembled at a point in the parapet where a couple of sandbags have been removed. The word has just gone down the line from sentry group to sentry group. Our return is judged for one o'clock. From time to time the sergeant of the watch is to throw up three Very lights in quick succession as a place signal.

We three make a curious study in contrasts as we stand with the captain in a disused bay ankle-deep in water. My gas-bag, Sam Browne belt and tin hat have all been discarded, and for weapons I carry a revolver and a short dangerous knife which I have plastered with mud to avoid any possibility of shine or flash in the murderous dark.

This is my first visit into No Man's Land itself, and I am nervous and jumpy, but the excitement which I hope I hide under an air of official composure does not communicate itself to the other two.

My corporal is a bronzed, wiry little man, a 'regular', who has been at Mons and the Marne; service in India is also told by a double layer of sunburn and a spectrum of chest medals. A hatchet head, eyes twinkling like broken glass, a gullet as long as a Chinese duck, and a nose like Nero. He is a Cockney and almost stone-deaf. He speaks in high-pitched tones as though we others shared his affliction.

The bomber, a big fellow, has seen much active service in France and is years younger than his corporal. He has unorthodox views on military discipline and the distribution of the world's wealth, and carries six Mills bombs. He is the only one of us who has not smeared his hands and face with mud to avoid detection in the dark.

The captain gives us his final instructions. "Keep along the ditch, walk slowly up to a hundred yards of their line, then down on your bellies. After that, stop every ten yards for a good listen and a long look round. If you meet any Fritzies, follow. But your first job is to find out what their working party is up to. Now over you go. Good luck."

And so over the sodden sand-bags into the unprotection, the mystery and the thrill of No Man's Land. After days behind the shelter of a parapet I feel stripped naked and dumped out-of-doors into a world of chillier hostility and nearer nearness to death. Once the plunge is taken, however I feel a strange elation and I call up visions of capturing whole platoons of Germans and leading them back in triumph!

"This way, sir", says the corporal, and we find ourselves sliding down a muddy slope into a maze of wire entanglements. The numerous barbs catch at puttees and tunics as though not to let them pass into the valley of lurking death beyond.

Suddenly there is a rending of cloth and the corporal's voice shrills in a mighty curse about his torn tunic. "Shut up! Do you want to get us all killed before we start?" I grumble, but the tall bomber is grinning, while from the trench behind us comes the sentry's laughter.

As we leave the wire, the corporal ties his handkerchief to a stake at our exit point. We make our way leftwards towards the ditch where, overstepping the bank, I flounder knee-deep in water and mud. This time it is the corporal's turn to laugh. His great guffaw seems to go echoing to the German line itself.

Then the first adventure. For overture, a thin sibilance, high to one side, an unrobust tot of sound that marks the first bullets from a traversing machine-gun. Next moment we are all belly to the ground with a hail of them whistling over us. Two feet above our kidneys it sounds – though the volley was probably three times that height. That first hiss has multiplied, and like raindrops spitting down a wide chimney flue, tsip, tsip, tsip, the bullets prick through the air above and away into the solidity of the sand-bag ramparts.

For a brief fraction of eternity death seems very close. I bite my lip hard and try not to sweat. My heart thumps, ready to burst. In imagination, as I lie so close to death, the metal seems to be tearing along my spine. Lapped in my own moisture, I know myself in the grip of Fear and am helpless, grateful to the dark which hides my shame from other eyes. A thousand thoughts of dying, suffering, safety and flight are in my brain whilst in my ears the tsip, tsip, of that frenzied fusillade! It is a great adventure. Two feet from nasty death!

To and fro for about three minutes the gun sings in its traversings, slinks to its place, and then, just as we are stumbling to our feet, barks out again. A minute more it makes its grim music and then again moans back into the tranquil caves of night.

I clamber up, wondering resentfully if my hair has changed to snow or perhaps to some handsomer military tint of grey. I feel a little sick and every puff of breeze seems for a while to hiss with those metallic dartings.

"Better get on with the band now, sir", says the corporal.

In that fraught silence his high-pitched tones sound as though from a megaphone. Later, in the Company Mess, they said that his voice could be heard by our sentries from at least half way between the lines.

Slowly, with frequent halts, we follow the ditch bank. We keep a keen look out as we stumble through the reeds and long grasses.

Every dark patch seems to be death, every rustle the crawling of an enemy!

From the enemy behind comes an occasional flash of fire followed by a rifle bark. At intervals tired flares worm their way into the sky, casting a weird effulgence like a rather sickly search-light. For the rest, an eerie silence in which every slow and careful footfall seems crammed with peril.

The strain is terrific, even for young soldiers like ourselves. Through constant peering into the darkness our eyes seem to be starting from our heads. Each yard seems like a hundred advanced. Now and again I half raise my hand in warning, only to let it fall at the more reassuring sight of thistles or rushes.

Every time the flare rockets go worming into the night we stop and stare tensely round, probing the darkness with what we wish were cat's eyes. Then up and forward again. Sometimes the corporal side-slips into a pool and then the night hears all the blasphemies of Job.

Suddenly from far in front comes a tremendous flash like a huge arc-light switched on and off . . . and two seconds later the expected boom, boom of the 'heavies' firing their timed salvoes, timed, prearranged and mechanical as the evening meal itself. Far away on the right flank also we can hear a faint murmur from far guns in action. These seem to make the tense silence and the darkness more dark and eerie still.

We seem to have slow-walked for miles and are just beginning to wonder if we have lost direction when suddenly the corporal grasps my arm. "Listen, sir", he whispers. From straight in front comes the sound of voices and laughter, the slithery digging of spades, the hammering and clanking and rough orders of a working-party.

Down we go on our bellies. I am panting with excitement, but the corporal, quite unconcerned, pretends to be snoring as in sleep. He grasps my arm again. "There's one of them", he whispers, "over to the left. He's seen us. Look, he's crawling away."

I stare into the dark, see what I take to be the spike of a helmet, or top of a tin hat, receding to the left. Snatching at my knife, I crawl over the corporal's legs and away like a seal for the sea in chase. I slip and slither through the long grasses and in imagination, see a grey-clad back beneath my knife, the gleam of steel as my hand strikes, a vast hiccup and then the drip of very wet blood. A cinema version if ever there was one!

The helmet seems to be no more than ten yards away. Moving slowly I squirm along in deadly chase, reach the edge of a morass, sail into the slush and ooze, and seem to see my quarry halt and raise his threatened head.

Next moment I fling myself forward and in an instant later I am lying helpless with laughter. The spike has vanished! In its place is a bunch of reeds with one upstanding stalk!

Drenched to the bone in slime, I crawl back to my companions and motion them forward. For thirty or forty yards we snake through the reeds and we are then almost on top of the German working party. We can hear spades biting into clay and see earth come shooting out of a hole in which some Germans are working. There are guttural curses and laughter and some of them are singing in a sort of chorus.

"Digging a new trench, sir", is my corporal's rather obvious comment. "Expect they mean to try to bring their line forward about fifty yards. Better get back with the news before they spot us."

The whisper has scarcely left his lips when from the hole shoots up a flare turning night into artificial day. We three push our faces into the damp grass and lie tense and motionless wondering if we have been spotted. Ages pass; the flare grows gradually dimmer and at long last friendly darkness again.

Just as our eyes are beginning to get reaccustomed to this, an angry shout rings out followed instantly by a flash and a double report of rifles at close range. This time I am certain that death has come. I feel a spattering as of mud on my head, but curiously warm. I lie in suspense, like a man trussed up with thongs of fear, incapable of thought and even action. Next I feel on my outstretched hand something dripping, sticky, horrible. From the bomber at my side comes a queer grunting noise, and then silence.

The German working party are now making off to their own trench in alarm. There is a scurrying of feet and a clatter of picks and spades.

Raising my head a few inches I stare at the dead bomber by my side. His face is hidden, his body contorted, rigid, grotesque, like a felled ox. Skull smashed, arms and legs spread-eagled in mud . . . a shape, lifeless, meaningless in its winding-sheet of slime. On the shoulders of his tunic is a spattering of something horrible, his blown-out brains perhaps.

The corporal and I manage to lift him up between us. There is nothing further from the German trench, and now, without pretence of concealment, we begin our return journey. Back across No Man's Land we stumble, half carrying, half dragging the corpse to its burial.

In silence, in darkness, seemingly across wastes of space and ages of time, our strange funeral draws to its appointed place. The three signal flares serve to guide us safely home, and where the handkerchief has been tied to our wire we leave our burden for stretcher-bearers to retrieve.

In our trench we hear the sentries laughing at some jest of their own. The patrol is over, the reconnaissance complete!

The Fifth Close-up
A TRENCH CHRISTMAS

An abnormal rushabout quality was the curse, yet also the charm of front-line life. The hectic existence which the front-line infantryman had to endure, sometimes for months on end, might compare with that of a fighter-pilot, with added discomforts though. The only commodities you did not have to go short of were 'changes and choppings about', spiced with frequent danger.

There wasn't much Christmas fare about the Christmas I am now describing. Christmas Eve, for instance, was celebrated in a train jolting and racketing slowly across Northern France. In our particular carriage are five infantry officers. The windows of the carriage have long ago been smashed in and an icy and continuous draught cuts through like a knife. A shortish man in one corner has succumbed to war weariness and lies immobile. In the other corners are myself and two of the usual type of boy subalterns who went from school to France. At full length on the floor, and the only one really asleep, is a long man, snoring.

"Hi, you in the bottom berth, stop that damn snoring!" grumbles one of the subalterns, but his words are caught up on the icy wind tearing from one side to the other. The only more or less draughtless place is the floor. On the carriage seats sleep is impossible. We unlucky ones, in spite of thick khaki mufflers and 'British Warms', twist and wriggle and turn in an attempt to forget that we are half frozen with cold.

There are no lights, no heating arrangements. Supper is a thin memory of the past, breakfast a feast of the problematical future. Meanwhile the long winter night drags on. I call up memories of happier Christmas Eves, of feasts and roaring fires, of parties, dances, girls. . . . "God, what a life! What a war! What fool was it smashed these damn windows? Suppose he wanted a 'painless' war! Why does this lousy train keep stopping? Who put all the bumps in these b. . . French railwaytracks? Wonder what sort of a hell of a Merry Christmas they are having at home?"

In answer come the grampus snores from the carriage floor and queer little hiccupy grunts and sighs from the small man in the corner.

"Ours is a nice war, ours is", chants one of my companions, but we others pay no attention for already the dawn of another Christmas Day is turning the darkness into a dreary grey. Soon there will be the rush and bustle of detraining, the stretching of stiffened limbs and possibly hot tea from the Company cooker . . . and then the march up through the snow to the front line.

Christmas night in a front-line dug-out. One subaltern is on duty outside whilst we other two subalterns, a captain and a full ' loot' are all four sprawled on plank seats waiting for our dinner. The skipper is shouting out orders to the Mess cook somewhere behind us in an inner gloom. "How long do we wait to feed, professor?", he calls, "I'm due on duty upstairs in half an hour."

The 'professor' shuffles in – a thin, sandy, woebegone individual with an outsize in noses and an outsize pair of spectacles which have earned him his Mess nickname. In one hand he holds an empty sandbag and in the other two forks and a few spoons. "Someone scrounged our silver, sir. Must 'a been while we were held up in the C.T. by that outgoing Company. Even the tin-opener's gone!"

With this he grins feebly and waits for the torrent of abuse which duly descends and sends him back in hasty retreat to his 'galley'.

Next minute we are all joking about eating our Christmas meat with spoons. Dinner appears – tinned soup, tinned herrings, bully beef rissoles, tinned apricots, tinned milk and tinned coffee to follow. Quantity unlimited but quality not so hot! The batman who is acting as Mess waiter sweeps the last crumbs off the newspaper table-cloth with his sleeve and leaves us to our pipes and coffee mugs.

An orderly enters with a chit for the captain who bends over the candle to read it. "Plenty much strafing tonight, chaps", he says. "Battalion on our right is doing a raid at ten. We are bound to get the backwash. Fritz will put down a barrage on us just to keep us quiet. His line is lousy with trench mortars."

"Ten? that's my stretch", I say, "Hope old Fritz forgets about that barrage. Wonder if . . . ?"

I get ready to go on duty, adjusting the bag of my gas-helmet, and putting on a tin hat, belt and revolver-holster. "Cheerio, old bean, we'll tell them you only done your dooty", calls out one of them as I slowly clump up the dug-out stairs. "Merry Christmas to Aunt Annie and all at home!"

In the trench above I lumber along the duckboards, my great laced trench boots slipping and slithering on the frosty wood. In the bay at the top of the communication trench I meet the subaltern I am relieving on watch. "Anything happening?" I ask. "Nothing, but it's cold as charity up here. Any dinner left? I'm for below. Cheerio."

I do my round of the sentry posts, and, meeting the sergeant of the watch, warn him of the coming raid. Towards ten o'clock we take our stand at a place where the firing line joins the communication trench. "Any minute now", I say, glancing at my wrist-watch.

Next moment the deafening roar of artillery smashes the quiet of the night. It is the three minutes strafe prefacing our raid. "There they go, sir", shouts the sergeant, but almost instantaneously the answering German trench mortar barrage crashes on our line. We duck low and cower in the trench, protected by the sandbags, Trench mortar shells by the legion, whizzing down at a steep angle, seem to shake the earth to its foundations. They burrow deep into the soil before exploding and rive its very heart out. There is a stink of sulphur. Mud and rubble are flying in all directions. The Germans have ranged our line to the inch and soon the sergeant and I are both covered with earth and fragments from the shattered parapet. We crouch almost on our bellies on the duckboards, wondering when the shell that is earmarked to land exactly on top of us shall arrive.

With the fusillade at its thickest, up the communication trench stalks a tall figure, carrying a long stick – possibly a Staff Officer from way back – we never did know, then or afterwards. He hurries not and his courage and unconcern are superb. Giving a glance at our crouched figures, he steps up on to the firebench, where his head and shoulders have no protection from the parapet and where he stands at full height, staring across to where the mortar shells are coming from. Mud and soil spatter him and the barrage never slackens.

A little shame-facedly the sergeant and I step up beside him on the firebench, wondering what it is all about and what good we are doing by so exposing ourselves. The tall figure takes no notice, the barrage goes on, the earth itself seems in agony and night hides our thoughts. Eventually the tall figure steps down and without a word walks back along the communication trench whence he had come.

From below us in the trench a voice says for our benefit, "Must be Father Christmas himself!", but there is a note of admiration in his wisecrack.

The Sixth Close-up
WE GAIN AN OBJECTIVE

Our battalion was one of the hundreds of battalions detailed to take part in the first Somme offensive of July 1916 – up to that time the biggest offensive the British Army had staged and our biggest for the whole of the Great War. For six weeks we trained on the rolling downs of Northern France, and then about the middle of June we moved up to the Somme area where we hung around, anxious and impatient, in villages behind the line for two weeks.

The whole of those two weeks we listened day and night to the near rumble of our guns in front. This was our planned barrage to soften enemy resistance before the actual attack. What a barrage! It never ceased and scarcely ever dwindled. When later we moved up to the firing line we passed our field guns by the hundred, axle to axle, in a long forbidding line stretching away east and west as far as our eyes could follow. Thank God we were on the right side of them during that fortnight!

And yet in spite of the seemingly all-destroying barrage, when at last, after weary waiting, we filed up to take our part in the actual attack we found that the first attacks had already taken place in our sector and had been anything but successful. The German trenches in front of us were still intact enough to house machine-gun nests which had mowed down the first waves of infantry as they climbed out of our trenches for the attack

True, some advance had been made on the first and second days, but out of all proportion to that terrific artillery preparation and to the thousands and thousands of troops of all kinds which we had seen collected in and behind the battle area. It seemed to us that the biggest, best-equipped and best-trained army that Britain had ever mustered was gathered together for that mighty offensive. Everyone knows the story of its success and failure – whether success or whether failure, perhaps history will one day enlighten our descendants.

About June 30th our Colonel had called all battalion officers together to issue final orders together with detailed maps of the trench positions. 'According to plan' we were on the second day – that is, July 2nd – to mop up that gaunt mass of jagged stumps and trunks which was named on the map as Mametz Wood.

In point of fact, we were not moved up until the third day, and then we found we had somehow changed our division for the time being, and that in any case, we were still only in Fricourt village – and that between us and Mametz Wood there was about another fortnight's battle.

For the next two days we were moved here and there, detailed to go forward and dig a trench, detailed to retire and do carrying fatigues, and finally sent back to the nearest village for a night's sleep. That was the first sleep we had had for more than forty-eight hours and we had to tramp six miles to get it. But we did sleep. I seem to remember sharing a French four-poster bed and a filthy mattress, but praise the Lord, no bed linen, with about four other junior officers. We just sprawled out one alongside the other and fell asleep.

We did not get a great deal to eat during those days, but we had plenty of action and excitement. We saw a complete German battalion brought in with their arms high above their heads at one point. Yet at other places, a few Germans were holding up whole battalions for days on end.

Back we went after our night's sleep to approximately the same place. We heard that attacks by other divisions had failed to dislodge Jerry from Quadrangle Trench, about half a mile the wrong side of Mametz Wood. My platoon had the job of carrying up Mills bombs to the front line in pelting rain, and it was still pouring when we tried to snooze standing up in a support trench that night.

In the afternoon of July 9th our Colonel called all Company officers to another pow-wow, and this time we were certainly for it – 'over the top with the best of luck'. We were to capture the trench which had so far eluded all attacks.

Things had seemed muddled before. They now developed a super muddle.

When the orders for this attack came round then Incoherence came with them. The earth and the laws of the earth now reveal themselves as one vast delirium, in which the individual stumbles along half hoping to escape the annihilation which is everywhere befalling his fellows.

Nothing more unlike the average novelist's, playwright's or cinema version of an attack can be imagined. The heroism is not individual, but communal. It is certainly not spectacular; rather it is the heroism of simply going forward, forward, when every cell in your brain, every drop of blood in the body, calls on you to drop down in your tracks, and hide like Adam from the eyes of God. Hand-to-hand fighting – there is none. The artillery has seen to all that. In fact, we go 'over the top', attack and capture the trench, without coming to grips with, or even seeing, a single German.

As tribute to the God of Muddle, it was in the pitch darkness that our battalion moves forward to attack this trench still sixty yards short of the edge of the wood, which, as I have said, should have been mopped up on July 2nd.

In the failing evening light our company comes trooping up from the support trenches, down the weary length of a communication trench which smells of the dead and is jammed with the living, and out over what had once been a pasture field, into the shallow trench from which the attack is to be launched. Somewhere on either side of us are two other companies of our battalion who are to share in the actual 'over the top'.

So far as the individual 'attacker' is concerned, however, these other companies might just as well be in Heaven or in Asia Minor; for he can see and hear nothing of them, and he has no thoughts to spare for them. All his thoughts are centred now on his own particular platoon, his own cherub-faced subaltern, his own sergeant and corporal. These are the only pillars he has for guidance in the new life of incoherence which has come upon him. All his months of training, of saluting and sloping arms, are now boiled down to the one solid fact that he must follow his officer whenever and wherever he shall lead him into the crazy darkness ahead.

Ten minutes before zero hour, the rum ration is served out, half a jar to each platoon. The last man has hardly swallowed his tot of the raw choking stuff than the word comes down, "Prepare to advance".

The word passes down the line like a great thrill running through the general consciousness of the whole company. Imagine us standing there in the tense darkness, rum and excitement as joint rulers of our bowels and emotions, waiting in silence for the whistle which shall send us forward to face a one-in-five chance of death, and a four-in-five chance of disablement. Already grotesquely isolated from everything which had made up our former life, we are waiting there, more like vague ghosts than solid men, for the signal which shall launch us into chaos.

Exactly on time the whistle sounds, the barrage crashes down on the enemy trench ahead, and our line moves forward slowly, automatically, and in silence. For the individual, of course, the line, except for the men immediately on either side of him, does not exist. He merely walks forward into the darkness, towards the flash and thunder of that brief barrage ahead, trusting that the rest of the company is doing the same.

Happily, the enemy artillery has been smashed to hell, and there is no answering barrage. At first then, our casualties are few, but as we advance up a slight slope, there breaks out from the wood a tremendous rifle and machine-gun fusillade which sends many screaming to earth. We break into a trot, and someone starts a cheer and soon we are all running like mad for the enemy trench, shouting the name of our regiment as we run.

The unit now is no longer the battalion, no longer the company, no longer even the platoon, but simply the individual alone, blundering, stumbling along, shouting, semi-insane, in an unhinged, fantastic world. Into the darkness ahead we run, scarcely noticing the men who drop like logs on either side of us, hearing, as in a tortured dream, the screams which come everywhere from the ground about us, and realising hardly at all that we are trampling on and stumbling over dead or dying men as we go forward. Nor, happily, do we appreciate the shuddering fact that every second bullets must be missing us by inches, and that the next second, we too may plunge to the ground, wounded, dying or in complete oblivion. The actuating thought is to go forward . . . forward, but the great obsessing desire is to drop in our tracks and hide the flesh of our bodies from that whistling hail of bullets. Thanks to such innate courage as in us, and thanks to even more months of discipline and training, and perhaps even thanks to the generous tots of rum, we go on advancing.

After a few seconds in which we have lived through a few eternities, a halt is called – at least by some mysterious process the line gradually slows down to a halt, and we find that we are standing on the edge of what is left of the enemy trench. There is no enemy left to tenant it, and we simply slide over the remnants of the parapet and take possession. Our objective is gained; the attack is a success.

It is true that in the total darkness we are not quite sure whether we have captured the right trench; it is true that when we have improvised some sort of hurried roll-call, barely thirty out of a company of one hundred and sixty remain; it is true that the enemy are still bombing and enfilading us and treating us to fireworks from the edge of the wood; it is true that all round and from every side come the groans of the wounded and dying, the call for stretcher bearers, and the curses of those whose temperaments tell them to curse at death; it is true, above all, that at dawn it is found necessary to retire and leave our grimly won trench in the possession of corpses – but still, our objective has been gained.

Not heroism, but Muddle was the dominant impression. It was an incoherent muddle which brought with it such revelation of the meaning and meaninglessness of life that those few seconds of attack altered one's whole outlook and attitude to God and His Universe, finally and utterly. The man who had gone into attack was as dead as if he had been actually shot through the heart. The man who survived and came out of it was another being, a being endowed with a new understanding, and stripped right down to his soul of all save the great fundamental facts – that life is good, death is good, but to face death fearlessly and without question is best of all.

The Seventh Close-up
ARMENTIÈRES

Our First World War was not all highlights, even for a front line battalion. We were not always up in the front line among the mud and muddle and "crowded hours of glorious life". The Tin-Hat Country had its quiet suburban retreats as well as its hectic Sommes and Salients.

Such a vale of tranquil bliss was the township of Armentières – inevitably known as Armen-tears to the infantryman and all others in khaki. Although the little town was only two or three miles behind the front line, yet for the first two years of the war, it went unscathed and unshelled. Much of the civilian population was still unevacuated, shops were open and doing business of sorts, the streets of picturesque old buildings were whole and intact there were unmentionable places which catered for the troops, and there was, in fact, Peace.

Rumour had it that our artillery had a working agreement with Jerry not to shell Lille, in return for which abstention he did not strafe Armentières. For some time after the Germans had occupied Lille, it was said that the British in Armentières used to receive electric current over the mains from the power station in Lille. "I'll bet old Jerry weren't half wild when he found out", as my platoon sergeant put it.

However that may be, Armentières was a sort of dream town to all sojourners in the line. Next to going on leave, a spell in that nice, quiet, 'cushy', warless area was what he daily prayed for. And great was his sorrow when the spell was eventually finished, and he had to return to the flares and fireworks. This temporary armistice also extended along the line for some way north and south of the town.

It was while our battalion was doing the 'Armentières rest cure' that I was told that I had seen the Right Honourable W.S. Churchill. Another second loot and I were feeding in a largish sort of French restaurant called 'Les Boeufs' when a Major wearing some sort of naval cloak came in with a group of officers. My friend said that this was Mr. Winston Churchill and that he was with a battalion of the Ninth Division a mile or so north of Armentières. Later we heard that he had returned to England in a destroyer.

All sorts of rumours used to float round this area, mainly about the spying propensities of the native population, and how they used to creep towards the front line at night, hide up in trees, and shoot our men from behind. I never came across any such business myself although one evening we were told to keep a sharp look-out for two spies who were supposed to have passed over from the enemy trenches. Another favourite rumour was that Jerry was about to launch a big attack in that area, but that didn't materialise either.

Very often we could hear the rumble of artillery from up towards St. Eloi and the Ypres salient, and more than once we heard huge mines blown up from the same region, but everything in our own particular garden was lovely.

Many things I remember about the Armentières of those days. I remember marching into the place on a mild April night with a draft of two hundred men from base camp. We had detrained at Pont Nieppe and we had a march of some miles before I finally delivered the men to the West Yorks Colonel in the Houplines sector of the town.

That was my first introduction to the war, and that tramp along the pavé cobbled road in the darkness with the flare lights worming their way into the heavens in a wide semi-circle north and south of us, the occasional crackle of machine-gun fire, the dull murmur of a 'heavy', or the milder 'plop' of light field artillery, the clatter of the men's feet on the stones, our progress into a country of unknown landmarks and unpredictable events, all had for me a feeling of premonition and doubt, yet also of thrill and adventure.

I parked my sleeping-bag that night, or rather in the early hours of the morning, on the stone floor of the Battalion Headquarter master's stores in the heart of Armentières. Next day I made my first trip to the front-line

I remember being also on a bombing course in the premises of one of the local schools. It was there I nearly killed a perfectly good sergeant instructor. We were receiving instruction in a rather touchy little weapon known as a rifle grenade. We were supposed to place the rifle-butt firmly on the ground, insert the grenade, which had a sort of stock, or rod, into the muzzle of the rifle, and then fire the rifle by means of a special charge. I had seen men firing these grenades, not from the ground, but from the shoulder, as in firing an ordinary bullet. I thought I would do the same, and I did. Unhappily, the grenade, instead of flying gracefully a couple of hundred yards in the required direction, simply exploded in the muzzle of the rifle, as I was holding it.

More happily, most of the metal flew down into the ground. I was untouched, and the only casualty, by great good luck, was the sergeant instructor who had a tiny piece of grenade just to say draw blood from his chest. I am afraid my Company Captain was none too pleased about this incident when I returned to my battalion.

It was at Armentières also that I did my first patrol between our trench and the Germans. It was there that I saw a man accidentally shot through the face with a rifle at about six inches range – a sickening sight, and it was there that I saw a private of another regiment dancing about on top of a dug-out and waving his fist at the enemy just as dawn was bringing new light to the trenches. His dance lasted about ten seconds and was ended with a bullet neatly through his heart. Very good shooting at four hundred yards in a dim light.

At Armentières also, I remember several champagne binges, and particularly one in which every officer in our company mess had to drink two bottles of champagne. We had just marched out of the front line and we drank the stuff like water to quench our thirsts. I am afraid I was disgustingly sick later on, and as we were sleeping in a convent dormitory with proper beds and clean bed linen, that binge is not one of my most exalted memories.

Of life in the front-line at Armentières I remember much, even though it was quiet and cushy. The only tricky part of our sector was a place called the 'Mushroom', and here we were only eighty yards or so from the Germans, instead of three or four hundred as elsewhere. One of our many permanent rumours was the Mushroom was being undermined by Jerry, and that it was liable to go up skywards any night. Naturally one felt a little uneasy doing a spell of watch in the Mushroom.

I managed to get some fun out of it one night. Enemy snipers were so good in this sector that any small piece of white paper or other object, if lifted above our parapet of sandbags, would be shot down within exactly one second. Our trench periscopes and bits of mirror which we used as periscopes – in the same way as you will see Londoners using a bit of mirror to see over the heads of a London crowd – were all shot up in no time, and supply could not keep pace with losses. Even at night the slightest movement around our parapet in the Mushroom would bring a hail of very accurate bullets to the exact spot.

We had our special snipers too, but the ordinary platoon men were, not unnaturally, just a little shy of perking their heads and rifles above the sandbags. I, accordingly, got one of the men to fire from one end of the firing-bay, but keeping his head down, whilst I stood four or five yards away at the other end. As soon as his rifle flashed out in the darkness it was answered by a flash from the enemy trench. Taking as good aim as I could in the darkness I fired at this answering flash. I think I may have done some execution because there was a loud shout from their trench, followed by a perfectly infuriated hail of bullets smashing into the sandbags above my head – by this time lowered to tactful safety.

The track into the Mushroom also had its thrills. It was a crazy duckboard affair bridging a wide swamp. There was water, water everywhere in the Armentières sector and we used to fish in one wide ditch by exploding hand grenades in the water – not very successfully, however. The track I refer to was not properly covered by our parapet, and anyone passing along it to the Mushroom came into partial view from the German sniping posts. Wherefore the knowing and the wary were careful to bend very, very low when crossing this duckboard death-trap. Also all newcomers were kindly warned to do the same.

One of these newcomers happened to be a tall and lanky Staff major – it was a quiet part of the war – and he, like others, received the warning. He saw fit to ignore it, however, perhaps thinking that no mere German sniper was going to make him duck down to duckboards. We got his body away at night, but it was an awful job with such a tall man and such splodgy ground.

I also had the experience of being sniped with field-guns when passing down the long communication trench to the support-line, I and a working party, that is. We were returning from a morning's work in the front-line, and some of my men were carelessly carrying their shovels and picks high over their shoulders. I suppose some gunner observation post got on to them, for half-way down the trench a dozen or so light shells came along. I got a fair-sized piece of shrapnel in my British Warm, but no one was hurt. We did the next couple of hundred yards at the double though, and picks and shovels were carried at half-mast for the rest of the trip.

Still, it was a quiet bit of line. I remember particularly one lovely Spring evening. In the cool, clear Maytide twilight our Company Mess were gathered round the dug-out entrance in attitudes of various abandonment, costumes of divers khaki, and converse of feeblest intenseness. We slacked and we sprawled around on duck-board and sandbag, consuming the peaceful pipe or the serenely insipid cigarette, as happy and assured as though we lay amongst the plush and boiled shirt specklessness of a hotel lounge.

From the dug-out came the clink and welcome chit-chat of our tableware under the hasty, irresponsible ministrations of the mess boy. Our own chatter was no more than a meagre murmur, an indolent matter of grunts and half-finished phrases, of smokerings and appetising sniffs. From the cook-house wavered down on us the aroma of soup, toasting cheese and dexterously poached chicken. The labours of the day were oblivion, the watches of the night as yet a jest. Not the single crack of the sniper, or the spit of straying metal disturbed the cream of the settling dusk. Silence and the spirit of sweetness lay on bird, beast, bush, and the six British officers of C Company mess.

"And there will be wars and rumours of war", chanted Frost from a perilous post over the dug-out lintel. "Personally I think this is quite one of the best-looking wars of the last few decades. It's one of those quiet affairs, no fuss, no fire – the children like it". Frost had the luck in fatigues, and had spent his day restraining three men and a corporal from over-exertion in revetting the Major's latest dug-out.

"This war is a matter of mechanics, man-power, efficiency and regulated work", muttered our second-in-command, who had just turned twelve weary hours to account amongst staves and sandbags. He was stretched full-length along the duck-boards with his back to a biscuit-box.

"This war", began our Captain ponderously, "is a fair . . .".

He failed to finish the dictum, for from the paling light of the North swelled an interruption, bodeful, and arresting as a passage of Valkyries. On the vernal evening rose the roar, the grind and the rending apart of a thousand blasting quarries, quavering at first as though a trifle diffident of this shattering of shattering, but growing swiftly with impulse irresistible until the still corridors of space resounded and echoed again and again with the fury of its advent.

The Boche had inaugurated his nightly strafe.

"Then, there is a war to be waged after all", said Frost, jumping down into the traverse. "My forefathers, those Canucks, are catching it tonight, in the Bluff. Remember St. Eloi, last February. I never felt so grateful for three miles of sweet wholesome space between me and my colonial brothers before, as I do tonight."

"Only hope they stick it. The flare and the flop of the ferocious five-nine is no mean argument. There's a rumor round the men that the Canucks have lost the Bluff, and all the trenches we held, up in front of the five craters."

Apt, but nonetheless grimly terrific, came response from the North. A crash, tremendous, quick, volcanic, smacked clean through speech and sense. Followed a tense moment's exhaustion of all sound, and then the long rumble, roar, and rolling thunderclap. Like the triumphant retreat of a grand tornado. Reluctantly, burdensomely, the air settled to its former comparative mild fury of calculated cannonade, unremitting bombardment. A mine had been blown, and the war was still waging.

"There are now six craters", asserted Frost, "And there was much grass in that place."

"Wars and rumours of wars", murmured the second-in-command, "Wonder if the Canucks can stick it?"

"Ha, ha, ha, that little mine-blowing will do 'em a lot of good", laughed the Captain, who was sanguine and full of stature, "Oh, a lot of good." He was only twenty-three, and had seen ten month's trench warfare.

I also remember Marie-Louise.

Marie-Louise of Armentières was known in all the regimental messes and beloved of the whole British Army. Platoon commanders pined for her, company dittos called on her, battalion dittos bowed before her shrine, while brigade, division and corps dittos threatened to duel and die for her. She was the one sprig of beauty in Northern France – a rose in the wilderness, a blossom springing from a ruined wall.

For months they had toured the trenches, lined the lines and held off the enemy from the Salient down to the Somme. For months they had refreshed their hungry eyes with nothing more pleasing than odorous farm-girls and broad-beamed 'aubergistes'. Women had become for them an abstraction, a memory, or a dim impression of photographs and sketches in illustrated journals. Then one happy day they had marched into reserve billets at Armentières and settled down to forget for a space about the war.

There they met Marie-Louise.

In the early hours they had tramped to their billets, sore, stiff, drenched and unappeasable. They struggled out of slumber in time for late lunch, attended to their men, cursed the quartermaster, blessed the C.O., and sallied forth for tea. They went to the Café – everybody did – and the marvels began to unfold. They who had subsisted for all time on tinned bully, tinned milk, tinned butter, tinned cake, tinned chocolate, tinned soup and tinned jam, who had quaffed from tin cups, chewed from tin plates and failed to cut with tin cutlery, they who had almost developed tin intestines by tinny adaptation, these wearers of the Tin Hat – survivors of the Tin Age – discovered themselves ambushed by all the luscious delicacies of Parisian confiserie. Bonbons, croquettes, éclairs, meringues, marzipans, and all sorts of creamy things were piled high for their regalement.

Madam, in pearls and silk, smiles a welcome from her paydesk. From the inner room the chatter and clack of tea and the jazz thumpings of a piano transport them back to those misty days when a shillingsworth of taxi sufficed to land them at the doors of some gilded restaurant. They enter, and find themselves in a skirmish of khaki and conversation, colonels, captains, smoke and white-apronned waitresses. They beat about for a seat, trying to look as though this were a little thing to them, and that to tell the strict truth, they had just blown in from some expensive flat in Mayfair. Months of mud, centuries of sandbags, the rat, the flea, the beetle, the enemy, even the gas-helmets on their belts, vanish as a dream. Then comes the seventh wonder. She is at their side with a tray – "M'sieu?", she says. They look up, they see her, they are smitten, are dumb-struck, and tout de suite become devotees at the khaki-crowded shrine of Marie-Louise.

She is tall, yet not scraggy, plump, yet not boorish, she is a waitress, yet not menial, a queen, yet not forbidding, a goddess, yet condescends to earth. Her skin is exquisite, pink as a baby's foot, her hair is full and dark like shadows on the hill-tops, her eyes brown as a rifle-butt and as straight, her bosom rounded like ripened fruit, and the lines of her build were drawn by a genius. She is fair as France herself, and walks royally as becomes an angel – adored by the most exclusive messes in the British Army. Her deftness makes the welcome tea taste like nectar, and the éclairs like honey in desert places. Her voice makes divine music, as sweet as molasses, as invigorating as 'Mountain Dew'. So magical is her influence that one stout and sentimental subaltern consumed twenty-nine 'petits gâteaux' at a sitting in order to secure her witching attention.

She is pure and untainted withal. This stands for the marvel of mankind. She is practically isolated from her kind, she is beautiful, she is surrounded by men living rough, primitive lives, with primitive passions, and primitive conventions, and yet she stays pure and untainted. Marie-Louise represents to our officers all that is good and great. She is fearless, she is modest, and she has suffered greatly.

Marie-Louise has her history – her home was in Lille but she is sparing of speech. She has her coquetry, her glances, her management of the jocular optic for spiky-moustached subaltern, captivating captains, martial majors, and captious colonels alike. She fascinates all, and favours few. If, however, you should be a chaplain, or a corps commander, or happen to have any slack moments at all, you may manage to wheedle her into casual conversation, and extract her narrative in small portions between the courses.

She is alone in the world, on her own resources. Her father and two brothers went to Verdun, and will not return. She is befriended by ' Madam' of the pay-desk, her aunt many times removed. "What can a girl do?" she says, "My father's property was all in Lille – not a sou left. The war has left me nothing. Aunt is very amiable, and I help her with the ménage, and serve messieurs the officers, and the work helps me to forget things. I am quite safe here".

She speaks of the enemy not with hate. "We have had dealings with him. May the English serve him as he served my Mother and my cousin Haydée. You will pass forward one day one, two, three, four years, n'importe. In the end he will burst, and then will come revenge and the cleaning-up. . . . Encore une glace à vanille, m'sieu? Mais, m'sieu, nous n'en avons plus jusqu'à midi. Vingt minutes, m'sieu, vous attendrez, n'est-ce pas? Merci, m'sieu".

"I have lived in Lille, formerly, m'sieu. My friends and relatives were all there till the enemy came. I remember that – women screaming, men shouting dementedly, the neigh and clatter of horses, the shots and whistling bullets, and everywhere the grey hordes of German soldiers – horrible, horrible. I was sick with wonder – I was only seventeen, m'sieu – and blind with terror".

"I escaped, I was lucky. My mother and my cousin Haydée, they were lucky too, in a way – they died, no worse".

"All day we had watched your army retreating through the town, marching hurriedly but regularly and strongly, as though to a parade. Most of them were singing, as they went in step, others shouted to the crowds on the pavements, "We'll be back soon, don't worry". They had very few officers with them".

"Whilst the last stragglers were still passing, my father ran in, very excited. "The Boche is coming", he shouted. "We must prepare a hiding-place. Quick, you girls and mother, down in the cellar. You can hide amongst those old barrels". He gave each of us a small phial with a heavy liquid in it. "In the last event", he said, very gently. We all went down the wooden steps into the musty cellar, which was littered with straw and papers, and crammed with lumber – old bedding, broken chairs and tables, crockery, bottles and barrels."

"The place was damp and smelt evilly. I was pushed into a cask in the far corner, behind a mattress, and some torn screens. Haydée and mother were nearer the ladder, in a huge piano case, turned on its side. We talked in whispers for a time, till my father called down from the trap. "They are here". Hours seemed to go by. I had cushions and a fur rug in my barrel, and soon began to feel drowsy. I went to sleep, and was roused by a stamping overhead, and some shouts and oaths. I heard my father protesting, and then his voice grew fainter as though they were dragging him away. The stamping came again, and there was a creaking of cupboard doors, and drawers turned out, and a general ransack".

"Eventually they discovered the trap of the cellar, and a couple of them descended. One of them slipped on the top step and fell the length of the ladder. Those above guffawed and squealed at this, and he jumped up in a great rage, and sprang at his companion who was laughing like the rest. They closed and floundered about the wet flags, till one of them slipped, and they both fell heavily across the piano-case. Next moment, mother and Haydée, screaming with fright, were dragged up the steps and the door of the trap crashed down. After that, a babel of curses, laughter shrieks, and stamping feet and then, later, everything was quiet".

"Many hours passed, and eventually, long after midnight, my father returned. We slipped out of the town, and crossed over by the fields to Armentières, where my aunt made us very welcome. Father told us that Haydée and mother were dead. They had drunk their phials".

"Afterwards he was called up, and went like my two brothers, to Verdun. They are all dead".

Very few of her admirers heard this story from Marie-Louise. As her stout, sentimental, and devouring devotee said, "You can't get a word out of Marie-Louise. Been chipping her all tea-time, not a word. I asked her what she thought of the loyal troops, and she only answered, "M'sieu, British soldiers no bon", so I said, "Splendid. How's your father?", and dashed if she didn't almost start crying. Funny kid, very".

Such was the legend of Marie-Louise of Armentières. We believed it at the time, but looking back after the lapse of years, cold common sense tells us that it was extravagantly untrue. The proverb tells us that after he has been hunting, after he has been courting, after he has been fighting, we should believe no man. Women are unbelievable at any time!

The Eighth Close-up
SECOND TIME OUT IN THE TIN-HAT COUNTRY

When I returned in the summer of 1917 for another spell in France after being wounded on the Somme and invalided home, I was very much more nervy and 'windy' than I had been on my first trip.

Thousands of others, of course, had the same experience, and they usually explained that, whereas, on their first trip overseas they had only second-hand ideas of what they were in for, yet on the return trip they knew they were for hell with the lid off.

In my case this was not quite the full explanation. I had few 'nerves' on my first trip because I had convinced myself that an infantry second 'loot' had virtually no chance of coming away whole and alive, so why worry? But on my second trip it began to dawn on me that perhaps after all I might scrape through the war if I kept my head down and wasn't too keen on turning Germans into corpses, or too officious in pushing myself forward for patrols, wiring parties and so forth. Hence the nerves, which fortunately were of the hidden variety.

For the first few weeks of my return, the war was pleasant. We crossed the Channel by the Dover-Boulogne route for some reason best known to U-boats, and at the French port I was dumped on a train which wandered round most of the great democracies and finally stopped at Rouen. It was lovely summer weather for a holiday, so I didn't mind this a bit, especially as I soon found out that I should have gone to Calais!

I spent an interesting ten days in the city of the great Joan, marred by one short spell of orderly officer duty, but I don't now remember much about camp except that it was a cyclist corps depot, and that every evening, after closing time in Rouen we had an enormous hill to climb before we got back to our tiny two-man huts. I also remember a large white bridge and a brand new cinema, an officers' club, a church with a big round window which I mentioned in letters home, and other places which I did not mention.

I was genuinely sorry when my revised orders came through and I found myself returning whence I had come by the most roundabout route and in the longest train that the tourist agencies had to offer. This time my ticket was correct and I found myself in the camp outside Calais, sharing a bed with two other second loots, though it was about this time that suddenly I found I had become a first loot by virtue of service.

The weather remaining summery, Calais, like Rouen, was really very pleasant. The crazy narrow gauge tramway with its strings of rattling, bone-shaking, one-deck cars, was always a joy, even if it did close down far too early in the evening for practical purposes.

No one ever seemed to know what the correct fare was on these tin leviathans, least of all the conductor, and we used simply to hold out a palmful of small French coins and let him do his worst.

The curse of the base camps in the later stages of the war was the night bombing. Every night we could hear them bombing Dunkirk, and our own camp was bombed several times during the few days I was at Calais. There is nothing I like better than lying in a canvas tent and being pelted from a great height with large bombs. You have no sense of protection at all such as a trench affords from shell fire. You have just awakened from a sound sleep and your faculties are all at low ebb as you lie there with a heart pounding like an engine while you listen to the crrrrump, crrrrump of the bombs smashing into the earth only a few feet away. You would prefer to jump up to take a peek at what is going on, but the fear of being branded as 'windy' by your tent-mates keeps you lying there pretending that you don't give a damn for a spot of bombing or so.

In Calais itself was an excellent restaurant – I believe it was called 'The Continental' – where they served a splendid dinner of several courses, all good. I was there one evening with a boy just fresh from public school, when a group of officers, mostly red-tabbed, and at least one fair sex civilian entered from the street and passed through the main dining-room and into a private room. The whisper went round that the Prince of Wales was among them, but as we had finished our meal and as someone started dropping bombs round the restaurant at that moment, we did not wait to confirm, but beat it back to camp.

I had rather an odd little adventure at that same restaurant a night or two later. I was looking in a shop window in the street when an engineer captain, a man about thirty and goodish-looking, came up to me and started a conversation. There was nothing odd in that, of course, as we were all in the same boat out there, but I noticed he seemed to be keeping a keen watch on the entrance to the restaurant, though keeping up a flow of conversation with me all the time.

Suddenly he grasped my arm and said, "Would you care to take dinner with me, or have you to go back to the mess?" The prospect of a free dinner and a good one was not especially painful to me so I murmured, "Delighted. Thanks very much."

Soon we were seated at one of the tables which the captain had been at some trouble to select, and I for one was thoroughly enjoying the first courses of the meal, to say nothing of a bumper of wine. My host, however, hardly touched his food, and I soon spotted that his attention was all for a pretty young woman seated at a neighbouring table. She had on a grey raincoat which she had not troubled to remove, but no hat to cover her bonny fair hair. Somehow I gathered that she was a nurse – perhaps I caught a glimpse of uniform beneath her coat.

Anyhow, she lost me half a good dinner and half a bottle of good wine. For, having consumed a vanilla ice, she took her 'addition', paid it like a man and went out. Scarcely was her foot over the step than my sapper grabbed my arm again and said, "Let's go". He left a bunch of French notes big enough to pay a month's mess-bill and off we went. He didn't say a word to me about the young woman, but we followed her all the same. After five minutes walk she tripped up the steps of a large new building which might have been a town hall or might have been an hotel. Apparently it was the latter, for we climbed the steps after her and seated ourselves in a kind of circular gallery overlooking the lounge below. The girl was at another table. There was no one else on view except a very elderly war-time waiter whom the captain ordered to fetch cognacs.

I did finish my drink this time, but it was not in the company of my host. The girl got up from her table, climbed another short flight of marble stairs, and with a backward glance at him, disappeared down a long corridor. With a hurried "Good-night, old man", he vanished also in approximately the same direction. I never saw either of them again.

I have often since wondered about that little war-time intrigue and what became of it, how it started and who the principals were, and, above all, why that sapper captain should have adopted such a round-about method of cornering his quarry.

One other thing I remember about the Calais camp, and this had tragedy for a sequel. We did a certain amount of training of course, in the 'bull-ring', and the first morning I went across there I recognised one of the of officers in charge of a training section as a young fellow about my own age and of my regiment, with the familiar black 'Blob' on his tunic sleeve. His name was Gale, and in earlier days we had been at the same depot on Cannock Chase, about the time when Cannock was first thought of.

Gale told me that he had had this job at the base for some months, and that he thought his luck might hold for several months more. I thought he was in luck too, but, as it turned out, I had the luck instead. In the following October, when our battalion was training to go into the Paschendale stunt, Gale suddenly arrived from Calais just a few hours before we moved up. Our Colonel decided that he should take my place as platoon officer in the coming attack. As only two officers and two sergeants per company were going into the scrap, this let me out and instead of going over the bags, I spent my time at Corps depot with other details. Gale, who took my platoon, was killed.

I could have put up with a few months at Calais myself, but had to satisfy myself with a few days. I soon learned that my battalion were in the line at Arras in much the same sector as the one they had attacked in the April push of that year, and lost about three quarters of their strength, platoon after platoon being held up by the wire and simply shot off the ground – same wire having previously been reported destroyed by gunfire.

My name, along with other returning officers, duly appeared in the training depot 'ordres du jour' to entrain at 10.00 hours and was the occasion for one final good meal at the famous restaurant. Next morning it was even wetter than it had been the night before, and our spirits were damper still when we piled into a first-class compartment in a train so long that it must have been put together for travelling round the fat bulgy parts of the globe, like the Equator.

I don't recall a single thing about my fellow victims except that conversation and drinks were both nil. We had some sandwiches and arrived at St. Pol far too quickly and detrained for Corps replacements camp, a canvas affair just outside a tiny village.

Here we did a little more mild training and I was told that the Arras sector was now quiet and 'cushy' with first-class new trenches and dug-outs. Later I decided for myself that the 'quiet' was perhaps a little exaggerated. It was quiet enough at the replacement camp, however, except for a very talkative and rather elderly Irish major who was, I believe, mess president. We had planned a lorry jump into Doullens, but within a couple of days we were on another lorry and driving up into Arras. Before leaving I had my hair cut by the world's worst barber, a private who had wangled himself a soft job on the strength of a pair of scissors, half a comb and a crazy chair borrowed from the mess. The chair was placed in the sun outside a bell tent and the barber's victim had all his work cut out to keep his temporary throne upright long enough for the scissors to do their job.

After the April push Arras was now well back of the line and there was no active sign of war when the lorry took me through the town and about half a mile out on the west road where it dumped me and valise on the side of a wide, hedgeless field. A hundred yards inland from the road I found our battalion transport lines and Q.M. stores. I knew both the transport officer and the Q.M. of old, though not very intimately. It was too late to go up the line with the transport that night so, after a sketchy meal, I bedded myself out under a small section of curved metal roofing, finding the ground pretty tough to the bones after so many months in civilised beds. I slept well enough, although I never did like transport lines, there being something hostile and aloof about them to the ordinary company officer.

Besides being more remote from Fritz, Arras had improved in another respect since the push – it now had a good Officers' Club. I and two Lincoln second loots went down there for lunch the following day. The town itself was quite whole and upstanding after some of the villages we had seen suffering from an overdose of iron tonic.

I said goodbye to my two friends, promising to call on them up in the line, as we were all in the same brigade, and late in the afternoon made my way back to our mule lines. The Q.M. was taking the ration party up to H .Q. himself that night and he had a staid old nag for me to ride. However, she could get a move on when occasion demanded, as later events proved.

We had some dinner and then towards sunset started with our mules and limbers towards the front line. The Q.M. was leading on his fat old charger and I was just behind. It was a good road with a steepish, grassy hill on the left side and long stretches of canvas screening on the right. The canvas was about nine feet tall and I suppose it was painted to represent grass or something on the side away from the road and facing Fritz.

We hadn't been in the saddle long when the earth seemed to shake and quake beneath us and there was a thunderous boom in front together with the usual tube-train noises associated with the firing of a heavy gun. It turned my dinner over but the horses were used to it apparently and they just kept on jogging along.

The Q.M. turned round in his saddle, "There's one of our big naval guns on the hillside just off the road about a mile further on", he informed me, "Fifteen inch, I believe, and fires a shell about the size of a tram. When it fires it shakes the whole parish and saves the waiter at the club the trouble of shaking his cocktails."

"Sounds like the end of the world to me", I answered, to which he said, "So it will be if Fritz is trying to find the emplacement with some of his heavy stuff as we go by."

And that was exactly what Fritz was doing when we arrived at the top of a long rise about a mile further on. Happily, the German shells were clearing our road and landing in the chalky hill beyond it. Still, there was no knowing when the next one might fall short and bust up the battalion's provisions, to say nothing of the men, horses and mules escorting them. The Q.M. seemed in two minds whether to halt his circus and wait till the shelling had stopped, or to push on at the double. He decided on the latter, put his fat beast to the gallop and away we went, my nag following and the limbers rattling after us. I took back all the nasty things I had been thinking about my old piece of cattle flesh as she made the next half mile in evens. Probably she had been a Derby winner in real life. Anyhow, she was Signoretta to me for the rest of the journey.

It was dark long before we reached Battalion H.Q. in a dugout facing on to the road. A communication trench entered the road at the same point and there was a group of ration parties from the companies lounging about in the dark and waiting for the limbers.

I made my way into the dug-out which was not dug downwards but into the side of the bank, and reported to the Colonel who was seated there with the Adjutant, the doctor and the second-in-command. He was a little man, very likeable, with lots of guts, and had been continuously in France for more than two and a half years in command of the battalion.

Up at St. Eloi during the winter of 1915-1916 he had, I was told, been reprimanded for taking undue personal risk, meaning that he preferred to be up in the line amidst the platoons rather than sitting in H.Q. dug-out in the support trench. No doubt a bar to his D.S.O. sweetened the reprimand a little.

He looked rather tired and worn out on this particular evening and I think he was sick to death of the war and the trenches. At any rate he left us a month or two later shortly after the Paschendale slaughter. The war had lost most of the glamour and adventure which it had held for the new troops of 1915 and 1916. The old personalities and leaders had disappeared and a new type, probably more efficient in actual modern warfare but less interesting and picturesque, had taken their place.

Of the four officers in the dug-out the Colonel was the only one who had held his place since I was with the battalion. The doctor and the adjutant were new to me whilst the second-in-command, now a major, had been a company captain in the old days.

The last time I had spoken to the Colonel had been right in the middle of the most exciting night of my life, the night of July 9th 1916, during the first stages of the Somme battle. Our company and another had attacked and partially captured Quadrangle Support trench on this side of Mametz Wood. There was nothing but darkness, death and disaster anywhere within shooting distance, and not many of us had reached the objective trench, or what was left of it. The captain wanted some more bombers and I went back to our jumping-off trench to get them. I found the Colonel with his reserve company eagerly awaiting news of our attack, and it was in the din and darkness of that battle that I had last seen him. I took my bombers back across the field of death, lost my way, reached the trench at the wrong place, where another company were having a hell of a time, got knocked on the head with a stick bomb, and finished up in hospital in London.

The Colonel now asked me to have a drink and complimented me on having gained my old 'rotundity', and asked one or two questions about London and the 'home front'. After consulting with the adjutant he ordered me to report to A. Company who were short of officers in the front line. He added that the line was quiet enough in that sector except that Fritz had scores of trench mortars in front of us and these were the bugbear of the company in the line. He detailed a runner to guide me to A. Company H.Q. and I saluted and backed out through the gas-blanket into the roadway and then into the communication trench.

It was a queer feeling to be going back into the front line again after more than a year amongst brick walls and safety. Yet it was pleasant, too, in a way to be back in the Tin-Hat Country where human history was being made before one's eyes and where one lived and fought alongside men who were the pick of the nation as regards physical courage. At any rate, the rest of the nation were glad to have these men represent them in the line of death and battle, and it was good to be amongst them, to be one of them and not a mere 'also ran'.

Against that, I must admit, it was not so hot to know that I was entering a region where infantry officers like myself were being killed and wounded at the rate of hundreds a week.

The communication trench was strong, deep and stoutly-built with plenty of timber and well floored with duckboards. In fact, from the little I saw of the Arras sector at that time it must have been the strongest trench system in the whole British line, and there is small wonder that the Third Army were able to hold on to it during the great German onslaught of March, 1918, when the Fifth Army gave way in the feebly-trenched and poorly-manned area of Cambrai.

Except for the occasional Very light and the clatter of traversing machine-guns, the war had ceased for the time being whilst the H.Q. runner and I trudged up the half mile of communication trench to A. Company dug-out in the immediate support line about fifty yards behind the front line proper. The three officers in the dug-out were all new to me as was the fourth at present on duty upstairs. They made me very welcome especially the two junior ones who had been doing four hours on and four off for several days.

The one who had just come off duty was busy with a bully beef steak on a tin plate at a newspaper-covered table. There were wire frame bunks, covered with equipment at the moment, and the mess kitchen was behind a blanket curtain at the far side of the table.

I have never known a man so reckless of personal danger as my new company commander turned out to be. He was rather older than most of us – getting towards forty perhaps – and had come into the war latish because he had been farming in the Argentine at its outbreak. Already he had been in several scraps, including a trench raid and the Arras stunt of the previous April, and had been slightly wounded five times altogether.

His one ambition seemed to be to throw bombs at the enemy from close quarters. A few nights later, for instance, he filled his tunic pockets with Mills bombs, climbed over the parapet of the front line and announced that he was going off to capture a village which we could see in the day-time and through which part of the German line ran.

He came back an hour later with empty pockets but what he had been up to during his hour in No Man's Land no one ever heard for he simply drank himself silly and the second-in-command of company put him to bed – or to bunk.

That indeed was his great trouble, for, although he was one of the boldest men I met in France, he was also one of the most unsober, and when you have said that you have said a mouthful!! Practically every night his second-in-command, who nevertheless had a great admiration for him, had to put him to bed in his cups. He always carried a long six-foot pole about with him in the trenches and he was still carrying it when a shell carried him away for ever on the morning our battalion did their attack at Paschendale. A fool, you may say, but a brave one.

Having been allotted a batman, a young Irish boy and a devil for doing that which he ought not and leaving undone that which he ought, and having had a drink of lime juice and a bite of supper, I went up into the line for my first spell of duty. I make no virtue of drinking only lime juice, but it was all I could get, whisky being scarce and already spoken for, as it were. However, it never bothered me one way or the other and never has.

In the line I had a very pleasant surprise in the person of Sergeant Bricknell, my old platoon sergeant of D. Coy. and now company sergeant-major for A. Coy. He had been battalion since it was formed, and, like the C.O., had been with it the whole of its time in France without break, except for short leaves.

He was an old Boer War soldier, a quiet, unassuming man and a splendid one to have beside you in the trenches. He is one of the figures I recall most easily from the long cavalcade of wartime friends and I am proud to have known him. He was also killed in the Paschendale stunt whilst walking back to the dressing-station with a 'blighty' wound, and, as soon as he had got it, a shell came along and put paid to it.

Anyhow, on this particular night I was very glad to see him and to talk about old times. My 'watch' was dead quiet, without any incident at all. One curious thing about being in the line was there was nothing to distinguish one day from another, and usually you had only the sketchiest idea as to which day of the week it was. 'Stand to' and 'stand down' were much more important than Sunday, Monday, Tuesday and so on.

I know that my first watch must have been Saturday night because I am dead sure that the next night, a very eventful one, was Sunday. It must have been Sabbath morn then when I was relieved and returned to the dug-out for a shave in half an inch of tepid water, a breakfast of bacon without 'oofs', and a sound sleep on a wire bunk.

After lunch I did another spell of front-line watch which was enlivened by some trench mortar stuff from over the way. One of our own T.M. emplacements was blown in but none hurt. You could watch the cruel little cylinders tossing up from the German trench, curving high and wide in the air and finally crumping down on our sandbags or thereabouts. He had our line beautifully ranged, but we also had his T.M. emplacements spotted. Each had its special name with us, like Prince Eitel, Kaiser, Bertha, Seven o'clock, and so on. When any of these seemed to be getting too lively we scribbled 'Strafe Bertha' or 'Strafe Kaiser', or whichever it might me, on a scrap of paper and sent it along to the signallers' cubby-hole. They wired it along to Brigade artillery and the guns usually sent a few eighteen pounders along on approval to the address stated.

At least, such was the theory of it. In strict fact, on the one or two occasions that I sent a 'strafe' message along, nothing at all came of it, and Fritz simply carried on peppering OUR front trench with Tok-emmas until he was tired of it – which was none too soon for us.

The man I had relieved on watch told me that our guns had the trench mortars nicely 'taped', but, as I have said, there was no visible proof of it. I had to take it on trust.

Meanwhile it was a pleasant Sunday afternoon of early Autumn and this war of attrition didn't seem at all too bad in the light of a sleepy, mellow sun shining down on a dry and roomy trench, deep and well-timbered and full of loyal troops, all wishing they were about fifty miles to the south of elsewhere.

At any rate, there was no outward indication of the hectic events which were due to crop up later in the evening. The day was warm and drowsy and the war seemed to be dying on our hands with no regrets from all present. The mild excitement of the trench mortar peppering had died down especially as everyone, without exception, had taken good care not to be 'at home' as regards the piece of trench into which the shells were dropping. Tea had been served round and, save for those on sentry duty, the men were free to amuse themselves as best they might, no amusement park having been provided for the holiday campers.

Most of them were gathered in small groups, chatting and smoking, laughing and chaffing one at another. Some were cleaning up rifles or equipment while others were stretched out asleep in shallow cubby-holes under the parapet.

Many who have written of their experiences during the Great War seem to take the view that the companies had been recruited from nervous wrecks throwing hysterics at every bursting shell and shivering at every whistling bullet. This is especially so with European writers, but our own also are not free from criticism in this respect. Not only in novels but in plays and on the cinema you can see the fighting soldiers of allied and enemy armies portrayed as poor rambling wretches who sit about in the dug-outs and hold forth to all and sundry about the horrors and the idiocy of war.

In such stories there is usually one character who goes quite insane – more

so than the others, that is – and he hares off to the nearest shell-hole shriek-
ing something about his aged mother or his infant children. He then gets
killed while the mighty Wurlitzer plays a simple hymn.

Such characters and such soldiers must have existed solely in the author's
study. We had, of course, the 'windy' ones amongst both officers and men, but
they were well recognised as such by the rest of the company, and far from
making scenes, they were only too glad to keep very quiet about it and to lie
'doggo' as much as possible.

If anyone in the dug-outs and trenches ever sat around and discussed the
horrors and wickedness of war, it was not in my hearing. The horrors and
wickedness of the ' brass-hats' was a more usual topic of conversation, also
smutty stories. Why are all the funniest stories the unprintable ones? I suppose all the smutty stories from the four corners of the earth used to collect
together in the trenches. And there were always plenty of laughs to go round.
In other words, the 'spirit' of the troops was good, whatever post-war authors
may have to say to the contrary.

Just as far from the truth in another direction are the jingo boys who write
as though all our front-line soldiers were thirsting for blood and glory whilst
officers and men simply revelled at being shot at, maimed and converted into
corpses.

Most of us, I believe, strongly disliked the front-line trenches. We had a
particularly strong dislike for 'going over the top' and for intensive bombardments. We preferred our section of trench to be quiet and orderly and, in
fact, 'cushy', whatever might be happening elsewhere – I don't think the
ghosts of dead heroes will arise to call me a liar, and I doubt if many surviving ones would care to contradict me.

It is about an intensive bombardment that I am now going to write, or, as
some would call it, 'a bloody strafe' . At six o'clock of that Sabbath evening
I was relieved, and I trotted down the short length of communication trench
to the Company H.Q. dug-out which, as I have said was in the close support
line about thirty to fifty yards behind the front line proper. I was due for
another spell of watch at midnight.

Down in the dug-out I was greeted by a heavy smell of officers' dinners
in course of preparation and an active buzzing from the H.Q. telephone. By
the time I had unloaded my revolver, box respirator and tin-hat on my bunk,
the message had come through. The captain was scrutinising it, a trifle
unsoberly, by the light of an improvised petrol lamp, constructed from a milk
tin, a piece of rag and some scrounged tank petrol, and strictly against
regulations, of course.

"Strafes, strafes, strafes, nothing but bloody strafes", announced our
commander. "Listen to this. At nine o'clock, or in other words, twenty-one
hundred hours, battalion on our immediate left will raid enemy trench, also
on our immediate left. Two officers and thirty other ranks to take part. At
midnight battalion on our right with two companies and three-minute artillery barrage will attack enemy trenches, also on our right. Object: to secure

prisoners and ascertain exact enemy strength in this sector. What do you think of that, boys? And what do you think is going to happen to poor old A. Coy. sandwiched in between these two stunts?"

"We'll be strafed to hell", answered the second-in-command truthfully and with some feeling.

"How come?" I asked, more for the sake of something to say than because I didn't know the answer.

"We may miss it the first raid", said the captain, "because it is only a short, sharp raid with no barrage, but as soon as the second show starts Fritz will put down Hell's own block barrage of trench mortars on this desirable bit of trench at present in the occupation of good tenants – live ones at any rate".

"You'll be on duty, just in time for the second show", the second-in-command told me, "better go up a quarter of an hour before midnight and go the round of the posts before it starts".

"Sure", I said cheerfully but there was a queer feeling in the space reserved for my dinner.

The dinner was the usual type of trench dinner in a quiet part of the line. There was fresh meat, as tough as horseflesh, and potatoes and tinned peas. Also fresh apples, stewed, custard, and some sort of cheese savoury specially manufactured for uncritical appetites. Tinned coffee, tinned milk, tin plates to eat from, and tin cups to drink from. Newspaper for tablecloth and Perrier and whisky for thirsts. There were also, strange to say, newly-fallen French walnuts as dessert. I suppose the apples had been wind-falls from the same orchard, but how they either of them arrived at A. Coy Officers' mess in the front line is best known to our ration party.

After the last plate had been cleared away and the 'tablecloth' carefully swept with the sleeve of the mess-steward's tunic, I unlaced my trench-boots and clambered on to my wire bunk for a few hours sleep before my spell of watch. The captain climbed the dug-out steps and disappeared into the outer and forbidding regions above, while the second-in-command busied himself with note-book and pencil, making out some returns and indents for battalion H.Q.

I seemed to doze for about five minutes, though I suppose it was really two hours, when I was roused by the captain's voice calling down the steps, "All of you, come up. Stand to".

He had to shout loudly to make his voice heard above the crash and clatter of shells which were bursting somewhere outside, though not very close, it seemed to me. I glanced at my wrist watch. Two minutes past nine. So the first raid was on.

I hurriedly resumed my equipment and made my way upstairs after the second-in-command, the mess steward and batmen having also ascended, but by the other flight of steps. It was pitch dark up there and rather chilly after the fug of the dug-out. I could make out that the trench was crowded with men. Away across No Man's Land the usual hectic flight of Very lights and coloured rockets was swarming into the sky. There was a continuous clatter of machine-guns and rifle fire, and faintly we could catch the popping off of Mills bombs as our raiders scrambled along the enemy trench.

Shells were dropping on our trenches, but some distance away from our sector. Altogether I didn't see much reason for having been roused from a perfectly good sleep, and there seemed too much 'wind up' altogether about the 'stand to' order. Not only was it not necessary, but, by crowding the trench with men, it endangered scores of lives to no sensible purpose. I said so with some vehemence.

The captain must inwardly have agreed with me, for a few minutes later, the noise from across the way having died down, he gave the order, "Stand down". Later we heard that Brigade considered the raid quite a success, for though we lost an officer and half a dozen men, yet we captured a couple of useful prisoners.

For my part, I scrambled down the dug-out steps and into my bunk to finish my interrupted snooze. At half past eleven my batman called and after we had swallowed some scalding hot tea, we both went up to the front line. We found the Company 'standing to' again and every available man up in front. This seemed poor tactics from two points of view. It made the men more 'nervy', and it gave the German trench mortars a trench packed with human lives as an excellent target for their shells.

The plan which the Germans often adopted of leaving as few men as possible in a bombarded trench seemed to be more sensible.

The man I was relieving met me at the top of the C.T. and I never saw a man gladder to be relieved. Evidently he had his own idea as to what we were in for at midnight. After he had gone I made my way along the trench, found my sergeant and inspected the sentry posts.

Sunday night; and what a Sunday night! A Sabbath without rest and a night without peace. The air was warm and in the sky above hosts of stars seemed to be smiling at these little men at war. There was a wonderful silence which, had it been less ominous, might have reminded us of the peace of the English countryside and the fields bare from the lately garnered harvest.

All along our line the men were bunched together in little groups, whispering about the coming strafe. Each one probably has that queer chill feeling in the pit of the stomach which comes with imminent danger. Some are crouching in shallow cubby-holes in the dry soil beneath the parapet. They have some sort of feeling of protection with their bodies and their tin-hats pressed close to mother earth.

Two, I notice, are squatted under a small pane of galvanised sheeting about as helpful as a paper parasol against the storm of hot steel which shall soon riddle it through and through. Yet they are laughing and joking as though sheltered by proof steel and armour plate. The one was a tall ungainly lad from a town in the Potteries. He had been wounded in the Gallipoli landing. The other is a corporal, small and wiry, and wearing a

Boer War ribbon. His home leave is due to begin next day, and he is joking about his chance of a 'blighty' wound.

Close on midnight the platoon sergeant and I take up our stations at the head of the communication trench. From No Man's Land comes a light, spasmodic breeze, bringing with it the smell of water-logged ground, of decay and death. A great hush has settled on the earth, and in it we can almost imagine the sound of gently beating wings, the gathering of angelic hosts to arbitrate the question of life and death which shall shortly be set before the courts of night.

Then suddenly night gives itself up to chaos! The signal is the belching forth of 'heavies' from far behind. Our barrage has begun. The air is split, the silence smashed, in one appalling tornado of sound. The barking and booming of the guns and their echoings through the corridors of night, the whining of shells, the thud of explosions, proclaim the might of armament and deride the sanity of man.

The shells have no sooner left the mouths of the guns than the German strafe has fallen on OUR line. Every trench mortar in his line has spoken tensely, swiftly and with the coolest accuracy. The heavens are raining steel and explosives. Earth and mud spatter on our helmets and on our backs as we crouch under the parapet. All around and about us the shells are tearing into the ground, thudding against the heart of the earth itself, and upheaving great grabfuls of soil with each explosion. From the other side of No Man's Land we can catch the faint 'plop, plop' of the mortars as the cylinders go spinning into space.

All along the parapet in front, all along the parados behind, the shells are pounding down, and each one is like the blowing of a mine. It seems we stand on the rim between two eternities waiting for it to cave in. It seems impossible that death can keep us waiting long, that our small patch of trench can go unscathed. The stink of sulphur is in our nostrils like the first harbinger of hell to come.

Black fumes and wisps of smoke have half blotted out the stars. Along the trench comes stumbling a man for whom the stars are blotted out for ever. A handful of shrapnel has smashed against his face and left him eyeless. His helmet has dropped off and he is pitifully trying to hold the stripped remnants of his face together with his hands. His silence is more terrible than the howling of a multitude. The blood comes pouring between the fingers pressed against his face, running down his wrists and dripping on to his tunic, his boots and puttees.

As he reaches us the poor wretch reels in his tracks, stumbles and falls upon his knees, still dabbling with his hands at the horrible mask which had once been a human face. Even as we move to help him, he collapses and lies outstretched on the duckboards, groaning a little, his fingers clenching and unclenching like the claws of a cat. In a second it is over, and he lies very still, very quiet.[1]

---

1. See the poems 'Manslaughter Morning' and 'Ghost of the Somme'. (Ed.)

The strafe does not slacken. Time and space seem to be made up of the whistling of shells, the shock as they crunch into the ground, and, almost simultaneously, the pent explosion. The shuddering din, the nerve torture and the strain seem to have been part of our lives for all time. We crouch lower in the trench, almost praying for a direct hit – anything rather than maiming, blinding, dismemberment. If it is cowardly to be afraid, then we are cowards; if it is heroic to stand our ground and stay sane, then we are heroes.

The end to the delirium seems so obvious that soon our minds become numbed to further thought, in just the same way as a man in agony reaches a point where mere physical suffering has no further meaning. Oblivion must sooner or later seek us out; and meanwhile why not rejoice in the magnificence of that torrent of shells, the prodigality of the music and the thunderings?

And so, in all this frenzy, the strangest irrelevances creep into our minds. Pictures of the main street of a provincial town, the giggling girls, the groups of young lads eyeing their legs, the shop-lights and the gleaming tramlines. . . . Pictures of the seashore, the crumbling red cliffs, the gulls screaming and sweeping in the wind. . . . From these, switch off to some minor absurdity: "Wonder if I have a pair of dry socks in my valise? Wonder if we'll go back to rest billets next week?

Wonder if I'll get a trip to St. Pol. . . ?"

Smash! It has come at last. A roar like an express train, a jagged tongue of flame, and next second we are both on our backs with rubble and soil tumbling all over us. We scramble to our feet, unhurt. A couple of shells have dropped clean on the parapet above our heads, crumping it in and filling half the trench with debris. As we shake off the mud and dirt, another shell goes screaming slap into the communication trench not two yards away, but does not burst. "A dud, sir", grins the sergeant, but his face is white and his eyes strained and unsmiling.

A few minutes later the tumult stops as suddenly as it had begun. Never was there a silence so benign, so rich with unheard harmony, as that which follows. The pendulum of feeling swings from hell to heaven itself. The angel of destruction has swept by and left us whole. Our nerves relax; we take assurance from the very stars, smiling there as though war were dead and bombardment never had been.

Never could there be a peace so ecstatic, so crammed with contentment as that which comes after bombardment. Life becomes a miracle, the earth a thing of glory. It is a peace that is filled with the sheer gusto of living, a peace snatched from the imminence of death.

Yet the bombardment has taken full toll. As we pass along the trench the stench of explosives, the stink of the slaughter-house, mingle with the crude smell of newly-turned earth. At many points the parapet has been smashed, the trench piled with earth and sandbags. The stretcher-bearers are carrying off the wounded, while here and there are corpses half buried in the soil.

Crawling over a small mountain of earth, we come to the spot where the boy and the corporal had sheltered under the iron sheeting. They are both dead. The stretcher-bearers have placed them side by side on the mound. The corporal's Boer War ribbon is hanging from his tunic by a thread.

"That's the last leave for him", says the sergeant, reverently.

The nightmare is over, the furore at an end. In silence beneath the stars, we stand alive in a land of death. The silence is no longer bland and consoling, but bitter with the aftermath of bombardment – the peak of human progress in scientific destruction.

The Ninth Close-up
CHRISTMAS AT CAMBRAI

My final front-line Christmas, that of 1917, was spent in the Cambrai sector shortly after the famous British tank push of November 1917. The town of Cambrai was still in German hands, about three or four miles distant. It was a Christmas of mud and muddle, just like any other time of the year in the war zone. There was very little sign of peace and goodwill, and less of Santa Claus!

I never had been in such a lonely and isolated piece of the line as the Fifth Army occupied in those months before the disasters of March 1918. For miles on either side of us seemed to be utter vacuum, and we seemed out of touch with everyone and everything except loneliness and depression – and snow. It was zero hour for the souls of Tin-Hat Country

From the rain, slush and eternal strafe of Paschendale, our Division had withdrawn to rest billets about a fortnight before Christmas, and we fondly hoped to spend the festive season in more or less festive surroundings. Our battalion had been badly smashed up in the Paschendale slush push, and, like most others, we were healthily glad to see the last of that dear little Ypres canal. A fleet of London motor buses had obligingly picked up all that remained of us – a few basketfuls of poor fish looking for a loaf – and here we were, far, far away, right in the heart of the downlands of Northern France, and not too far from the Officers' Club at St. Omer to boot.

True, we were billeted in lonely farm-houses, and the nearest village was a good two miles away, but our Company Mess had been allotted an almost ideal farm-house, very clean and comfortable, with all the livestock outside, and not in the bedding. It seemed like a lovely dream of Santa Claus, but, alas, it was not to be. We had already selected a fat goose and several likely-looking chickens from the flocks in the yard outside, when, phut! the whole 'think' flew away as though Jerry had dropped a bomb on it! Our orders came through for immediate entrainment at the nearest railhead, and that after only one night in those idyllic beds! We didn't even have time to steal the goose.

In my own case it was a double deprivation. My orders had just come through to attend at Brigade Headquarters with a view to my being appointed Brigade Gas officer – a job which I rather coveted, particularly as my qualifications were nearly nil, so that I was bound to be a success if I had a good sergeant. Anyhow, it would have kept me out of doing spells in the line, but, once again, alas! it was not to be!

I did get a good lunch out of it, however, at the Brigadier's table, and, as soon as it was over, I had to push off with the Brigade Transport Officer to meet my battalion which was entraining late that night at a rail-head some miles away. The transport officer was an affable fellow and we had a pleasant journey on one of his lorries to the rail-head in question, where, to beguile a long wait, we dined and wined a little in a local establishment patronised by the British army and the French villagers in some numbers.

About ten o'clock I rolled myself up in my British Warm and dossed down on the floor until my own people should arrive . The hum of voices, French and British, above me, and all the perilous nearness of heavy boots on either side, robbed me of all save an uneasy doze.

About midnight someone tapped me on the shoulder and I was glad to get up, bid good-bye to my affable friend, and make my way in the dark to the little station where our men were already piling into the cattle trucks.

War was a great maker and a great spoiler of friendships, and, I suppose, it still is. You met a man you liked one day, became intimate, listened to his young life-story, and he to yours, thoroughly enjoyed his company, and next day, perhaps even the same day, you parted for ever, and his comings and goings never again crossed your comings and goings. While in the army you seemed to meet and become acquainted with half the male population in Britain – to say nothing of the female – yet when you returned home, you could take a stroll through the hub of a universe and the heart of the Empire, and not come up against a single person whose face was familiar to you. It may be a small world, but there are a hell of a lot of people in it!

There seemed to be a lot of people piling into that rickety French train that particular midnight of mid-winter. Rumour had already decided that we were to join the Fifth Army near Cambrai, and for once, rumour was right. It was no small journey, of course, taking us, as it did, from the extreme North to the extreme South of the British line. On that December night, in the light of electric torches and flickering hurricane lamps, the men, with no great enthusiasm, chalked up 'via Iceland' on their 'forty oms weet chevooks' French cattle trucks.

Certainly, the all-night journey which followed seemed to be in the direction of the Polar regions, but much further. This was a foretaste of bitterly cold weeks to come. Our Company Mess of five officers occupied a first-class carriage, but it seemed many years since it had really smelt first-class. No windows and no heating of any kind! The cold was intense. To this day, whenever I hear anyone complaining about a draught, I think of that windowless first-class carriage.

The floor was the popular berth, and so we shared it out, securing an average of about one hour's icy sleep each. Berthing on the seats may have been healthier because of the gusts of undeniably fresh air which chased through the darkness from all angles.

The platoons, in their closed-in trucks, may have been a bit less frozen, for they had mostly managed to scrounge one of those charcoal bucket stove affairs, and the fumes were at least easier to stand up to than the iciness of our compartments de luxe. Also they made themselves tea, which, though without a lacing of rum, kept them going until morning.

By the time we saw first light we too were glad of a mug of 'char'.

We had been stopping and starting again all night through like a South-end excursion, and when we finally stopped more or less at the correct final stopping-place I was glad enough to jump down on to the track, and beg a mouthful of that tea. It tasted good. As I was gulping it down from the tin mug, I saw a poor devil being lifted from one of the cattle-trucks in a state of collapse. He was carried pick-a-back across the railway line. He looked pitiable, and died later that morning from pneumonia.

Our hutments were close to the siding at which we detrained and we were as yet some miles from the front line. Our strength was now made up with new drafts from the base – mostly 'Derby' men – to a battalion figure of 450, or rather less than half full service strength. That's how things were in those later days. The average platoon mustered about 25 in place of 60 men.

The huts were comfortable and they enclosed a large quadrangle on which a good football-pitch had been prepared. This was hard with frost, but several games were organised between the various units of our brigade. At one of these I recovered a British Warm which I had never thought to see again. A second loot was wearing it, and when the bitter wind blew it partly open, I spotted my old rabbit-skin lining, the only one like that in the B.E.F. I had left it behind, according to orders, when we moved into the Somme attack of 1916, and its adventures since then made quite an interesting, though perhaps a trifle unsavoury, story. Anyhow, a batman brought it round to my hut that same afternoon. Verb sap.

Within a few days we were moving up again, this time on foot, across the open, shell-marked countryside, into and through Havrincourt Wood with its famous sleeper-built road, until we came to rest at the deep cutting of the Canal du Nord. Havrincourt Wood was a large affair and actually possessed a Town Major. I met him later in hospital.

The line here was very higgledy-piggledy. No one seemed to know much about its general run and direction. We were in the support line which was partly trench and partly just a matter of dossing out in the open under rubber sheets or lengths of galvanised iron. Such trenches as there were had formed part of the famous Hindenburg Line before our tank advances of the previous month. The country was broken with fairly steep slopes and embankments, and the trenches ran mostly just under the rims of these.

There wasn't a sound from the front line proper, not the pop of a trench-mortar, not a whistle from a whizz-bang, not even a chirrup from a stray rifle bullet. The war had bedded down.

Mostly we also just bedded down on any piece of old France that appealed to us as looking a bit softer and drier than the rest.

Our Company Mess was a matter of canvas sheeting and flimsy poles, but the wind had no respect for either of them. There was more gap than canvas, and more wind than warmth. Some of the Companies had Messes in dug-outs in the trench itself, and these were more homely but had the disadvantage of facing the wrong way – a detail of some moment should any shelling crop up.

Whilst our batmen were erecting our precarious shack, the men were using their ground-sheets to make themselves little bivouacs, each supported on any sort of rods they could scrounge, and each large enough to shelter two, with a hard shove and plenty of optimism. The cookers rolled up and the limbers, and some sort of hot meal was dished out before the brief December day closed down.

This was an eerie bit of the line – an uncanny, isolated, dreary and desolate place. We had been in trenches where one would have preferred to be left alone, but here we were left alone too much. A Territorial Battalion of the Warwicks had marched out as we trailed in. They were cheery enough – they were marching the right way – but after their going we seemed to be miles and miles from anywhere on earth. The war seemed to have parked itself elsewhere, our platoons were only semi-platoons, and, altogether business seemed to have gone bad on us.

Better lose a war than lose your sense of humour. As I walked round our impromptu camp at 'stand-to', I noted the names which the men had stuck up on bits of board beside their two-feet high bivouacs – 'the Ritz', 'Sea-view', 'Sycamore Farm', 'North Pole Palace', and so on.

Next day we merely pottered about, holding some sort of parades and inspections, and next night the snow came. It was in a blinding snow-storm that we marched on again – first across open country, then for a little way up a half-finished wide road into the remains of a village, through the basements of some houses, and so into a concealed communication trench on our way to the front line. We breakfasted in the close support trenches, which were no more than a continuation of the communication trench, and late on the following afternoon, relieved the battalion in the front line. They, for their part, dispensed with the quaint formality of waiting for us to 'take over', but instead they shoved past us half-way down the trench as we moved up.

They were in a hurry to quit, and I don't blame them. As they passed us, one of their officers slipped a scrawled list of trench stores into my hand. This was in lieu of showing them to me in person and handing them formally over, but it didn't matter a jot because they all turned out to be non-existent. Anyhow, it wasn't my funeral – I hoped.

In the snow-storm of the previous night the world's worst tragedy had occurred. Our Mess Orderly had dumped a sandbag full of plates and table-ware on the parapet whilst he rested and lit a cigarette. When he turned to resume his march his treasure-bag had disappeared – scrounged, of course, by that crowd we relieved. Such was his pathetic narrative, and it may have been true. On the other hand he may just have got tired of carrying the damn things!

For the rest of that spell in the line we four or five officers had to take our meals in relays with the help of one fork, two spoons, and, worst of all, no tin-opener. What a war! However, there was not much to eat, so it did not make all that difference. In any case, we always had to feed in relays owing to the need for one or more officers being on duty.

The front line was ankle-deep in snow and slush, especially slush and the country all round wore a white mantle. What a line! I never wish to be in a more uncanny spot. We seemed to have marched about a couple of continents away from the war. There was no shelling, no rifle-fire, no bombs, no nothink! Fritz seemed to have disappeared and we missed his company. It didn't seem natural for him to leave us in the lurch like that. We would have welcomed even a little mild shell-fire as a neighbourly act.

The snow kept on for two days, and it was as though we were living in the heart of a silent, white desert the whole of that time. After it ceased we did begin to get an occasional shell over which was a relief of sorts. Our sector seemed miles long, and we had only about eighty men to the Company of four platoons. I never did get in touch with whatever unit was holding the line on our left flank to the North. I had to take it for granted that higher-placed officers than myself were actually in touch with them, but considering how that piece of line crumpled up in the German attack of the following March, perhaps even that was doubtful.

To the South, on our right flank, was another Company of our battalion, and beyond them and far, far away, a battalion from some other division.

Previously we had been used either to a continuous trench system or else to a continuous series of posts and pill-boxes, but here we had a marvellous mixture of gaps and trenches and posts, but mostly gaps. What front line we held had been part of a German rear position, whilst our present communication trench had been part of a German support line. No one seemed to have the vaguest idea of the general lay-out, and very often we preferred to climb out of the trench and make our way about in open country, as being simpler and more direct, and not much more dangerous.

Nothing in the way of signallers or artillery observation officers or trench mortar or machine-gun or Staff wallahs from the back portions of the war seemed to think it worth while to give us an occasional call. One exception to this provided a tragedy. A party of trench mortar men, making their way up to the line in the dark, came across a good pavé road which they followed with the best intentions. Unhappily, this road ran right up to our line and then across it and on into the German positions. That is where the party must have landed up for we never saw them again. Whether they were shot down or taken prisoner, we never discovered.

Our Company Mess was in a dug-out in a practically empty support line about three quarters of a mile back. Either you took the risk of travelling overland, or else, if you stuck to the trench route, you had to cover three sides of an oblong to reach your meal and bunk. We mostly preferred the overland.

The best we could do up in front was to man a few very small posts connected by a shallow snow-filled trench with no parapet. The great and popular feature of the line, however, was a long and very elaborate underground gallery which had once been used by a German heavy artillery unit. There were still on view at the mouth of the gallery high stacks of shells without fuses and some dismantled guns. This didn't worry us. The place was deep and safe and comparatively warm and cosy. It ran perhaps fifty to sixty yards underground and emerged at the point where our series of posts began. There were rows and rows of rabbit-wire sleeping bunks and there had been electric light and current.

Orders were that no one was to stay for any length of time in this God-sent gallery, but these were cheerfully and sensibly disregarded. No one came along to see that they were enforced. In fact, no one came along from anywhere except our own ration fatigues with an inadequate supply of food – it was mainly cold boiled bacon. Just the diet for a snowstorm, as the men were not slow to remark.

Our tunics and trousers, socks and boots, were sopping wet, but after a time we got used to it and didn't notice any more, except that sitting down was rather squelchier than standing up. I was wearing cold breeches. They took some time to get soaked, but once the job was done, they stayed soaked for weeks, clingy and clammy and totally non-West-endish. Our feet, of course, had long ceased to take any interest in anything.

Eventually the snow stopped. By that time we didn't give a damn whether it snowed or not. However, we were now able to look round a little more easily and to take some rough bearings. We could make out the buildings of Cambrai about four miles ahead and slightly to our left. Nearer at hand was a largish sort of village, whilst directly in front of our bit of trench on the crest of a slight ridge were three beautiful tanks – scuppered and abandoned. We couldn't make out any line of German trenches, and to our rear there was nothing but a white wilderness.

Our posts were so spaced that the officer on watch had all his time cut out to visit each post once during his spell of duty. The Company captain did not take a watch in the front line, of course, and we had lost one officer sick, so there were left only myself and another subaltern to take the watches, apart from the second-in-command. This did not leave much time for fun and games.

The position, in fact, was one of semi-open warfare. Our High Command had been praying for 'open warfare' during the past three years, and now, in part, they had got it. It was now almost time for that long awaited 'cavalry breakthrough'. I do not know how many million times we had been told what glorious things were going to happen 'when the cavalry got through'. The only cavalry I ever came across were some troops of Indian Lancers behind the lines at Fricourt, waiting for the smash-through which never occurred, and secondly, a lot of dead horses near a sugar factory at Arras. At one time also we had a number of dismounted yeomanry serving with our infantry Brigade.

Our general at this time was very keen on 'thrusters'. He wanted all his officers to be 'thrusters'. This was a sort of communal joke in the company messes, as was also a pamphlet which was circulated round the regiments instructing officers how to be 'offensive'. Apparently you had to ask yourself every now and again, "Am I being sufficiently offensive?" What with 'thrusters' and 'offensive' we had enough jokes and catchphrases to last the battalion humorists for months. I also heard tell of one Divisional General who insisted on shouting, "I want blood!", every time he addressed an officers' pow-wow. He didn't mean transfusions!

One of our Mess had the Military Cross, and he, too, had mild ideas about being a 'thruster'. His particular plan at the moment was to patrol the three stranded tanks in our No Man's Land, which, he asserted, were used by Jerry as advanced posts at night. There was no real evidence of the truth of this, and I, being chilled and wet through to my innards and full of cold and depression, did not welcome the idea of hiking on our bellies through the snow in order to throw bombs at three scrap-iron monuments. Nor did I hesitate to say so, much to our 'thruster's' distaste. He had some remarks to make, but I managed to round him off by telling him that I would go any place at any time that he would. With that the debate was closed .

Jerry certainly did not occupy those tanks during the day, whatever his plans may have been at night. During the brief hours of light, he did not seem to occupy any line at all. There was no sign of him, neither scent nor sound, and no firing anywhere except to say that we could just see parties of Germans in their ring caps skating on a pond more than a mile away. We potted at them with Lewis-guns but the distance made accuracy hopeless, and they did not seem to appreciate our efforts very much.

At any rate, it didn't stop the skating. The Lewis-guns were all choked up with mud and snow and rust, and quickly developed every stoppage in the handbook, and some not yet in the sergeant's vocabulary!

Another reason we could not define the enemy line exactly was that he did not send up any of the usual flares at night. A popular theory was that he had gone home for Christmas, and we wished to Hell we could do the same. As I have said, during the long winter nights, we made a habit of using the cross-country route to wherever we wished to go. We quite commonly lost our way, covering plenty of landscape before we found the trench again. One of our own ration parties was said to have followed the same pavé road as the trench mortar men already referred to, and with the same disastrous results. I will not labour the yarn by saying that they had the Company rum ration with them.

If we saw little of the one enemy, we saw far too much of some others in this depressing bit of line. Colds and coughs were the rule, not the exception. Conversation had sunk, for the most part, to a thin whisper or an exchange of husky grunts, much to the disgust of my corporal who was rather given to his own particular brand of ripe and full-throated profanity. A fruity cold had put a stop to all that.

Our ranks were so thin that every man dropping out was a major tragedy, yet trench feet robbed us of several more. I remember helping to cut one poor lad's boot off his foot which immediately swelled to the size of a melon. He had to be sent down, of course. It looked as though we should soon be left without any men to hold the line at all. That would have made it evens, as the line was non-existent!

In the Mess three of us had raging colds, but it was unthinkable that any of us should report to the M.O. At this distance there does not seem much reason why we should not have gone sick, but at the time it seemed to be one of the most important things on earth that we should remain on our feet and with our company. Incredible, really, when you think of feather beds and real bed linen!

Perhaps the most terrible enemy of all, however, was that overwhelming sense of isolation, of being out of the war, out of the army, out of the world, in some frozen inferno of dark and desolation. The short December day was followed by seemingly endless night, and breakfast and daylight seemed to be waiting in some far distant parish entrenched behind an impassable horizon. Slices of fat boiled bacon taken cold between unbuttered bread were no antidote to well-founded depression.

As I have said, there seemed to be neither enemy in front not friends behind. Ordinary service activities seemed suspended; engineers' wiring parties, sandbag fatigues, were all 'napoo'. We didn't even have any rats. Never was there such a rotten, uninhabitable bit of front line.

The quartermaster seemed to have lost his lorries and his imagination. Rations developed a sort of ragtime irregularity in time, if not in kind. Perhaps he was busy inventing sledges to send us supplies. Our Christmas letters and parcels were waiting somewhere in that eerie, uninhabited hinterland behind us, but meanwhile, isolation had engulfed our persons and swallowed up our Christmas as well.

The reason for this 'hung-out-in-the-snow' feeling was that the Cambrai attack had been successful only up to a point – in spite of the fine work of the tanks. It had taken place late in the year and the bad weather had come before we could consolidate properly or establish a strong trench system. There had been a sharp, sudden advance followed by a short retreat which left us about three quarters of the way we had meant to go.

The line, consequently, was in a frantic state of undefinement – all zig-zags and salients. To the North the enemy line seemed to be behind our own so that they seemed to be firing at us from our rear. Also, as far as we could judge, the Fifth Army was poorly served in the way of reserves and reinforcements.

Nevertheless, in spite of all this confusion, desolation, slush and snow, hunger and cold, we still managed to get a laugh out of it. Better lose the war than your sense of humour! ! Our platoons had taken possession of the German underground gallery – 'verboten' though it might be – and there, deep beneath the snow, and encompassed with a thick fug from steaming garments and blazing charcoal, they kept up the unstemmable stream of cross-chat and banter with an occasional chorus song, as though they were still in those beautiful billets miles behind the lines. That's what I call practical optimism under difficulties.

We laughed through that Christmas as we had laughed through the whole war, albeit on empty stomachs and with wet breeches. In truth, I have spent many a less cheery peacetime Christmas. Eating fat, boiled bacon with a teaspoon can be screamingly funny, especially on Christmas Day!

By New Year's Day we were already back in the support trenches and here we received our letters and parcels. There were puddings and also a cake. There were also night fatigues. I had the job of overseeing about fifty men who were transferring a mountain full of petrol cans about a mile back from where they had been dumped for use by the tanks. We carried them – or rather the men carried them – across country to a spot where the lorries could collect them. I sat by the dump and watched, feeling none too comfortable at the prospect of a stray shell in amongst all that petrol. However, it didn't happen.

Our next move was at night back to our shack beside the canal and near Havrincourt Wood. My platoon and another walked into a spot of shelling in the ruins of the village already mentioned. It must have now been more ruined than ever, but it was too dark to see, and nobody was hurt. We might have avoided the shelling if we had waited a short while, but the other subaltern with me thought we ought to push on, so we pushed on and were none the worse for it. A month or so later he was shot dead through putting his head over the sandbags. He was no more than nineteen, and from the Midlands. In great confidence he once showed me a photograph of his young lady – a very pretty girl indeed. He was a very likeable boy, but perhaps too rash for the cold-blooded type of modern war.

Everything was the same at our canal shack, even the snow.

We slept in the snow several nights. It is wet and not even soft, since it melts with the warmth of your body and lets you down on to the earth beneath. My cold became a raging tornado, and my temperature a nightmare. I spent the nights being sick mostly, as my stomach would not hold my food.

I did manage to take the company to bathe at the village of Havrincourt, however, and I remember vividly what a feverish thirst I had. I stopped a carrying-party on the road and one of the men gave me a marvellous drink of water from a petrol can. There was plenty of petrol left in it, but it was cold, and my throat was a furnace.

Still, neither the march nor the drink did me any good. I was awake and sick all night, and next morning I sought out the doctor in H.Q. dug-out. He sent me to a field dressing-station in an ambulance. After many adventures, including a night-trip on a miniature railway, and a day's bombing of our hospital tents, I landed at Tréport Hospital.

In the evening of the day I had left the line I arrived at a Casualty Clearing Station in a big house in a village street. Here I found other casualties, some of them being wounded officers from the battalion on our right There was also one German officer with a shattered foot. My new acquaintances told me that they had been wounded in a novel type of raid, and one appropriate to the season.

Apparently Jerry had been making snatch-and-grab raids on many parts of the Fifth Army Front and he knew how thinly it was populated. One night hordes of white-clad figures, scarcely distinguishable against the back-ground of snow suddenly swept down on the battalion to our right. The little groups of posts of three or four men each must have thought they were face to face with companies of ghosts. However, these ghosts proved more deadly than the story-book type, and the posts were soon overpowered.

The Germans in their white sheets, or whatever they were, barged inland for a hundred yards or so, and then turned back and disappeared once more into the desert of No Man's Land, taking several prisoners with them. This was what modern reports would no doubt call 'lively reconnaissance activity'.

It was all over in a few minutes. The enemy left behind one or two dead and a few wounded, like the officer with the smashed foot, but, for the most part, his white camouflage served him in good stead, and kept the Christmas party clean, as it were. Nor did we have many casualties, because there were not many in the line to be casualties.

From this account of a Fancy Dress show I learned that other parts of the line were not so lonely and neglected as ours had been. Our Christmas with the Fifth Army was uneventful enough, but all the same, I never wish to spend a wetter Christmas – externally, at any rate.

In the following March, when I was back in London and working at the War Office, I learned that nearly the whole of our Battalion, and also Division, had been killed or made prisoner in the great German push, which promised to go so far, but which eventually turned against him to his utter destruction.

The Last Close-up
BLACK HARVEST

I am glad I was a soldier, even from a selfish point of view. There were laughs, thrills and adventures which I would not have cared to miss. I am not glad that later I was an ex-serviceman of the First World War. The laughs and the thrills had gone in those between-war days, and there did not seem much more than a grey grievance left for some of us. God knows I am ready enough to laugh and be friends with anyone who has laughter and friendship in them, but, like some others, I seemed to reap black harvest from my front-line service.

Perhaps we expected too much from it, perhaps we looked for more reward than we were entitled to for risking our lives and shedding our blood. Perhaps we were wrong in thinking that wars are the inevitable portion of any great nation and that men who serve such a nation in stress of war are entitled to at least as much as those who serve it only as citizens and workers of peace. For, after all, other wars will crop up, and the nation will need those warriors or their children, again.

It may be argued that we had grown swollen-headed, some of us, with all the petting and fuss we received while in uniform. Maybe so: quite naturally so, in fact, but that was our fault or only our bad luck. Wherever the fault may lie, it is certain that some of us became victims of tragic neglect and disillusion. Speakers on all platforms have admitted this. In the Second World War, there is every reason to believe that this immoral mistake was not repeated when the conflict ended. Let us hope that those who shed blood will not have to shed their illusions also, and will not have to rely solely on virtue producing its own reward. Let us hope that they reap a more substantial harvest from the dividends of victory.

It is not a subject which anyone of average goodwill would care to labour. Some blame the vagaries of the Press for all their misfortunes, but I think the soldier of the First World War was more inclined to laugh at the newspapers than to curse them. I remember one Autumn we were in a quiet part of the line, and for that reason gave praise to the Almighty, and lesser authorities. To the reserve line about two miles back came a newspaper man of some fame [Horatio Bottomley, see Letters passim]. One heard casually of his being there, and of the Staff pulling his leg and 'putting the wind up' to some purpose. He, however, was well behind, whereas we were well in front, so we did not call out the battalion band or wax very enthusiastic. In the reserve line some wag fixed up a notice, after the great man's departure, saying, "Mr. X stood on this spot such and such a date". Alas, an even waggier wag capped this by sticking up alongside an ordinary trench board – commonly used where bodies had been buried – with the wording, simple and terse, "Foul ground".

There does not seem much point in that story except that it is true. Some weeks later the newspaper to which the great man belonged – or which belonged to him – began to bear fruit of its kind, being a sensational weekly journal [John Bull], and we began to realise the minor horrors of the war. There were descriptions of trench warfare which certainly surprised us who were taking part in it. We had never heard or experienced anything like it. Much of it was so incredible that we would throng round in the Company

Mess to make sure it was in print. We took it in good part, however.

Not so easily laughed off were the multitude of war articles, 'expert views', and 'specialist's reviews', which appeared in the ordinary run of papers. These often aroused resentment amongst all ranks because they seemed to get so far away from the truth of the war as the individual in the front line saw it. He didn't want to be called a hero by anyone in Fleet Street, or elsewhere – not even by his best girl. He didn't want to see it in print that he was killing and capturing Germans by the thousand all day long, because he knew darn well he wasn't.

A suggestion one sometimes heard was that the whole Press should be amalgamated into one Official Gazette. We did not object to a plain statement of fact, and we saw possibilities in a plain statement of untruth but the recurrent comment and prophecies and criticism got our goat.

The obvious question is, "Why did we trouble to read this stuff?" Well, we didn't. We were too busy, and continually on the move, and newspapers represented so much surplus kit. Yet we guessed that this stuff must be having its effect on some of the people at home. Think of the tragedy of spending fourteen days' rare leave in wiping from the minds of Mother and Father and Mabel all the aftermath of months of reading the views of 'Our Military Expert'.

We had exceptions in the platoons, of course, but ninety per cent of the men were simply the standard infantryman The infantryman had no time for 'views'. He had to think of his gun, his pack, his meals, his fatigues, his parades, his raids, stunts and shows, his rum issue, his 'gaspers', sleep, shaves, and dodging 'minnies'. Give him a good cooked meal, a can of tea, a pipe, a dry dug-out, and a quiet part of the line, and he didn't give two hoots for debates and discussions. If he discussed anything it was either his last leave or the reckless bravery and mental genius of the 'Brass Hats'. The only things he wanted 'expert views' upon were the date of the termination of the war, the chances of Division going into rest billets, the best shows in London, the safest bit of the line, and, "Where's that one coming to?" To him the remarks of his platoon officer were more vital than the most ponderous pronouncements of peers or premiers.

In my opinion none of the writers of those days that I read came anywhere near expressing the real minds, the real convictions, hopes and aspirations of our 'Tommies'. The latter were certainly not the shell-shocked neurotics, flying off the handle and screaming up and down the trenches, as depicted by one school of novelists. Nor were they grim, relentless heroes, thirsting for Teutonic blood, as depicted by others.

They were normal men doing an abnormal job of work without any previous experience of same. I don't think they were bloodthirsty, nor had they much hate in their hearts. They regarded the enemy as a fellow in much the same boat as themselves, enduring the same discomforts, facing the same risks. They were ready to shoot him off the earth, and they knew that he was waiting in the trenches opposite to do the same to them. That was all part of the job. But by paradox and by contradiction and every irrevelance they knew that the men of the two lines of trenches were really of the same fraternity – for the time being at any rate.

I don't think the men in the line had a great hate of the German, but he often had a deep contempt for stay-at-homes of his own nation. Perhaps he was illogical too, but then everything in war is topsy-turvy.

As a matter of fact, in ordinary trench warfare, you never saw the enemy from day to day. Personally I did weeks in the trenches before I saw a Jerry. The first of the species I saw were prisoners.

This was at a village railhead near Corbie on the Somme, and the prisoners were the fruits of our trench raids preceding the big attack. There were four of them and they were waiting for a train to take them down to Army H.Q. for further interrogation.

They were nondescript of appearance and belonged to some Bavarian regiment – friends of Corporal Adolf Hitler, perhaps. Their drab grey uniforms were muddy and stained from weeks in the bombarded trenches and the drabness of their uniform and general dejection gave to their faces a peculiar pasty tinge. They had Blücher boots with their grey trousers tucked in at the ankles, and round ring caps of the 'pork pie' variety, with a button or emblem in front, and a red ribbon round them. One of them had the black and white ribbon of the Iron Cross sewn above the button-hole half-way up his tunic.

They were stocky, well-built men about twenty-five years old. About this time our newspapers were telling the nation that all the prisoners we were capturing were either extremely old men or else infants fresh from the nursery. That pastiness of skin was a feature which I noticed among lots of German prisoners whom I saw later in compounds behind the 'push'. I could never make out whether it was due to the drab greyness of their uniform, or perhaps to some vagaries of continental diet. It may merely have been imagination on my part, or lack of ablution water on theirs!

There was a jabbering ring of French villagers round my four enemies at the railhead. Over the heads of the civilians I could see that the prisoners were being served out with rations for the rail journey. Then they were assisted by three North-country 'Tommies' to the waiting train. These French trains stand high from the platform and the prisoners made rather a hash of climbing in. So much so that the 'Tommies' with their fixed bayonets, jumped up and began to help and haul them into the carriage, rations and water bottles as well. One German had been 'dished out' with a long, pointed, French loaf of bread, and the end of this was protruding from his tunic pocket. As he clambered into the carriage, his friend behind, a large, fatty youth, gave one quick look round, thrust forth his paw, broke off the protruding half of the loaf, dexterously transferred it to his own pocket, and at the same time managed to give the man in front a jolt with his shoulder which precipitated him on the dust of the carriage floor. He jumped up, however, and gave the thief a ringing smack across the face by way of revenge. The whistle blew and away went the train at about two merry miles per hour.

A week or two later, and much nearer the front line, we watched incessant strings of German prisoners passing down the dusty roads to the compounds. From there they were passed on in batches to the railhead on their way to English prisoner-of-war camps. The crossroads where we stood, with their constant stream of men, mules, lorries and guns, rattling rapidly one way, and equally constant streams of dusty, grey-uniformed prisoners trudging the other way, was a regular Hyde Park Corner of the Tin-Hat Country.

The prisoners' compound was also interesting. Here were hundreds of the very men we had been fighting for years and never seen, except perhaps for a chance glimpse through a precarious periscope. We chatted to some of them through the barbed wire fence, and gave them 'gaspers' and matches. They had been in the front line for a fortnight under bombardment, and that is no small joke, believe you me!

Such were my personal impressions of our enemy of the trenches. Yet, in newspapers I could read this kind of thing:

"There is something unpleasant about the face of the Boche which goes deeper than the cuticle, something more insidious, subtle and fundamental, and that is the lax, unfocussed shiftiness of his eyes. His glances slip from side to side, noting, observant, vigilant, like so many jabs of poisoned fangs. You feel that each individual is ready to stab you in the back. The Boche is a born schemer, a filcher, an evader, a furtive soulless thing, and the proof thereof is writ in the eyes of his head. You grasp in a flash the meaning behind the old biblical allegories of 'the Brand of Cain' and 'the mark of the Beast'."

Really, what a racket! Makes you think, don't you think?

Still, it takes all kinds to make a good war. In our platoons we had all types from plumbers to poets. Yes, they were all in puttees, which seems to be the major difference between the 1st war and the 2nd. Our crowd must have spent untold hours in winding puttees. Nowadays they just button their gaiters.

What sort of job did gaiters make of it? After all, puttees did not do so badly. They won a victory which lasted twenty years, which was something. Tanks and aeroplanes were hardly at a beginning in those days, to say nothing of submarines and aircraft-carriers. It seems inevitable that when Man makes a new invention he must try it out in war. Will it ever be otherwise?

When I joined the war as a cub second loot, I had great plans for winning it. When I reached France I almost expected a telegram from the Kaiser: "For God's sake, remain neutral". I dreamed of deeds of valour and personal hauls of captives of high rank which should bring medals and promotion. And yet, when I was actually in it, what I looked forward to most was a spell of leave.

When I joined the peace perhaps I had something of the same unpractical ideas. After all, we had been promised many things, including kisses and a royal welcome when we returned to the land of our birth. Caste and class distinctions were to disappear, snobbery had been dissolved in the acid of war, equality and brotherhood were to reign supreme in the new, brave, post-war world. We who bore the equal brunt of peril should share the equal fruits of victory without reference to rank, privilege or birth. And so on.

Do we hear echoes of these same things years later, and are gaiters going to be any luckier than puttees?

Dead heroes are, of course, suitably rewarded with cenotaphs. But dead heroes are so much more tactful than live ones. They do not complain. The millions of live heroes and live heroines who return should have no reason for complaint. A cenotaph in every village will not serve as a slogan. Those who go to save hearth and home must have hearth and home to come home to.

I remember some years after the armistice visiting a Bureau which found jobs for some ex-officers. I did this on the advice of a man who knew another man who thought he had heard of another man who once heard that there were jobs to be had there.

The liftman seemed a trifle surly. He seemed to regard me as so much loose dirt. I decided that he had seen ex-officers before. I never saw a room quite so unfurnished as that Bureau. There were neither chairs or carpets, not even lino, just bare walls gracefully draped with typewritten sheets. There was one rickety table on which sat three ex-officers, very 'ex', and a long time out of food. One average well-fed wartime of officer would have brought that rickety table to the floor by sitting on it.

The typewritten sheets referred to vacancies. These were all for engine-drivers in tropical climates or for attendants at mental hospitals. As I read them I also gave a sidelong examination to the other people in the room. The bare place was crowded with 'applicants'. Very interesting they were, too. Slipshod and down-at-heel, they wore old trench coats and slouch hats. Some of them, rather pathetically, carried their army canes with a mild attempt at wartime swagger. It was a jauntiness which hid nothing but despair. It was hard to believe that this was the same sturdy crowd I had mixed with in camps and clubs all over Northern France. There was a hang-dog, furtive, 'unwanted' air about them which contrasted badly with the squared shoulders and 'sergeant-major' carriage of the Ypres days.

Apart from obtaining this unhappy mental picture, my visit to the bureau was so much waste of time. It may be that these were the exceptions, the unfortunates, and perhaps even 'the unemployables' amongst the surviving 'heroes'. Yet these same unlucky ones were not the ones who opted out from death and disaster in the front line!

So much for Black Haloes. "Their name liveth for ever", as the cenotaphs say. What thought they of the Great War, those who fought it? Their hell had many mansions and all those mansions were in the front-line trenches. Their word was the word of Courage. Their birthright was their deathright. Their job was slaughter, but not their faith. They were not heroes, and they did not hate anyone – except perhaps 'Brass Hats', mildly.

The human being is an extraordinary animal. He cooks, laughs, and he gives names to things. We of the Tin-Hat Country were also extraordinary animals. We didn't cook a lot, but we laughed hugely and often, and we certainly gave a wide variety of unprintable names to one damn thing after another.

Our God was the God of Battles, and His habitation – MUD!

Part II
War Poems

Introduction

One of Tomlinson's first published poems appeared while he was still at Cambridge, in the short-lived (1913-1914) University literary magazine, *Mandragora*. The May 1914 issue contained a remarkably catholic range of writing, from the most conventional type of rhapsodic sub-Tennysonian pastoralism to an avant-garde Futurist poem in French. The first type of verse is exemplified by D.F.G. Johnson's 'June'. In the magazine's section reporting successes at Emmanuel, mention is made of Johnson's winning the Chancellor's Medal for English verse: a poem on the Southern Pole. On the southern wall of the Chapel cloisters Johnson's name appears among those of other Emmanuel men who died in the 1914-18 war. He was killed on 15 July 1916, and is buried in Bouzincourt Communal Cemetery Extension, France. 'June' begins:

> Sweet month of love and roses, hail!
> Queen of all joys that never fail;
> The grasping fingers of fern are open,
> The Mays still blossom adown the vale.

At the furthest possible extreme to this is 'Pont' by the leader of the Futurist movement, F.T. Marinetti. It ends:

> crrrrrraaaak trop tard enfer malheur au diable le pont angle obtus arc tendu bombe son ventre souvrrrrriiir aaaaie *pataboumpatatraaack*
>
> malédiction canailles canailles crier crier, hurler, mugir *joie joie délire les turcs* à tue-tête *hourrrrrrrrraaaah tatatatatata hourrrrrrraaaah tatatatatata* POUM PAMPAM PLOUFG *zang-toumb-toumb-toumb-toumb hourrrrrraaah tatatatatatata hourrrrrraaaah*

Apart from these violently contrasting contributions there is a poem ('Gust of Spring in London') by Harold Monro who founded the influential poetry magazine, *Poetry Review* in 1912, and who started 'The Poetry Book-shop' in 1913.

A further contrast is supplied by Tomlinson's industrial poem, 'Furnaces' (see Appendix D). Such a poem, aggressive in form and content, would have stood out in stark contrast to the norm of undergraduate verse being written immediately prior to the First World War. Already, some of the characteristics of Tomlinson's later war poetry are apparent: an angry, bitter tone, and a preference for long, ponderous lines. The same poem appeared later in Tomlinson's collection of poems, *Candour,* published by Elkin Mathews in 1922. Tomlinson has annotated his copy of the book in the College archives, and he has written at the top of the page: ' Cambridge, March 1914' . It must have been one of the first poems about the industrial North of England to be published in Cambridge. 'Furnaces' is Tomlinson's spirited riposte to Rupert Brooke. In Tomlinson's lengthy, unpublished diatribe against Brooke he chastises him for ignoring the industrial world as suitable raw material for his poetry:

'He was born with the Public School affliction. Others catch it along with the English Stare about the age of twelve, but Rupert had the growth from birth. His father was housemaster at Rugby. They make locomotives and mechanic electric modern things at Rugby too, but Rupert was diligently winning Waterloos with his patrician stablemates, and never worried about chimneys and triple-expansion eight-cylinder trifles of the twentieth century. Tom Browne for him, and Tom Dickonarry of the N.U.R. [were] not on Rupert's visiting list. He may have observed that the L.N.W.R. main line had managed to score an inner on his native village; he may have seen a large-size station complete with several platforms and electric lights; I dare say he didn't have to ask when he saw the Irish Mail whipping its stallions through the astounded night; but he never let on about all this. On the contrary, he wrote quantities of verse at Rugby, including two of the most priceless prize poems – one, 'The Bastille', two, 'The Pyramids'.' [See Appendix A for further extracts from this polemical article.]

Candour contains an even better industrial poem, 'The Mineshaft' [see Appendix D], written at Middlesbrough in December 1921.

Of the thirteen war poems in this section, the first seven appeared in *Candour,* where the place and date of composition are helpfully provided. The remaining six are published here for the first time. *Candour* was widely reviewed by national and regional papers and journals in Britain (e.g. *The Times,* the *Spectator,* and *The Writer;* the *Glasgow Herald,* the *Yorkshire Post,* and the *Western Daily Press),* and by a remarkable number of foreign newspapers as well: *Cape Times, The Illustrated Buffalo Express, Evening Sun, Baltimore, Boston Evening Transcript, The West Australian, The Standard,* Buenos Aires, and by the German *Literaturberichte.* There is a striking unanimity in these reviews about the qualities of Tomlinson's verse. They point out his virtues and his faults, and they all agree that if he could remove the rough edges, and tone down certain obsessions, yet still manage to retain his undoubted originality and vigour, he could look forward to fulfilling the potential that is manifestly there.

Here are some of the critical comments which, when taken together, give a fair and balanced assessment of the worth of Tomlinson's verse:

The poet has ideas, vision and courage; but he flings all three at us pell-mell; . . . [he] is blunt to the verge of vulgarity, which is not in itself a defect if a purpose is to be gained; but as often as not it springs from a tendency to be carried off his feet by the spate of his own speech. . . . there is an excess which kills the poet's aim. Nevertheless, the book has genuine vigour, . . . There is promise in him. *(Glasgow Herald)*

He crowds together with a ruthless haste surprising and violent phrases; . . . but a nucleus of odd burly power, of passion, illustration, and word-harmony is left behind, demanding to be seen. [His] problem is that very old one, the wood and the trees. We may mention one or two war poems in this volume, as cases in which his theme finds his manner most appropriate. *(The Times)*

It is rather amusing to read, like going out in a high wind, but it is also tiring, because so often it seems equally senseless. [He] has energy, and he seems to be sincere, but he really must ration himself strictly in polysyllables. *(Yorkshire Post)*

A strong personality dictates this verse, even at its most crabbed and caustic moments. *(Yorkshire Observer)*

. . . a promise and an achievement. . . . There is an almost brutal virility . . . constantly chooses words and phrases of power and cyclonic ruthlessness. He has a healthy hatred for the mean shifts and compromises of hypocrites, and a swingeing desire for stark frankness. At times his rhetoric is intense to the point of becoming hectic. . . . Of war poetry we have had more than enough; but this volume is above the average. *(Western Daily Press)*

There are forcible lines in almost every poem, there are striking words, and there is imagination. . . . There is a feeling of too much straining after effect in the manner of these poems and in the words selected to express the author's thoughts. Nevertheless there is much evidence of power and the possibility of cultivation of gift. *(Northern Echo)*

He leaves nothing to the imagination and tries to bludgeon rather than persuade you into accepting his point of view. But he has a point of view and something to say and insists on saying it in his own way . . . A keen, sensitive mind. . . . He hates old men, lewd women, lust, greed, – above all spiritual and intellectual denseness, and he lashes them with a command of language and imagery that are at any rate vigorous. *(The Writer)*

[His] hatred of old men dominates much of his poetry. . . . The roughness, the rather blatant virility of the earlier Kipling is recalled at times. . . . more important . . . as a promise than an accomplishment." *(Evening Sun,* Baltimore, 1 March 1924)

Vigor is his speciality, rather than restraint. [He] exhibits a healthy hatred of sham and hypocrisy in high places. . . . A more temperate outlook, a clarifying philosophy which will turn the turgid and terrible in life into more verisimilar shapes, will help this man of indubitable gifts to conserve them and convey them to his readers in a less revolting and wearying medium." *(The Illustrated Buffalo Express,* 2 March 1924)

Finally, in *Literaturberichte,* we find Karl Arns assessing Tomlinson in the following terms:

A humanely as well as poetically important speaker is belatedly being driven to stirring condemnations of war by his enlightened social conscience. From this powerful experience he has created poetical images which glow with the fire of his honest, youthful personality. He pulls the romantic mantle off war with ruthless candour . . . original and linguistically creative power, . . . his abundant inventive ability, his daring flights of fancy . . . occasionally his poetic display errs towards a fantasy that is hard to fathom . . . at times his meaning drowns in a flood of words.

Of the *Candour* war poems ' Sed Miles' stands apart from the rest. Here Tomlinson's satirical bite is all the more effective because he is in control of a much tighter, more condensed line.

Two of the unpublished poems, 'Men of the Line' and 'Their Friendship was Mine' should be considered together, since they share the same theme, expressed in similar language. The message of common experience and humanity that bond the poet intimately with his fellow-soldiers is expressed with unquestionable sincerity.

Two other poems, 'Ghost of the Somme' and 'Manslaughter Morning', are inspired by the same horrific incident witnessed in the trenches, and must also be set alongside each other (see the 'Eighth Close-up'). There is some shared language, but they are significantly different: 'Manslaughter Morning' is purely descriptive and narrative, whereas 'Ghost of the Somme' is more expressionistic, with its chilling addition of the supernatural element.

'The Strand, 1917' shows Tomlinson in ferociously puritanical vein, and the anti-Semitic sentiments he expresses make uncomfortable reading.

In his parody of Brooke, 'If I Should Die . . .', Tomlinson is determinedly set against heroic gestures and sentimental attitudes. Behind the burlesque there is a serious, honest, and down-to-earth standpoint .

His most effective war poems are those that lack the negative features, that is, the lumbering metre, the polysyllabic turgidity, the over-elaboration, the excessive alliteration, and the blustering tone. At his best, he imbues his work with an invigorating freshness and ruggedness.

Tomlinson's later published verse, for example the books of poems he wrote after the Second World War when he was living in Lowestoft, such as *Suffolk in Verse*, *Lowestoft Men*, and *Waveney Sonnets*, is markedly different from his earlier Great War poetry. The brashness, the satirical bent, the audacious metre and vocabulary, have all disappeared, to be replaced by a much more timid and traditional approach. Many of these poems were originally published in various East Anglian newspapers and magazines, and some were broadcast on BBC radio. The final two poems of the twenty that comprise *Waveney Sonnets* are Second World War poems, 'These who Fly', and 'Vapour Trail' (see Appendix C). It is hard to believe that they are by the same man who wrote such vitriolic poems as 'Sed Miles', 'Bellicosity', and 'The Strand, 1917'. 'These who Fly' is particularly insipid as a tribute to the R.A.F. 'Vapour Trail' is better, and does have one or two effective images that heighten the description: "a flask of smoking wine", and "a tin of scarlet dye". But what brought about this transformation? How was it that this gritty young man from the North with his pugnacious, risk-taking approach and readiness to take on the world, toned down so drastically, and became such a bland and conventional poet in his later years?

Sed Miles

All the best
Have long gone West;
The East is cursed
With all the worst;
In this, at least,
Our Farthest East
Is London Port,
A sick resort
Where all the blood
Of Mametz Wood,
And all the guts
Of Mesnil Buttes,
And that slight Hell
At Poelcapelle,
Are suet and duff
For a journalist puff;
And the whole damn War
Little more
Than "Latest News,"
And "Our Expert's Views."

It's often said
You're a long time dead,
And the grey worms eat,
Through the nails of your feet,
Through the white of your thighs,
To the whites of your eyes;
You feel pretty cheap
As a drab little heap
Of powder and smell;
For a Fritz gas-shell
Leaves more behind
In the way of rind.

But when West you go,
It's nice to know
You've done your bit
In spite of it;
And Blighty's name
And Blighty's fame
Will find in your
Demise, manure,
To sprout and spread

Till English red
Is the favourite hue
For Bartholomew,
And his maps all blush
With a porty flush,
And only Mars
And the minor stars
Are beyond the zone
Of the next War Loan;
When West you go,
It's nice to know
You've done your bit
In spite of it.

London, December 1916

The title is taken from Sir Henry Newbolt's poem, 'The Island Race, Clifton Chapel'.
Part of the poem reads:
> 'Qui procul hinc', the legend's writ,
> The frontier-grave is far away
> 'Qui ante diem periit:
> Sed miles, sed pro patria'. (Ed.)

Bellicosity

Babel of Bellicose Man;
Ancient fanfares of slaughter hubbubing the rotund earth;
Babel of statesmen and cretin, butcher and pulpiteer,
Whose din, catarrhic and gobbed with its phlegm of self and self-worth,
Lets three primary blarings persist from its formless blear.

Blare of the Patriot:
Downright as boiling of beef, and clean as his "Bedford cut";
A rosy rainbow of ribbons, a hygienic tad-polish norm,
Fond of brave meals and bad women, intolerably fond of good form,
Treating the baboonish nations to bayonets and twiddled gut.

Blare of the Pacifist:
A meatless, euclidean fool, flushed from his foozled clutch,
Clucks plush-covered peace to his hen-run, while Englishmen,
Clamouring like riderless stallions for goal, bung into touch
These that love all in the Cosmos, and spike Krupps with the nib of a pen.

Blare of the Scuppered:
A sob from the slain of all nations, the million passers-by
Who saw the empurpled placards roaring for war;
And stood from the mother's fender, and stepped out to die,
Shot down like a tenpenny rabbit, or gassed like an obsolete whore.

Babel of Bellicose Man:
But the hubbub lifts like a fog at the fresh-tapped hearths of dawn,
When the sad, bored voice of the Englishman thrashes in from the deep,
Scrubbed by the salt of his Englishry, pure from the covert and cheap,
Cleaning the world with his cleanness, English and gentleman born.

France and London, 1916

"Soldiers"
By a Pacifist

Drilled into Denseness;
Dressed by the drum in line, like grimacing cockshies at fairs,
Like dough, like Lot's old harridan, 'cept there's red in our veins;
Worked by the whistle like newsboys, or trams or tongue-lolling curs,
Till all we're worth is a clothful of suet and scrambled brains.

Gorged on to Glory;
They pad us like pythons with cow and vermilion carrion, and teach
Mess and the wet Canteen are the soldier's wings of Grace;
They suckle our heads with dumplings, and oil us with offal, till each
Swaggers the earth like its Maker, – with spots and a lavender face.

Cursed into Childishness;
In the Army a brain is an abscess, as proved by the Carmine Command;
Cursing is curing, and soldiers, like convicts or Borstal kids,
Must take their porridge and breeches, and God, of the Government brand;
And their spirits dry up like stale fish-heads to the size of baccy-spit quids.

Back to the Brute;
If famished, like fangs of the jungle, we'd rip the liver from Hell;
We'd bivouac in snow, if weary, or impartially doss with a whore;
If thwarted, then, heedless as apes, we'd spit on Death's beard, and tell
Brigadiers, and bastards, and sergeants, what soldiers are soldiers for.

Afterwards;
As the berg grinds free from the floe, all nations will break from the years;
These canaille in field-grey and khaki have had flair of the red as it runs.
With that tigrish stench in its sweetness, they'll stir, when the tiger stirs,
On the Ox-heads who drilled 'em like dogs, and squandered their lives to the
guns.

Richmond, April, 1918

from: Spring at a Discount

Do they smell the Spring in the shell-holes?
The officer's carcase had dropsy, and its chops were lichen-green;
His batman's had splashed on the point of a dud: the sergeant's trunk
Was concertinaed like wire, with its cheek in a Boche latrine
Spring is lush in the sumps where four years of charnel have stunk.

The tight stark riftings of six-inch guns are a genial tune!
But sarcasms blue on a bayonet have crusted the blues of the Chase;
And a gunshot's clotting of blood mimics the ploughland's maroon;
The seasoned hearts of the shell-holes, they are the Spring of the race.

Richmond, Spring 1918

To German Soldiers
I
Overture

As we curse not the car for the smash-up, but the lout at the lever controls;
So khakimen curse only quitters, and field-grey bears not their grudge;
As funkermen snot you with untruths, one fighterman voice shall troll
A salt-fresh rune, like a headland to square-face the funkermen's sludge.

II
Field-Grey Fightermen

As the Dutchman is bold for his hearth, as the Cossack and Kurd for rapine,
So the Grey glues its back to the block-house, though skewbanked and stalled,
Sharing the sport of the killermen, sharing the right of the line,
Swinging no lead nor miking when the roster of courage is called.

Electric beavers of boudoirs, and sumptuous lovers of saps;
The sob of the soddish minny arrests not your sedulous spade;
For you, from your mouldy shoon to the crop in your red-ringed caps,
Are merlin-pioneers and moles of the sand-bag shades.

III
Fightermen: Writermen

Home-press, foe-press, they're pimps and they're ponces of gamboge lies;
Their insults are stink, and their praises prussic for you in your rage
Of war, you fightermen in the fight, for you that despise
These fly-blown critics and liars, and the printed manure of their page.

Four years you've free-traded fatality, and paid to the perishing guns,
That spray such juice on the sandbags, cracking your skulls like cane;
Four, and your masters still slash you, you myriad surplus sons,
Like gads on the steaming river, like locust pests on the plain.
Four summers, from Liège to Langemarck, the field-grey has thriven on lead –
Four springs has the grey goose flown from Stornaway, North to the floes –
If Verdun's the vale of Gehenna, the Somme has seen one or two dead,
Khaki and Grey together, ripe carrion for killerman 'shows.'

As crump-hole differs from crump-hole, as mire may be softer than mire,
As the cut of their tunics won't help much when the men are maimed yet
    alive,
So killerman Grey and killerman Drab are oafs of one sire,
Settling problems of population with Mills, Number Five.

IV
Turning Worms

The bear that dreamed through the cyclone will waken to cyclone the pine:
So will you, though mute through War's mistral, blaspheme when they cry
    for calm;
Then the gun-trail shall turn in the trench, and the breech shall make mistrals
    to whine,
Lament for the masters who sounded the killermen's tattoo to arm,

They were flung like putrescence, or stalks, to the middened field.
Field-grey and field-khaki, field fellows, articled mates of the kill;
They shall turn that trade on their tyrants, and richmen shall richly yield
Offal and life for the killerman, craving their sustenant swill .

The curtain falls, but the killerman keeps to his chaos track;
Stampedes the land that bore him, tumults the towns of his birth;
Until ancestral dazzle-lace generals pay bloodily back
Youth to the young, love to the lovers, hope to the earth.

Richmond, Spring 1918

A Hero

My father, when I went to war,
Grasped me with a pudgy paw,
  "Good luck," he said, "My precious lad
  "See you do credit to your dad,
  "You're no age yet, you have the spunk,
  "I'd hate like Hell for you to funk.
  "If I could march I'd slope a gun
  "And help exterminate the Hun.

"If my legs were twenty-five years younger
"I'd ginger up the German Junger."

"Stout words, old dad, perhaps you're right
"Pity you're too old to fight,
"Pity you're not Peter Pan,
"Your belly's like a beer-can;
"There's backbone in your senile chatter,
"As much as in a pot of batter."

"My boy, your simile's cheap and wooden,
"Batter bakes us Yorkshire pudden,
"And that's the stuff to give you guts,
"And make you putt those ten-yard putts.
"I'd try to 'list' as under forty
"But the Bible says deceit is naughty.
"Ah would," he sighed, "this ghastly war
"Had come but thirty years before."
"I'm with you there, I quite agree
"That date would just have done for me
"And incidentally done for thee."
"Your wits are keen, I once suspected
"Your moral assets were neglected;
"You intellectuals make me quiver,
"You load the brain, but bleach the liver.
"But now you've got a blood-hound's chance
"To find your manhood out in France.
"What finer finish to education
"Than perishing for your pater's nation?
"Go, and hold it no effrontery
"To croak it for your king and country."

"Good-bye, dad, a thousand thanks
"For giving me to swell the ranks;
"Your magnanimity's no small dose,
 "You run old Abraham quite close;
"God will requite our sacrifice
"With expensive seats in paradise."

"Good-luck, my lad, should you perchance
"Return a trifle soiled from France
"I'm despatching you upon approval,
"So keep me primed with all the 'nouvelles'
"My welcome will be unreserved,
"I'll shake such limbs as you've preserved
"And find the job that you've deserved."

Off I went and saw the war
And thought it all a bloody bore;
I clawed and scratched for home and beauty,
And tramped some hundred miles for duty.
I cursed and dug and dropped a limb,
And leaked blood enough to dowse my glim.
My father almost wept an ocean,
But bore up, for I'd won promotion.

Discharged at length as no more use,
I felt like Portland broken loose;
I came back to a grateful land –
They tactlessly forgot the band –
My father seemed a bit put out
To see the hand I'd come without.
His welcome was at best reluctant,
Altruism's not a good inductant.

"I'll make allowance for your loss,
"In spirit, not in filthy dross,
"But times are bad, and living high,
"The government's like a giblet pie.
"You can't expect with one hand dud
"To run a blasted racing stud.
"Perhaps if I have any luck,
"I'll find a job to suit your book."

He found it; deep down in a bank,
A concession to my captain's rank,
And now with sixty bob a week,
I lack a limb but got my keep.
Besides I've got a decoration;

I'm grateful to my pater's nation.

Middlesbrough, January 1920

March Past

The Staff heard music in the marching fife,
The dancing drumstick and the blared bassoon,
And when the flare-lit raid ran rife
It made them music to the sickening moon;
And in the purring shells and spattering strife
They heard such lullabies as culvers croon.
And white-faced death for them made harmony.
They thought a howling wound as sweet as honey.
The Sergeant-major thought it dulcet glee

To ring with blasphemy the non-plussed ranks,
To bawl obstreperous on each company,
To slang a mumskull [sic] at his flatfoot pranks;
He almost packdrilled him to atrophy;
His inflamed glottis never needed thanks,
Mellifluous to him the obsequious 'Sir',
Let Smith omit it if he damnwell dare.

The Quartermaster heard a barcarolle
Loosed from the 'bully' in the bubbling pans,
He loved his rations like his very soul,
And always scrounged himself a double man's;
Lush melodies came from the cheese he stole,
The milk played concert in its rusted cans;
His tuneful tunic drummed itself undone,
His apoplectic paunch was like a tun.

And Smith and others of the best platoon
Drank muddier beer though themselves were muddy,
And in estaminets heard a jocund tune
Rippling from lips a trifle over-ruddy;
And Mac said, 'Mon, isn't this reet boon?'
And Smith said, 'Norarf, why man, it's bloody.'
Such scherzos heard there they'd dance and laugh,
Belched from some tin-tuppenny flat phonograph.

And you and I sang duet in that score,
Arcadians both, though lackeys to the guns,
Faring unlovely through the lanes of war;
For once we heard up by the Menin Door
A cracked accordion of the entrenched Huns,
And held it as eery as the play Coq d'Or.
And once we heard an ousel sing at Loos,
 Like some pure girl entrapped in that carouse.

Men of the Line

Men of the line, their friendship is mine,
Friendship forced on rats in a trench,
The day has no night, night has no song
Save a handful of earth and a skinful of stench!

Men of the line whose friendship is mine,
The trench is our High Street, our town and our bed,
Through a periscope paradise staring at death.
Friendship is there though no word is said.

Ours is the friendship of suffering and laughter,
Some laugh, some weep with vultured breath,
Unsellable souls that pass through the sales ring,
Sugar meat of battle in shops of death.

The clarion of cash is not one they answer,
 For a franc per fool they hold on to the line,
These very civilian soldiers of quality –
Their ditch I share and their friendship is mine.

Their's is the hell and their's is the heritage,
These manhole midgets of modern war,
The slain are their's and also the slaughter,
Spare pity-dust then for the burden they bear.

Forget them not as forgotten these others,
The picked men of peace, the ditch-troops of trade,
Generations of peace have to be paid for,
This is one generation that paid!

What can life give to make it worth buying?
Only the courage to lose at call
Like dogs in a ditch they gave without whining
The answer of men to the last call of all.

Men of the line and the lean strength within them,
A pennorth of ploughman, a haporth of clerk,
Their friendship is mine, dear God, and the answer
That mouths without platforms give to the dark!

Manslaughter Morning

On Manslaughter Morning in Massacre Wood
I see a sentry shoot his best friend's face away,
Cleaning his rifle at dawn stand-down.

They take him away with a sort of kind contempt,
A death among deathless deaths, a name among nameless names
Duly reported to the ginger-haired captain.

In the Battle of the Somme
I see thirty khaki citizens
Carrying sandbags full of hand-bombs
Slung over khaki shoulders.
Resting on a green bank,
One citizen drops his bag carelessly
To rest on foreign clay.

The explosion blows his back out,
The small of his back out,
The small of his back and webbing and khaki!
I see his inside
Like an operating table model,
For he is dead but not quite dead,
And his limbs ache with war!
At midnight in murder time
Along Looney Bin Lane,
The Line is lousy with loose metal!
Sandbags quake, men cower and from world's outer end
Stumbles a figure, eyeless for ever!

Helmet-less, he tries to hold his face shreds
With both blind hands!
More terrible than multitudes howling
Is his last blind silence!
From fingers pressed against blood,
Blood comes pouring down his wrist,
Drenching boots, puttees, tunic;
Still dabbling at the petalled mask, once a man's face,
And stretched on the long duckboards,
He groans his last,
Fingers clenching and unclenching
Like a pleased cat!

Ghost of the Somme

A khaki phantom passed along the trench
No one touched it, no one heard its step,
And yet it reeled along a duckboard track
Filled with widening eyes!

Was it a fiend from Hell
Come to join the Hell already there?
That Hell already there,
That Hell where trenches run like trains
Under a hail of red-hot steel
While crowded figures crouch
Waiting for steel to smash
The warrens of their watch!

At midnight in Looney Bin Lane
The line is lousy with loose steel
From bumping trench mortars!
Sandbags quake, men cower, and from world's other end

Stumbles this figure, eyeless for ever!
The sulphur stink, the black fumes, the blotted stars
And a handful of shrapnel have left it unseeing!

Helmetless, the phantom holds its face
In two blind hands;
More terrible than the howling of multitudes
Is its strange blind silence!
From phantom fingers pressed against spectral face
Blood seems pouring down wrists,
Down dripping tunic, boots, puttees,
Yet no one hears its steps!

Reeling against the clay, it falls to earth
Still dabbling at the bloody mask,
The ghostly face!
Stretched on the long duckboards,
It seems to groan its last,
Fingers clenching and unclenching
Like a pleased cat!

We move to help it,
But we find nothing there,
No dying flesh, no drying blood, no carcase and no trace,
No evidence of what we've seen
No witness of its death!
Not only soul but flesh and bones have fled
In agony to face
The blandishments of Hell!

Their Friendship Was Mine

Who shall I praise for the days of my warring?
Who shall I thank for the friends at my side?
For there may be a god or there may be an ending,
But these men were men who fought there and died.

Their's was the friendship of glorious laughter;
They laughed at their wounds with their dying breath,
The pomp of the world and its prizes they laughed at,
Laughing at life as they laughed at death.

Their's was the flame and their's was the heritage,
Their's was the excellent scourging of war;
The slain were their's and also the slaughter,
Honour them, then, for the burden they bore.

Honour them not as ye honour those others,
The successes of peace, the stalwarts of trade;
Generations of peace have to be paid for,
Their's was the generation that paid.

Not for a coin nor yet for possessions
Those fools kept their compact up there in the line;
Their own self-respect was the whole of their profit,
Their folly I shared and their friendship was mine.

What is there in life that makes it worth keeping?
Only the courage to lose it at call,
Only the thought that you gave without whining
The answer of men to the last call of all.

To them came the call of the world in its warring,
Workman and farmer, shopman and clerk,
Their friendship was mine as they marched with their answer
From life in its sweetness into the dark.

The Strand, 1917

Theatre time.
A coralling of colts, of steers and of stallions,
Of youths in khaki and in chase of women;
Of women in little save the fragmentary,
Provocative dress of their trade.

And sprowling, Mediterranean-blue policemen to look after them.

Taxi-cabs, nettled because they are not permitted
On the pavement to knock people over;
To satisfy the bloodlust of machines.

Promiscuous strollers without collars or confidence,
Mingling with more vicious, more expensive,
Siphylis-dodging sharks; well-to-do,
Assertive sharks in white shirt-fronts.

Hebrews everywhere, like blackheads on the face of man;
Of a man who has overworked his nerves and blood
Into unhealthiness.

Hens of Jerusalem, too,
Gathered under the wings
Of the transcontinental ponces' board.

Humans massing for rubbing of backs and souls together;
For fear of balancing their odds in loneliness,
And recalling in solitude
The Ice which shall end Things.

A liquorous, lecherous pervadement of stench;
Body-stench, with a frangi-pani dash.
Like a verdigrised, rancid slice of lemon
In a beaker of very native-born fire water.
Small light, few lamps,
And a little obscured laughter,
Because there is a War.
And it behoves robust patriots
To remember the boys out There.

Midnight.

An unhealthy, devastating calm,
Where was unhealthy congestion.
And a discharging, vehicular stench,
Surviving fitly the folk-stench;
A silence more unnaturally, incestuously foul
Because of the furore that was.

And moonlight.
In sluicing Augean travail
To make Filth impossibly clean;
To render adulteries pure.

There are some drunken drabs, and sailors,
And reeling bow-legged men.
Unfits, indispensables,
Aliens and tipsy foreigners.
A shriek or so;
A warm wave of tittering
For the stomach's sake;
But patriotically subdued.

In camel-dung coloured uniforms,
Colonials with absurd hats.
The moon glares wildly on all,
Then, giving up her job
In a cloud of disgust,
Says, "Thank God, I am useful to guide
A few big bombs to this opened drain."

Dawn. Policemen and smells,
And one or two adornments
Of fish-heads still linger;
Some medals of orange-peel,
And ribbons from skinned bananas.
Soot-fungused walls, which once were white,
Grimace in the zinc-ointment light of the moon.

Disreputable heroes in stone
Gaze, rather woebegonely blue
About the eyelids,
On the remobilising traffic.
A red mail-van rumbles and grumbles by.
A sort of bleached, apologetic breeze
Tries to forbid the banns of daybreak and decay.
And, very soon, the latest news
Of a week-old trench-raid is on the streets.

The casualty list to follow.

If I Should Die . . .

If I should die just bury my flesh in any hole that lets an angel through,
On any shore that loves a stormy sea,
Down any street that isn't paved with gold,
In any land where no one ever comes,
In any wilderness where flesh can hide,
On any mountain that will make amends
For all the sunsets I have never seen!

If I should die just bury my flesh in any town of unassuming people,
In any land that makes an honest fuss,
In any box that's labelled with my name,
In any country waving any flag,
Or else in any cheering fatherland
That asks no loyalty of death but death!

If I should die just bury my flesh
In any forest that is full of leaves,
In any heaven that is full of shine,
In any shingle that is full of stars,
In any vineyard that is full of wrath,
In any firing-line my friends have filled
With long-dead lies that sent us to the fight!

Part III
LETTERS FROM THE FRONT
Introduction

Sixty-five of the eighty-seven surviving letters written by Tomlinson to his parents are included in this selection. Letters I-VII cover the period from April to June 1916, while letters VIII-LXV cover the period from late August 1917 to early January 1918. Thus the latter group of eighty letters (of which fifty-eight are given here) represents a remarkably sustained sequence of correspondence which works out at roughly a letter every other day.

The 1916 letters are addressed 'Dear Mother' or 'Dear People', while most of the 1917-1918 letters are addressed to 'Dear Mater', with just two addressed 'Dear Pater'.

Many of the letters are reproduced whole. From the rest I have removed the more repetitious parts, as well as certain references to and gossip about relations and friends which are obscure and add little or nothing to our understanding of Tomlinson's personality or of aspects of the War. I have, however, left in some of the repetitions regarding food parcels, the arrival and non-arrival of mail, and requests for tobacco and other items, as these were of great importance to all men who found themselves in the deprived circumstances of Front Line life. The regular receipt of letters, newspapers and little luxuries from home was crucial to the troops' morale.

From the letters we gain insights into Tomlinson's character, into his opinions about the War, and into his relationships with various members of his family. He is clearly closer to his mother than to his father. There are frequent reproving remarks about his father's apparent drink problem. His sister, May, is regularly criticised for what Tomlinson regards as her flippant and irresponsible attitude to life. For example, she is a long time responding to his demands that she undertake some useful War work. Also her obsession with buying an expensive fur-coat further irritates Tomlinson. He pokes fun at his brother Li[onel] for falling, as he sees it, into the trap of marriage. The letters contain his comments on the progress of the War, the way it is reported in the British press, and the attitude of civilians towards it. He writes about the varying degrees of comfort and discomfort that soldiers encountered in the trenches, in rest billets, at base camps, and on training courses. The problems of personal hygiene in harsh circumstances are alluded to: infrequent baths, and the constant battle against lice infestation. On a more mundane level, Tomlinson asks affectionately about Phil, the family dog, and inquires anxiously about the state of his bank balance.

He makes a number of interesting comments and comparisons relating to Belgium and France: the peasants, their farms, their way of life, the girls, and the landscape. This latter topic inevitably calls forth nostalgic memories of the landscape of North Yorkshire.

In letter XX there is a particularly fine description of the war-torn landscape of the Western Front. Tomlinson was especially susceptible to night scenes, and there are many descriptions of moonlit landscapes in France and Belgium.

There are a couple of brief references to Cambridge which give intriguing insights into his personality (XLVI and LIII). In the former he equates his social inferiority with his lack of inches; in the latter he displays his anti-clericalism. But Tomlinson reserves his harshest scorn for the notorious Horatio Bottomley whom he pillories in no fewer than eight letters (XVIII, XXV, XXVII, XXIX, XXX, XLI, XLVI and LXI). Other leading public figures of the day (political, military and literary) receive brief mentions: the Prince of Wales, Haig, Asquith, Siegfried Sassoon, Bertrand Russell, C.K. Ogden, and Lord Lansdowne.

Tomlinson writes many times about the possibility of a 'blighty' that is, a not too serious wound that would ensure his being sent back home to recover. His attitude towards this possibility is ambivalent. Sometimes he appears to wish devoutly for one, at others to regard it with apprehension. In letters XL and L he hints at his post-war ambitions.

In this revealing series of letters Tomlinson comes over as a complex individual: puritanical, censorious, sensitive to the beauties of nature, a mother's boy, a laconic fatalist, self-deprecating as regards his military role, but with a sense of self-worth as regards his future literary mission in life.

I

Wednesday April 12th [1916]

Dear Mother,

Thanks most muchly for the parcel, the first half of which I received this morning. The cake is splendiferous, and was greeted with great acclamation in the mess. The second half of the parcel has not arrived as yet. The cake you sent is far better appreciated than any of Buzzard's, or any other tropical bird of Oxford Street reputation. The chocolates also served to relieve the tedium of d[amned] long night watches. The magazine also is very welcome. Keep up the supplies and write plenty of letters. I get more letters than anyone, pretty well, and I am jolly glad of them. May's are most refreshing, and I hope she is growing slimmer and more presentable, and has passed her music exam with flying fingers. The Osbourne cigs arrived and the mess voted them excellent – could do with some more of them.

We are at rest now for eight days, and the weather has developed rather moistly. However, better be in billets for wet weather than in the trenches. We don't expect to stop in this quiet spot more than a month, but will be moved either to Wipers or Verdun shortly. That's when my blighty will arrive.

We had 'some dinner' last night: hors d'oeuvres, including olives, pâté de foie, sardines, and potato salad, six courses, fish cakes, omelette, caviare, and loads of whisky – quite a celebration. By the way, I hope you shoved that £5 in the bank for me this month. By the way, while I remember, what the blazes do you think I am going to do with a brown loaf, which May says she has included? I shall stand on the parapet and hurl it at the Hun, and see if it bursts.

You ask me how far I am from the Base. Well, there are about six bases, and I don't know which one you mean: St. Omer, Rouen, Boulogne, Etaples. You can find them all on the map, and then spot where I am. I hope the Zepps haven't been successful as yet. By the way, the local rag is much more valuable to me than the 'Maily Dail'; for instance, I received Friday's *Mail* this morning, whilst I was reading the *Morning Post* for yesterday, Tuesday. I received a letter from Ogden[1] rather late, but unfortunately he doesn't know any of the Birmingham Repertory people to whom I wanted an introduction.

There has been Hell's own strafe up towards St. Eloi[2] two or three times last week, lasts for 10 or 12 hours at a time. Boom, boom, boom, poor devils. I don't get any leave till June, and all leave is going to be stopped shortly.

There is not much sign of the war finishing up this way. The Boche has superiority over us as regards rifle fire, and our men get strafed like Hell if they put a single shot over, whilst the Boche blazes away as much as he likes, and just does what the devil he likes. Our battalion are not very great, except for D Coy who are the boys! In fact, the lads! I was up in the Mushroom all Monday night as I had been lent to another Coy. I had some fun doing fancy sniping, but the Boche is too d[amned] clever, and a splendid shot. He can split the top sandbag every time.

Hope you have a good time at Harrogate. The Great Push will be just about to commence then.

Write every other day.

Love,
    Bert

II

Thursday April 13th [1916]

Dear People,
Have not received the second parcel yet, but am writing for you to send on my spare pair of khaki breeches. My present ones are going at the rub. Send them off as soon as poss. You might also send one of Mrs. Gilbert's masks, if she would be good enough to send one. In any case, she would give you the pattern, and you might make one or two. I may be going to get the job of Company Bombing Officer, and have to do some raiding stunts. Send me a writing pad and envelopes, and a new silk knitted light khaki tie. Also a 3" broad piece of silk – black – for cutting out dabs for sewing on our tunics. We wear 2" circular dabs for the Stafford badge, so get some nice black silk and send it on.

There is no fresh news, except that the Hun has brought up some heavy gunnery opposite us, 12", I believe, same as they got at West Hartlepool.[1] We will see them next time we go up, next Wednesday. The post hasn't come today, so the parcel may be in it when it arrives. We are going to the baths this afternoon in the brewery.

There are signs of the Great Push coming off. Leave is stopped from April 18th, and the C.O. talks of sanguinary encounters to come. Wish to blazes it would come, and we could get the whole jolly business finished, one way or another. I have ordered the revolver you speak of, a Colt. Have to go on a fatigue tonight at 10 pm up the line. Life's a bore. We are going to have 'some dinner' tonight: chickens and whatnot. Will write again when the parcel arrives. Hope May has passed the music. Tell her to tell me all about the pictures and the snofficers [sic], and Doris. Glad to hear about the motor tour. Has anyone bought my bike yet? Put another advert in.

Love from Bert

III

Sunday April 16th [1916]

Dear People,

Have just been to Church Parade, and have all the rest of the morning for letter writing. The parson, or 'padre', as they call them out here, tells us they are going to administer communion in the trenches to everyone next Sunday. Some idea! I expect the Boche will walk across to join in. It is a glorious sunny day, and I am writing this on the window-sill of our billets. Lark song in the warmth. I expect you will be at Harrogate by the time you get this. Hope you have good weather and a Happy Christmas, or is it Easter? I don't think I should prefer to be with you all the same. After all, most of the good boys are out here with us, and think this is the best place till the rotten war is finished. Father wants to know what Division we are in: we are 17th Division, Gilbert's old Division, under General Pilcher.[1] There is no need to put this in the address. In fact I don't know whether we are supposed to reveal the fact or not. We are 2nd Corps of the 2nd Army. All leave has been stopped and everyone has to be back by April 18th. I don't know if this means anything or not. I have got myself a good revolver and plenty of ammunition, so feel ready for the fray. I go on a three days course in trench warfare tomorrow, and later I believe I go on a bombing course.

I received both parcels correct, and the Osbourne cigarettes. I don't know why you sent bread and butter – I'm not a bombardier or a lonely tommy. If we get into a bad part of the line where supplies are absolutely unprocurable I will let you know. Meanwhile you might send a pencil-holder with refill, and a shaving-stick, and some thin socks, and a pair of suspenders. Send one of those shaving-sticks that you rub on the face, and then use the brush. Both the cakes were much appreciated and disappeared forthwith. You may repeat with an iced one every three weeks or so. Set your friends on, and give them the address. I can get my cigarettes out here, and should prefer the money in the bank, say £5 a month. Don't send ordinary plain sweets, I can get those here, but nut-milk slabs, or marzipans, or so forth.

Father would be delighted with D Coy. mess, as we have the reputation of pushing drinks down the necks of anyone who has the temerity to enter. We had Hell's own champagne dinner on Wednesday. I went to bed slightly foxed at 11 o'clock, and had to get up at 12 to take a working party up the line and stop there in the rain until 7 am. I had some thick head, I can tell you. Our billets are four miles behind the front line, and when I say going up the line, I mean going from billets to the trenches. There is not much difference between the front trenches and the support trenches, in fact, the first are safer if anything. I had my first two casualties yesterday, both very slight from shrapnel. I don't like shrapnel. You can't hear it coming like H.E. By the way, you need never be anxious about not hearing from me, because if I were wounded or otherwise, the War Office would let you know within 48 hours, much quicker than I could.

Well, bye-bye and love, Bert

IV

Sun. Apr 30th [1916]

Dear People,

I am afraid it is more than a week since I dropped you a line but have been very busy up the trenches. I have received no parcels lately, except the breeches which I believe I acknowledged. I gave the tobacco to two of my men, and could do with some more for distribution. The weather here has been glorious for a week past; the sun is burning hot now. I am writing this in the garden behind the house we are billeted in, and the pear-trees along the wall are all in blossom. There are two little terrier pups sprawling on the lawn, and the birds are singing away in a big chestnut tree and brown butterflies are fluttering amongst the shrubs, and everything in the garden is splendid. We are in rest again, and I am going on a bomb course today for eight days, which means I shall miss our next tour in the firing-line. I was out on a patrol to the German wire last Monday night – some excitement and got it – wet through sprawling in the mud when the shell went up – the star-shells I mean. We had a man's head blown off accidentally by a silly ass who was cleaning his rifle. I was first in the bay after the accident, and it was some sight, I assure you – a bay is part of the trench where they fire from, as per diagram:

We expect to have more patrols next time up, and we are determined to bag a Hun this time.

Things don't seem too bright at home – what with Ireland[1] and Asquith[2] and what not. There's no sign of victory out here. The Hun sends over 20 shells to our one, and shows himself d[amned] smart and efficient all round. I think the issue is pretty well in the balance, and a piece of luck will decide it either for us or for them. I see absolutely no sign of that tremendous superiority the papers talk about. In fact our men would be d[amned] glad to be well out of it – which is not the spirit which wins wars. I'm afraid England hasn't sufficiently felt the pinch yet; and she won't wake up till she does. Has the old man's whisky supply been curtailed yet? – oh yes, I think not!

I suppose England must be glorious just now with Spring in full growth, and all the woods and gardens bursting with life – there are one or two woods out here bursting with death – I think I shall spend my leave, when I get it, on the river at Cambridge. I don't see any signs of the great Spring push yet – another newspaper legend, I think. Everybody here expects the war to go through another winter at least. Splendid!

I have just changed my billets, and two of us have a huge old house to ourselves, with a long rambling garden at the back with apricots, and palms, and magnolias, and big trees and a lawn like a meadow. I shall be here for a week while I am on a bombing course, so that I shall not go to the trenches till next Sunday again.

I should like you to make me two or three sleeping-caps of silk or something light and airy, not for warmth but just to keep my head from the rough of the sandbags, and to keep the flies off. Make a kind of bag with space left empty for nose and mouth. I had a run on a motor ambulance to Bailleul and back yesterday and quite enjoyed the little trip. By the way, my new billets have a lovely shower bath – no hot water, of course. Four things we miss out here – lights, hot water, water-closets and pure drinking-water. I haven't had a drink of simple pure water since I came out – daren't do it, too much enteric about. It's beginning to get dark out in the garden here, so shall have to go inside to finish the letter. There is a crowd of little French girls laughing and jabbering round the swing at the other end – there's an aeroplane up and the Archibalds[3] are trying for him. Those d[amned] trenches are a Hell of a strain, and you don't notice it until you get out of them and sit in a quiet garden like this again.

Have just finished dinner and am finishing this letter before going to bed – full of white wine.

The Boche bombarded our rest billets last night and a man brought the end of a six-inch into the café this morning that had gone clean through his bedroom. I wish to H[ell] your female labour in the shell-shops would send us out an adequate supply of metal, as the Boche seems to be the only one who is throwing his metal about at present. I believe all our stuff goes to Russia or Verdun or the Shetland Isles. It doesn't seem to come out here.

By the way, what a coincidence! I built a strong dug-out last tour in the trenches, and the girders we used were marked Dorman, Long & Co., Middlesbro – 6 in. channels – splendid!

Almost got the next train home to see about it. Has the old man been sacked yet, or had an increase in salary or been awarded the DSO or the VSO, or what-not? Bye-bye.

Love from Bert

V

Wed. June 8th [1916]

Dear People,

I was inoculated again yesterday and so get 48 hours rest. At present I am in bed waiting for the post and morning papers to come. The Navy seems to have done its share again very gallantly. 330 officers in the Roll.[1] It must be the depths of inferno to be shelled on a ship without shelter and no hope of dodging or getting under the duckboards. They tell me a good many go raving mad in a naval battle. When you've heard one or two 'heavies' slip purring overhead you'll compree why.

I received the cakes and vaseline all intact and still uncommingled. I think I've got about enough of the latter to last some time now. Thanks very much. The cherry cake was bon. I ate about half of it at one sitting.

The weather has broken for a time and we have marched to the training ground two days in the pouring rain only to be dismissed and sent back to the billets thoroughly drenched and delighted. I was in town on Sunday – quite a decent place with one or two good restaurants, pretty girls and scores of soldiery, and a park and pierrots. It's the first touch of civilisation since leaving England. As I wrote before, I expect my leave at the end of August, which is still a little distant. I have been out here three months now and am beginning to be quite acclimatised. I don't know when we'll move from this deserted village, but we can't be long before we move into the shocks and shells again. The rumour is that we are for Salonika, which would mean a sea voyage at any rate, but it's a very wild rumour, I'm afraid. By the way, you ought to know what Division we are, as I told father weeks ago. It's Gilbert's old Division, the 17th; Harry is with the 24th now, in the 1st Army, I believe. The first question you ask about a man at the front is his Division, and then you can generally fix his whereabouts, if you're not a layman. By the way, I don't think there would be much of young Clive Pickering left if a shell had struck his petrol tank!!! A piece of shell may have done so. You don't seem to have more than elementary ideas of what all the stuff in the newspapers really means. Exercise your imagination a bit. A bullet in his petrol tank would be enough to blow him up, never mind a shell!

I am sending back my woolly, and a scarf, and my watch, and a nosecap from our trenches. The shell to which the nosecap belonged knocked down three or four yards of parapet near my dug-out, a cement machine-gun emplacement, disused. The stamping die I found in a wrecked railway station at A------.[2] It will do for a souvenir. The shell above-mentioned is only an ordinary 3" whizz-bang thing. We are not supposed to notice in the ordinary course.

I want you to have my watch mended and re-forwarded. You might send me another thin long cigarette-case like the one I took away with me. I want another pad, pencils, and a dozen or so rubber bands. You might include a copy or so of the *New Statesman* in the next bundle of papers. The leather cigarette-cases are no bon, as the contents always get squashed.

I suppose you are saving money fast now that the old man is on the water-cart.

Well, cheeryo
Love to all,
Bert

VI

Officers' Mess, Army Cyclists' Base Depot, B.E.F.
Sunday [undated]

Dear Mater,

I am able to give you an address at last where you can drop me a line and anything else you fancy. I expect to be here a few days at least. Send me plenty of Gazettes and some Yorkshire Evening Posts. Tell Father to get me a writing-pad like the last one he sent out here, and send me a bundle of envelopes, and some plain p.c's. We are not allowed to send picture p.c's at all now. Don't forget to put my rank and regiment in my address. I don't know if the censor will let this pass, but I am at Rouen. It is quite the least dirty and the best-arranged French town I have been at as yet. The French are about the filthiest, unsanitary race that ever raced, I should imagine. The base camp here is very comfy, and the mess clean and good. There are plenty of young 'oomans' parading around, And as today is Sunday, I expect the town will be particularly gay. I hear there is quite a decent Officers' Club in Rouen, so shall go down and have tea there if I can get out of camp. The next parade to the Cyclists' Depot is full of Indians from the Lahore Infantry slouching around in twirled turbans and coffee-hued faces.

The weather is gorgeously warm and the sun shining as hard as he can go. There are plenty of flowers and orchards here, but the milk in mess is like warm water with a little precipitated chalk in it and the butter is about eight months gone. Thirty officers have just gone up the line from here so I don't suppose I shall stay long. Well, all the sooner for a nice 'blighty' and back to Angleterre.

I have just been on Church Parade, and had to read the lessons for the padre. Strikes me soldiering is an odd job kind of game. I don't think I have lost any more kit yet this trip. I forgot to bring my running breeks away with me, that I left in the wash. I had a lovely bath last night, after going 48 hours without even taking my big boots off. My calves and feet were quite swollen and sore. However, I hope I shall be able to get one or two night's decent sleep now before trotting up the line.

There is only one post a day and I shall have to hurry if I am going to catch it. Has May got her post in the office yet? I wish she would get fixed up. It would make a woman of her. There are hundreds of girls over here, and they look very smart in their brown uniforms and slouch hats. There are scores of V.A.D's[1] too, and there is generally a concert or something to go to evening-time. There are plenty of cafés and picture-shows too, in the Town. I wish I were back in the hospital there with just a nice little chunk out of the calf of my leg or something of that kind. I'm very fed with this darn war and army business, and think it about time someone developed a little common-or-garden sense.

My servant here is called Jones – can't get away from the name – and he lives on the banks of Ullswater when he's not in the army. He tried to give me a sleepless night last night by telling me terrible yarns about the number of officers he has held in his arms to die, with minute details as to the dimensions and sites of the holes in them. I kicked him out in the end, and told him my name wasn't Job. However, we shall see what we shall see.

Well, all love and the best of it,

From Bert

VII

Army Cyclists' Base Depot, B.E.F.
Monday [undated]

Dear Mater,

Just a line after breakfast, in time to catch the post. I was in the city all yesterday and had quite a good time. We went to a couple of picture-shows, and had our grub at the officers' Club. There are quite a number of English girls out here on different odd jobs – waitresses at the Officers' Club and so forth. They belong to the W.A.A.C. – Women's Army Auxiliary Corps and seem to hit it well with the Tommies. There's a rich conglomeration of nationalities and uniforms in this spot, and the scene along the boulevard on the quayside is picturesque enough – French, British, Belgians, Americans, Australians, Canadians, Portuguese, Hindoos, and Boche prisoners too. The French girls here are quite showy and decently dressed – compared with the old hags in the villages. We have all the street-lamps and harbour-lights going full strength at night, and the funny fat French tram-cars with blazing lights clattering down the streets and over the bridges, so that the city seems very giddy after the night-time obscurities of Linthorpe Road.

I will write again tomorrow. I expect to get moved to my own base in the North soon – where I took the draft.

Best love to all,

Bert

VIII

9th I.B.D.,
A.P.O. 24 Sect.,
B.E.F. France,
Wednesday 29 August, 1917

Dear Mater,

I have arrived up at our own base after eighteen hours in the slowest possible species of train. The camp is flooded, and as the gale has blown all the tents down and scattered their contents over France, we begin to think there must be a war on somewhere. However, as the Tommy said when the Boche were strafing his Company to Hades, "Thank God we're winning. I don't know what they'd be sending over if we weren't" – a remark not without humour to those who understand. I expect I shall be here several days, so hurry up and send some letters and papers and so forth. I think Father might as well send that mild looking Swedish knife. I would have brought it with me if I had remembered. I had a very good lunch in the town, then came on out to camp about four miles away. I think I shall go into town now I have reported. Life out here is much brisker than the mouldy old goings-on at home, and one meets a far manlier type of people altogether, so I am not fed up, yet I expect I shall be when I get into the middle of one or two good strafes.

Can you send me some of our apples and a box or so of dates? I hear the 8th S[outh] S[taffs] are away in the south, so I shall I have more travelling before I come up with them. However, thank God we are winning. How is the dog? Don't forget to send her to the vet for three weeks as soon as her time comes on.

I'm glad I managed that week at home before leaving, as it is something to look back on. That was a nice little walk we had on the Sunday night, and do you remember what a tremendous, lurid sunset there was, how rosy and fresh the hills looked?

We came through some lovely orchard country yesterday, with whole forests on every side, but it didn't come up to the hills and the heather to my mind. Don't worry about me. I expect I shall be alright, if they stop the war soon enough.

Best love to all, Bert

IX

9th IBD,
APO Sect. 24
BEF France,
Thursday, August 30th 1917

Dear Mater,

I suppose it will be a week or so before I hear from you, but I shall try to drop you a card or a letter every morning.

I was in the town most of yesterday, and had a good look round in the rain. The chief attraction there is a tip-top café, with very good chefs and a menu that would beat anything in the West End. I was there to lunch, and then an Engineer Captain took me there to dinner, and we tried to glide off with two French nurses, but it was no go owing to fierce competition from about forty other officers.

Peaches are very plentiful out here, and you can get great fat ones for a penny or tuppence apiece. We do manage to get fairly white bread, too. French pastry shops don't seem to take much notice of any sugar scarcity.

I had to sleep in my togs again last night owing to my valise not turning up to time, and I haven't had a wash or shave for a couple of days. However, it will be worse than that before very long, so no need to waste time grumbling now. I think I shall go to a picture-show this evening. I was through the trial gas-chamber this morning, but couldn't manage to get a Blighty. Well, best love for the present.

Yours ever,

Bert

X

9th I.B.D.
Monday Sept. 3rd, 1917

Dear Mater,

We had an air-raid last night, with usual paraphernalia. The Prince of Wales was in the café to dinner, so we had quite an exciting evening. The 'cocher' got the wind up and wouldn't take us to camp, so we had to walk it – about four miles. It was a gorgeous moonlit night, and the air-raid added a little spice to the walk. The tents in camp looked lovely in the moonlight, all ghostly and starch-white and silent. Camp always looks best and most romantic in the evening at sunset or at night, with the lights wavering behind the shut canvas. It is a splendid day now, full sun and a mild breeze, and the camp begins to grow a little less wet.

I'm afraid the Ypres business is napoo, however, as the weather is so frightfully bad and luck hasn't gone our way. However, I can tell you more about that when I see you in person, as one must not discuss military mush in private letters

I shall go to the Camp Cinema after tea – something to while away the weariness of things. There is nothing to do but read, read, read. How is May getting on? I must drop her a line. She will be wanting her fur-coat soon, I suppose. I think she would do better to get one from London, though you know best. How's the dog? Any stouter yet?

I suppose you are pretty busy with the Red X nowadays – something to keep you going – to say nothing of the worries of your young family. A Belgian aeroplane has just gone about two feet above the top of my tent-pole, making a terrible clatter. I don't think they think it's safe to fly any higher.

Well, I will get across to tea.

All love,

Bert

XI

Wednesday Sept. 5th 1917

Dear Mater,

I am writing this just before I turn in for the night. I have arrived at divisional headquarters and will probably not go up to the battalion for seven or eight days. We are about ten or twelve miles from the line, so no need to worry yet about shells and whatnot.

We had a regular game on Monday night with the air-raiders. The blighters kept coming over in relays about every three-quarters of an hour from 9.0 till 2.0 We were about fed to the teeth with them before they finished. We are in a very out of the way village at present – about three mud farms and an ancient church. If you address letters to the battalion I shall get them safely enough in a few days. I don't think I have lost any kit yet, but can't hope to keep the record up.

It is a gorgeous night again, a splendid saffron moon just coming up over the Eastern slopes. The sunset was mellow and cool, and full of calm and unwarlikeness. We had a very hot day today, though, much hotter than you would get it in England. The orchards here are full of little bright red apples and plums and grapes, and country as pretty as paradise.

All love to all,
From Bert

XII

Thursday Sept. 6th 1917

Dear Mater,

We have had a very funny day today. All the morning was gorgeously hot and summery, then about four o'clock we had a terrific thunderstorm which turned the camp into a very quagmire. The lightning was striking just over the tops of our tents, and what with the thunder, and the groaning of the heavies about five miles away, the uproar was satanic. The guns are at it all night and half the day too.

We are nice and snug about five miles the right side, and can afford to laugh up our sleeves. The trial is yet to come. However, it's a good death and there is not so much in life to cling on for after all. An overdose of work, an overdose of whisky, or an overdose of lead-poisoning isn't much of a choice, and I don't think the last is the worst of the three.

I think I should manage to last the winter out here safely, as it is not probable there will be much doing after the end of September. They seem to be having a merry time round Lens,[1] judging by the noise. They did some dirty work at Chatham[2] didn't they? They are not content with mere civilians nowadays.

Well, keep well and hope for the best. What about May's coat? Have had no letters yet.

All love,
Bert

XIII

Saturday, Sept. 8th 1917

Dear Mater,

We had night-training last night, so am knocking off just a line before we go on parade this morning. It was a very hot day again yesterday, but as there is not a great deal to do here that did not trouble us much. We get delicious peaches from the village and keep ourselves cool with their juices. Fruit is very plentiful out here, though the French people bleed us for it.

The village here is a pretty little place, but full of strange smells, of course, like every other place in France. The soil is very fertile and the crops and orchards do splendidly, but the farming of the land is painfully slipshod and a go-as-you-please kind of business.

I think I shall try to get into the nearest town today, but it's rather a long way off and I may not manage it. I must get on parade now, so will write you more fully tomorrow, when I shall be orderly-officer.

All love to all at home,

From Bert

XIV

Sunday Sept. 9th, 1917

Dear Mater,

In spite of the failure of correspondence from home – I haven't managed to get anything through yet – I keep up a daily epistle with commendable regularity. I am orderly officer today, so have plenty of time to catch the post, but usually I have to knock you off a line or two in a terrible hurry. I wanted to get to St. Pol yesterday, but just missed a lorry that was going by a quarter of an hour, so had to be content with a stroll round the neighbouring village, a place about the size of Stokesley with a few shops for 'British Officers', and plenty of dirty old yokels hanging around. There is an Australian Flying Squadron near us, and we went across there and had drinks and a 'yarn' with one of the observing officers. He advised us very strongly to join the F[lying] C[orps], but I don't think the change would be too salubrious. I like to have a toe or two on terracotta [sic].

The weather has been fairly bon for the last week or so, but today is misty and threatening. The Staffords have been resting for the last week or so but go up the line tonight. I shall *not* be with them. I may be here two or three weeks. One chap has been here nearly three months. It's quite a good way of putting in 'Active Service'. We have a big marquee between three of us, with home-made beds of timber, wire-netting and sacking. The mess is not up to a great deal – mainly rations – but we get plenty of fruit and groceries in the village. I am still taking pills but hope to be better in the tummy when I get a nice quiet time in the trenches.

They don't seem to be getting on with the war at all. I rather fancy it will fizzle out this winter. The loyal troops will stand a lot, but another winter in trenches won't strike them as very bon. Apparently there was quite a deal of trouble last year – censored.

I suppose you can't manage to beg, borrow or steal an old cricket sweater from anyone. Don't buy one, but if any of the good ladies at the Red X have one to spare, it would be pretty useful out here. I think I am safest out here with nothing to lose except my life. The blighted war has wasted three years of that already. I don't know how many more it will take. I suppose one mustn't mind as long as it doesn't take the lot. I don't think I have enough warm kit for wintering out here.

Best love for present from Bert

XV

8th South Staffords R.
Wednesday, 12th Sept. 1917

Dear Mater,

I am moving on another step today, towards the wrong side of the guns. We leave this depot at 4.30 and I expect to be with the old 8th this evening. There's one consolation – I ought to get a good batch of correspondence, for I haven't had anything since I left you. It is a nice, quiet part of the line I hear, and the division will be here for the whole winter probably. I shall have to get you to send me out some winter kit, but can let you know about that later.

It was a glorious day yesterday and I lay behind a hay-stack in the sun all morning and dreamed about home. The country just here is very much like the stretch from Linthorpe up to the foot of Dickson's banks, and it set my mind wandering that way. There was a big camp of Jocks just below me, and they were all out with their kilts swinging round their knees and the pipes skirling away like mad.

We have had a nice soft time here this last week, and I should not mind hanging on for another week or two but the Fates say move on, so up the line we go. Well, I hope I get a nice blighty one, but if it comes to the worst, we will just have to stick it, and think there are a good many better ones gone the same way. After all, I don't think human existence such a mighty special privilege that we need grumble to lose fifty years or so of its struggles and sweat. Anyhow, I hope I am prepared for whatever may come, because I know only too well what a mighty poor chance an infantry officer has.

I had a very bon bath yesterday, the first for over a fortnight, so I shall go up sweet and savoury. As a matter of fact, there are very good baths at Arras and swimming baths too. The trams run right up to the third line trenches, so you may see how quiet it is. I hope we don't get up towards Wipers as there seems to be old Nick to play that way on. They say the Boche is evacuating Belgium, but I don't believe that. I may not get into the line this time as the Staffords come out in about ten days time, and then the division go for a rest, but I expect it is more likely I shall go straight up to join them. I will let you know as soon as I possibly can.

Meanwhile give my best love to May and father. Has she settled on her coat?
From Bert

XVI

Friday, Sept. 14th 1917

Dear Mater,

I received my letters yesterday at last, just before coming up the line. I am in the frontiest [sic] of the front line at present, but as it is very quiet up to now, and as we have a fine deep dug-out, I had just as well be here as further back with carrying-parties to do, up and down the communication trench. I am on watch from 4 to 8 tonight, and as long as the Boche doesn't do any raiding we should be alright.

Little Barker, the C.O., was very nice when I turned up again and I should get on with him pretty well. The word of it is that he gives the officers he thinks most of the worst jobs. However, I think the best way is to make up your mind to get killed and then if you do come out so much the better, and if you don't, well, you are in pretty good company. The chances are not too good so it had better be faced out and met with a stout heart.

My old platoon sergeant is still out here and has been through all manner of scraps since I left them. We were jolly glad to see each other again as we had been through some queer times together. The battalion is not what it was, and is only at half strength, and the officers are not the boys we used to have. They've all gone to ground, worse luck. We had our first taste of shells coming up last night. I was riding the Captain's horse and we had a smart trot for it when they started throwing their old iron across the road. The horses didn't like it – no more did we. I shall have to tell you some of the sights out here when I am safe back on the other side. They wouldn't do you any good whilst we are still amongst it.

The postcards of Runswick set my heart aching for the good old times, and the cycle rides I used to have round and about the moors. I'm glad you got your holiday at Saltburn after all and in such delectable quarters. I would have given a pretty penny to be with you, with a new Sunbeam, and plenty of poetry to write, and a deal more to leave unwritten. How vividly I can picture the grand old moon coming up beyond Huntcliffe, and splashing the sea and the bay with silver, and all the cliffs standing gloomy and grim in the shadow. The sun setting down by the breakwater is another spectacle too sacred for the mouth of man.

Our dug-out is about as deep as the height of a house, and we have to have candles down there day and night. There are not many rats in these trenches, but the place is lousy with toads and frogs. We came across all the ground gained in the last Arras push, so we had a very good view of the operations, which you have seen described in the papers.

By the way, if I should go the way many of the good boys have gone, don't forget to claim my balances in Barclays at Cambridge and at Middlesbrough. Tell Father to shove £5 into the Cambridge branch for me at the end of this month as I am drawing from that all the time.

Tell May she can go up to £10 or £12 for a fur coat, and let me know.

Best love to all,

From Bert

XVII

Saturday, Sept. 15th 1917

Dear Mater,

It is Saturday true enough, but it is very hard to realise it down in this dismal deep dug-out. It might be Pancake Tuesday or Ash Wednesday or any other sainted or sinning day for all the difference it makes to us. Strafe and strafe, and watch and watch about in thrilling monotony, if such a thing exists. It's monotonous and yet it's exciting. I suppose it must be the wrong kind of excitement, or an overdose of it. Anyhow, it's not pleasant, not much better than boredom in fact. Nothing very remarkable has happened in the past twenty-four hours. There have been one or two aeroplane strafes and the Boche has thrown over one or two hundred trench mortars and we've given them back with interest, and so the war goes on. There is no water to get a wash and when I had try to clean my teeth the water was so mixed with petrol that it nearly made me vomit. Yet they say petrol is scarce. Why, we make our tea with it here, and glad to drink it too. It is a pretty rotten mess that I have landed into this time – nothing like the good old days of Wood and Snowie. However, I don't suppose I shall be with them such a very long time. Long visits aren't done in France nowadays. Life is short and sour. I'm hoping for a nice blighty again.

I didn't get any letters up yesterday evening, so contented myself with reading the old ones again. I wrote you yesterday, and I don't think I have missed a day since I came away. Very bon record, n'est-ce pas?

Tell May to send me some toffee de luxe, or caramels or something. I could do with a tin or two of cocoa and a packet of sugar too, just to make a cup of something to while away the dark hours of the watch.

I have had much more sleep so far than we used to get because we have so few men now. We can't get the work done. All the officers nearly are the new 'ranker' sort from the Cadet battalions, very decent chaps, but not like the old boys.

How's the dog getting on? I hope you are looking after her. Did you take her to Saltburn? By the way, I could do with those running shorts, as we may get plenty of football if we go into rest at all. We are due up here for a few days yet. I expect we will be about fed up by the time we do go. Well, I will try to write tomorrow if I find time.

Well, love to all at home, from Bert

Candles are running short, darkness descends.

XVIII

Sunday, Sept. 16th 1917

Dear Mater,

It's Sunday but not much sign of the peaceful Sabbath up here. There's going to be strafes and strafes tonight. There's not much quiet in the trenches nowadays. We are always at it and always in the soup, so, as I have remarked before, you must be prepared for any old thing that turns up.

There is a glorious sunset outside away back beyond our last lines, and a kind of pseudo-calm prevails for the moment.

Since I wrote the last page another twenty-four hours has gone west, and we have had a night much too warm to be amusing. We had two raids carried out, one by the battalion on our left, and one by the battalion on our right. The Boche responded with the devil's own bombardment, and I had forty minutes on my stomach with the fear of God well in my feet. The damn shells were dropping all over the place, not in ones or twos, but in dozens. It was enough to make you wonder how the hell a man's mind could stand it and not be deranged. To cap the lot our company captain was rolling drunk on the floor of the dug-out. I shall be glad when tomorrow comes and we go a bit further back. I can stand a joke, but this war goes beyond that.

I haven't had any letters or cards since I came up, but the post is pretty hopeless nowadays, so one just has to put up with that as with everything else, great or small, that may turn up, including your toes.

There's a couple outside the dug-out now with their toes upwards, waiting to go down to the cemetery.

Our old friend Horatio Bottomley[1] is up in this quarter on a Cook's tour. They keep him in the third or fourth line about three miles behind, and I suppose he thinks he's seeing the war – facing the foe, I should say so! He'll go home and tell the government to push on with the war and bring the Hunhuman Hun to the dust, and talk about the lads who are doing their bit, the vileness of the Boche and so forth. Personally, I'm fed to the teeth with the whole dashed outfit, and the sooner someone stops it, the better. There's a devil of a disturbance upstairs at present, so that I can hardly collect up enough calm to know what I am putting on the paper. I think we would want some No. I size kit-bag to pack our troubles, eh? However, once we get out of the trenches this time we ought to have a fairly decent rest, and then, God knows what we shall be put to. By the way, I am developing a kind of ague of shivering fever which comes on whenever I try to get a bit of lie-down, and puts the wind up me properly.

I am writing this on top of a newspaper on the table, and I have just noticed the advert, 'Richmond Hill Hotel'. It calls up some very happy memories. Do you remember what a day we had there, and how we were done down five bob for our tea, and got nothing for it, except the view? I wish we were there now to get done down another five bob. It would be worth it. As a matter of fact, I would much sooner have had the two weeks at Saltburn, but that too is very much denied us. Well, here's hoping we'll pull through and good luck to myself.

All love to all,
From Bert

XIX

Tuesday Sept. 18th 1917

Dear Mater,

I had a splendid batch of letters last night, which cheered me up immensely. They had been chasing me up and down France, but they have arrived at last, and all together. The last letter from you is dated Sept. 9th, the last day of your stay at Saltburn. I also had two lots of papers which I have read through and through, and a writing pad. You did not include any envelopes which would be useful. I had a letter From Li too, in which he recounts a very lugubrious and cheerless dream, wherein apparently he beheld me as a good-looking corpse with bedraggled locks and mud-stains, just as we see them by the dozen out here. Thank the Lord I wasn't a bit green and bloated with lying out in the rain for a week. However, dreams go by contraries they say, so perhaps I shall turn up radiant and blooming with only a limb deficient to mar my pristine beauty.

We are going out of this this afternoon, a little further back, thank the Lord, and shall be there several days. We have had our share of excitement this trip, and it's about time our nerves had a breather.

I am sending back a cutting from the *Post* about the good work you dear ladies are doing amongst the bandages. I suppose you will be able to retail me some of the gossip of the needle-room now you are back at home. I'm afraid you have neglected them somewhat since the summer time came on. You might make me one or two neat dressings for the fleshy part of the calf of my leg. I think a neat gash in that direction would just about suit my soup. I have had thrilling accounts of the deaths of most of our officers, and they have rather put the wind up me, but I shall have to trust to the God of Battles and your credit in Paradise to pull me through. The saying in the army is that "God will see you through", but I think he has his hands about full this trip, what do you say? The old Boche is very quiet today, so I suppose he is up to something. I wish he had got his bellyful, but I expect he is up to snuff for a while yet. Anyhow, it's a good job we are winning.

Our Company Commander is a bird, I can tell you – some No. 1 size ostrich, in fact. He goes strolling about No Man's Land by day and night, and waves his stick at the Boche and curses him an about umpteen different languages, including Johnny Walker's wildest. That kind of thing is very amusing whilst it lasts, but it doesn't last as long as a cake of Pear's in a sugger's hut. He's not sober when he's not tight, but that doesn't make any odds as he's always tight. It's funny how the fiends of alcohol seem to pursue me round and about.

I envied you your trip round Marske Mill, much more than I did the "music under ideal conditions". We get just a little of the latter out here. The Battalion band is pretty strong in 18-pounders, with one or two sixty-pounder bassoons and fifteen-inch trombones to give it a tang. No, I think the woods and the Mill would suit my taste for quiet just a trifle better than the pier orchestra, with all due respects to the band. Lord knows what we will be in for next tour — quick blighties, let's hope.

Well, bye-bye till tomorrow.

All love to all from Bert

XX

Wednesday, Sept. 19th 1917

Dear Mater,

I hope you get my yesterday's letter safely, as I had to stick it up with candle grease and trust to the tender mercies of the sergeant to get it to the dump. It's a perfectly glorious day today, hot and sunny and clear as in very mid-summer. Back here about a mile and a half away from the line we are on a prominent knoll and command a view of at least ten miles of the front. It is a sight worth paying a visit to France to have. A wide plain, bare and brown, broken up by long straggling lines of trench, used and useless and held or abandoned, as the case may be. Here and there rows of shattered tree trunks, leafless, without branch or bough, chipped, splintered, singed and burned and blasted to their roots. Here and there the vestiges of a wood and a little triangular coppice, or rather a congregation of stumps and streaks and planks and riven baulks. Here and there the remnants of a village, the ground floor of a factory, the rubble of a long-deserted villa or manor. No sign of crop, of cornland and root land, of pasture and strolling flocks, of farm or habitation whatever. It is impossible to make you feel the desolation and nothingness of all these miles of plain lying square and open to the gorgeous bounty of the sun. Here and there in its midst float heavy masses of white smoke marking the dire results of a few minutes bombardment, and the line of crumpled, tumbled trench. Those white fumes are mostly over the Boche lines nowadays, thank heaven. Up above the ceaseless air warfare is carried on in its high spectacular fashion. Down below we sit and shiver and wonder when and where it is all going to end, and what a glorious day it would be to spend in jolly old Saltburn or away on the moors. The wily Boche have just started shelling about five hundred yards away and I experience something akin to that shadow you speak of as marring the serenity of your holiday. I think I know how you feel as to that, Mater, and I only wish it were possible to dispel its blackness and foreboding, but this gloomy war has obsessed everything, and I suppose mankind must continue its walk in the valley of the shadow, feeling very much evil indeed. The time of repose and still waters will be all the more happy when it arrives at last after all these unspeakable horrors.

We mess out in the open out here but sleep down in an evil-smelling dug-out, just in case old Fritz bangs one or two heavies on to us in the night. It's rather a strain, this hanging about, waiting to be killed, but one gets used to it in a few days. I expect there may be working parties tonight; they don't leave us alone long as a rule.

Well, write tomorrow.

All love to all from Bert

XXI

Wed. Sept. 19th 1917

Dear Pater,

I was glad to have your letters, and the papers which I hope you will send regularly. You will note I write Mother pretty well every day, so there is not much time left for letters to you and May. However, you will get any news, of course, and my movements from Mater's letters. I'm afraid I cannot echo the war-like views in your second letter, as I am too fed up with the whole thing to entertain very much resentment against the wily Hun or anybody except the war itself.

However, I suppose you people at home get these fiery outbursts just to persuade yourselves you are doing your bit. I think a quarter of an hour's intense bombardment would just about alter your idea of things, especially when you collected bits of your dead comrades and wrapped them up in sandbags, which has to be done after every strafe. The navy, by the way, doesn't seem to be risking much just at present, since the *Daily Mail* persuaded them they had won the battle of Jutland.

I'm sorry the Saltburn trip was so expensive, but I hope that won't prevent you from shoving a fiver into the Barclays for me this month. It will come in very useful as the price of stuffs out here is fairly prohibitive. I note what you say about the development of the North-East coast, but it seems to me Tyneside always takes the lion's share in any activities and developments up that way. West Hartlepool seems to be more progressive and venturesome than the Teesside merchants. I see the munitions girls are going strong at football, and fixing up a regular league amongst themselves. Funny days we live in!

They say there is a chance of the Division having a rest in a few weeks. They have certainly made a name for themselves with the Boche for raiding and so forth. We got some prisoners a night or two back who would not give us any information, but asked, "When the Hell is this Division going to give us a rest?" I think the old Hun has just about got the 'wind up', and is ready to settle up peacefully, if we would meet them half way. I am certain I wouldn't object, but I suppose you fireside people will push it on till every decent boy is 'napoo'.[1]

Well, don't forget the fiver. Best luck,
From Bert

XXII

Thursday, Sept. 20th 1917

Dear Mater,

Still another fine day, and still the war. There was a very heavy strafe on yesterday evening and we had a grand view of it from our point of vantage, though we were a little doubtful as to whether we would be called on to go into it or not. However, we kept on the right side of it this time and thoroughly enjoyed the scenic and tonic effects for about a mile's distance.

We are busy just at present trying to fix up a bell from the mess to the cookhouse. There's a lot of wire in it and a long chain and a handle like a W.C. pull and an eight-inch shell-case and one or two other little items of military and domestic utility. I can't say it has been a success entirely, as we generally finish up by shouting after pulling the whole contraption down on top of the servants' bunks. However, it adds a touch of domesticity to the scene, even if its practical virtues are not over-great. There is a great strafe on up above us and one side or the other seems to be very angry with the airplanes up there.

I was up to the front line this morning to visit a working party, but did not stay too long, you bet. We have not had anything to do since we came from the line, and we are rather enjoying ourselves watching other people fight. I don't suppose it will last long. It's not the way of the war to leave you alone very long. We were all over an abandoned tank yesterday, and examined it with great interest. It seemed to have been in the war a bit and stank like a fish-shop.

Well, I will write tomorrow. Meanwhile, love to all,
From Bert

XXIII

Friday, Sept. 21st 1917

Dear Mater,

Still another grand day, and a very quiet one all along this front. We have come off very luckily the last few days and have nothing to do whatever, except sit about in the sun and smoke and watch the war. I'm afraid it's a paradise which won't have very long duration, but it's very bon so far. We seem certain to go into rest when we get out of this lot of trenches, so I shall be safe for a few brief weeks at any rate.

Our letters come up from the transport lines with the rations and mess-box at night, and we get them just after dinner, and very pleasant it is to sit and talk and read our letters in our little dug-out under the stars, and think it's a good war after all. You never know what the mess-box is going to bring you, as, for instance, when I received a dozen a night or two back. We get a good, long, uninterrupted night's sleep here, too, which is a decided improvement and eases the strain somewhat. It will soon be October, and that fur coat is due to May then, so I hope she has fixed up what she is going to have, and where to get it. I had a p.c. from her. Has she managed to fix herself on any office work yet?

There is little to chronicle in our doings at present, and our life is very much like life on board ship: reading, writing, eating and sleeping. We can't get away from our strip of trench, of course, and that makes it more than ever like ship. The men are quite happy back here and get plenty of good rations: oatmeal, rice, beans, fresh meat, bread, cheese, jam and tinned butter, and so on, and haven't much to grumble of as trench life goes. We have just had all the news through of a big advance at Wipers last night[1] so I suppose we are pushing on with the war a little. The weather is gorgeous and just right for wars or holidays. You would laugh to see me in my tin-hat and gas-bags and dirty old tunics, squatting here on a seat of sandbags. We have rigged up an A 1 bell at last, the only drawback being that it needs someone about umpteen feet high to reach it.

All love to all,
From Bert

XXIV

Saturday Sept. 22nd 1917

Dear Mater,

I have just come from a visit up the line. Am writing this in time to catch the post. It is still delightfully warm and summery and the weather has held splendidly while we have been back in the supports. There was rather a strafe away on the right while I was up in front, and I thought at first I had been caught in an attack or something, but it was well away over on the flank, so we sat down and watched it in peace. Then I went down a sap and had a game at poker, and finally came back for tea.

They seem to be doing fairly well up Ypres way according to the news we get through,[1] but it will be a long time yet. I suppose I shall be here for winter unless I am done in beforehand. I hardly know which is the worse of the two. A nice, mild Blighty would be the happiest solution, but we can't manage these things for ourselves.

The drink evil follows me about, as I say. My Company Captain is tight every minute of his life practically. We have to put him to bed every night, and he starts again as soon as he wakes. Of course, he won't last long, but I suppose that won't worry him, as the war will probably finish him before the drink. He is a very interesting chap when sober, and has knocked about the world a deal, but I'm pretty well fed up with the drink business.

I have had to drop some of my baggage already, but I didn't break much bone over that as I brought practically nothing over with me. I shall certainly have to get some winter clothing if I'm going to stay, as it is pretty cold at night already. I only have my greatcoat and that doesn't stretch as far as my feet by any means. My tummy is still pretty rotten and I have had a bad night or two. My pills have all melted and run into one another, so I want you to send me a tin of Glauber salts as soon as you can. I will have to write you more fully tomorrow as the post is in a hurry to get away. This kind of weather is much too fine for France, but I am in it now. Anyhow, it is better than Cannock Chase, and the boys are the boys here.

Goodbye and all love,
From Bert

[contd.]

Have just had a letter from you, written last Friday. As regards the watch, all I wanted was a five bob or 7/6 Ingersoll for the pocket. You must send some salts or another lot of my pills, unless you want me to be plugged up permanently.

I can hardly write this for laughing, because our Company Captain is as tight as ever, and is trying to give the Mess waiter instructions on how to meet a gas attack, if engaged in carrying a plate of fruit from the kitchen to the Mess. It's too damn funny for words, the servant trying to keep a straight face, and the Captain making googly eyes at him, just like father. I have just discovered that yesterday's letter did not go, as it got hidden behind an ornament, so you will get them both together.

As regards sleeping, if we are up at the war we have to sleep as we stand, but when we get back we get our valises[2] and pyjamas. I could do with some sleeping socks certainly, and with that sweater, too.

I have come across Yankee doctors out here and one or two Infantry officers too, but they are very quiet and chastened and soon get it knocked out of them if they are not.

I wish I could have shared the sunset with you, but I hope I shall live through to see one or two after the 'guerre', and to write about them, too. I'm glad you have plenty to do to keep you going, and I hope you will keep going whatever happens. It's a dull kind of day and not very auspicious, with all the leaves dripping rain and the fallen fruit all mushy and covered with clay. Well, I've got the 'wind up' properly, but that won't help much, so will close with all love,

From Bert

XXV

Sunday, Sept. 23rd 1917

Dear Mater,

We are being relieved in a few hours time, and have had rather a busy day, so am taking a few minutes opportunity after lunch to knock off the daily line. It is a gorgeous day once more, and good to be alive, but not much like Sunday as far as we are concerned. However, we are better situated than in the Hell we endured last Sabbath. We shall have a bath and a bed tonight probably, and a day's march tomorrow. However, we don't mind that, as it is in the right direction.

Is there any sign of the war finishing within the next three weeks? If so, I may have a chance of getting back to Blighty whole. By the way, you might find a letter in my dressing gown pocket from Hulton & Co. of the *Daily Dispatch*, and send it on with your next. I want the address off it. I must go along and get my kit packed now ready to move off, then I have to do an inspection of the trench and see that everything is left spick and span, and no tea leaves are left upon the sandbags. The British Tommy has to keep his cubby-hole as neat and sweet as your kitchen – or there is Hamlet to play. I have just read Bottomley's first article in the *Sunday Pictorial* about his visit to the boys. It's worth a good laugh, anyway, if no more can be said for it. I suppose he's helping to win the war. It was a scare about my kit, as, when it came to be weighed, it was just up to weight, so I didn't have to drop anything. Of course, I have got nothing with me, so what will happen when the cold comes I can't say. We shall have to eke out with the sandbags. Have you managed to worm an old sweater out of any of your friends or relatives yet? I have a very good boy for servant, the cheekiest young devil on earth, and he will look after me alright. He had his nineteenth birthday today, and I gave him ten francs for luck. Has Pater banked me that five quid?

Best love to all,
From Bert

XXVI

Monday, Sept. 24th 1917

Dear Mater,

We are on the move at present, so I have not a great deal of time for writing. However, I dare say I shall be able to write you a long one tomorrow. We are out of danger now, except for air-raids, which are pretty plentiful round here. We had a short march for today with the band blowing full steam ahead, and a scorching hot sun. We are settled nicely for the night in little huts, and I am just going to have a read before getting down to it. We are in a very pretty orchard with walnut trees, overcrowded with nuts and apples and pear trees and mademoiselles, and all the usual adjuncts. I don't know how these letters will get through to you as the post is always upset when we are on the move. You might write Bodgers and tell them I have gone to France, and shall not need the coat in question. My tummy is still bad, and my pills have all gone west.

Well, I will write much more fully tomorrow. Meanwhile all love to all,
From Bert

XXVII

Tuesday, Sept. 25th 1917

Dear Mater,

I have rather good news this morning, as I have just been warned for a month's course down at the Corps school all October, so that gives us a month to get the war over.

It is delightful again today with a warm summery sun and pleasant breezes, and I am sitting under the walnut trees inscribing this. The hens are cackling and the cocks crowing and the vegetables vegetating, and over-head the planes are humming steadily like the drone of an engine-shed in a great factory. We have a big Archibald in the next garden, not one of those puff-puff things you have on the golf links, but a pukka gun that makes things shake when they poop off. In fact, it's a damn nuisance, and ought to be suppressed. It has never hit anything in this war, but that goes without saying. There is a mademoiselle churning milk in the shed nearby, and the band is practising in the next orchard, so we keep things livened up. We have just had two Yank officers in the Mess from the Ambulance station, not very impressive, but anxious to please. The Mess steward has just brought me about a gallon of French cider, and I am swilling it out of an enamel tot with all the enamel chipped off. It is pretty vile, but it is wet, and we can't get lime juice for a day or two, and it's scorching hot, so I must drink something. The bugles have just blown Cookhouse, and the church bell is tolling for the dead, someone about umpteen years old. My servant's name is Gerry Delaney – sounds like something from Charles Darvis, and he's a very bright lad. He comes from Nottingham, and makes more noise than Robin Hood and all his merry men put together.

Your description of the Sunday evening sunset was rather spoiled by the thought of what we were going through that same night. I didn't appreciate the scenic effects myself, as I had the 'wind up' rather about the strafe which we knew was coming off at nine o'clock, and my God it came, sure enough. I would have preferred to spend the eve in blissful calm at home but can't say the night lacked incident, nor was it wanting in colour effect and fiery atmosphere. The stink of sulphur spoiled things rather, but the whole stage-dressing was well up to the standard of the strolling players of the Western Front.

I am smoking a great deal too much out here, as there is so little to do to pass the hours away, now I have given up my physical jinks. I think I shall have to get home again and get out of the army and then I shall be happy.

Everybody except the *Daily Mail* experts and Horatio Bottomley seem to be fed up with the war. I don't see why they shouldn't treat for peace if the old Boche wants to do so. I think he has had a bellyful to last him a few years, at any rate. Of course, we could go on till we are all killed if necessary, but that doesn't seem much of a consummation. I see Stockton has got a V.C., and a very gallant deed earned it, if the official account is correct. I'm not after medals myself, but I have every respect for the boys who get them, anyway. The weather still remains pretty well perfect. Though that is a good thing as regards comfort and so forth, I'm afraid it means the sacrifice of many thousands of lives. However, we seem to be doing well on the Menin Road, so I suppose we can take it for good fortune. Everyone asks when is the massacre going to end, and they get only the roar of the guns for answer. I haven't had a bath for weeks, but I changed my undies this morning and live in hopes. I haven't struck any livestock yet in spite of unsavoury quarters. There was a gorgeous moon last night, though a lot of clouds about. I had to get through the window to pay a visit as I could not find my way to the door through the mush of beds and British officers. One of the blighters tried to shut the windows on me, but I hastened back in time to thwart him. They talk a great deal about the Battalion going over the top soon, but if I get away on this course I should miss that pleasure, and perhaps preserve my miserable life a little longer.

Hope to have a letter from you tonight. All love to all at home,

From Bert

XXVIII

Thursday, 27th Sept. 1917

Dear Mater,

I did not manage to drop you a line yesterday as we were on the march all day, and then we were simply hours in getting our billets fixed up. Even now there are six of our beds in one room, and we have to feed in it as well. However, the farm is fairly clean and smells sweet, which is a miracle as far as French farms are concerned. The old girl has a little room opening off the corner of ours, and she has to march through our beds every time she goes to bed and gets up again. I tried to bag her room for myself, but she kicked me out in great indignation, with piercing shrieks and all the rest of it, while the others stood round and laughed rudely. Anyhow, she turfed me out, so now I have only a plank and wire bed, army pattern, made out of trench boards and rabbit wire. However, it's not lousy like the old woman's bed, even if it is a bit hard. We made such a row last night that I shouldn't be surprised if she gave up her room in disgust before long. This village is a pretty little place, simply hedged round and about with apple orchards on which we make forays, strictly against orders. We have plenty of fine russets, but they are hardly matured yet. I believe they should be laid by till Christmas really, but they don't get much chance of waiting when the loyal troops roll up.

I think May is not playing the game about the fur coat, and have a good mind to withhold my contribution altogether. I said I would buy her coat because I wished to save you the expense, not because I thought she had done anything particular to deserve it. It's a pretty monstrous thing for a family in our wartime straightened circumstances to pay out £20 for a bit of dress. Besides, I don't like the spirit of the deal at all. It wasn't sporting. I hope she's got fixed up for V.A.D., and when I hear she has I shall send the cheque, not otherwise. I shall have to reply to father's letter at more leisure. Glad to hear Teesside is going ahead. The local papers are a godsend, and I read them through and through, and I have the p.c. of Saltburn gardens that May sent in my bunk, and it sends my thoughts wandering to the prettiest spot on earth very often. I am getting a paunch on me these days, and I have to undo my belt rather too frequently. Still, one can't retain much elegancy in this kind of existence. We just live in the minute that is at hand and don't give much thought for the morrow or the day after, much less to our next visit to the trenches. It was a gorgeous night last night, and the stars were spangled in the sky, thick as the hosts of Midian. Old Orion is just beginning his winter tour and swarms up in all his glamour away in the south above the Boche sandbags every evening now. I expect you will see his splendours over the hills at home there. I remember I used to watch him all the winter through. He is the grandest constellation in our northern skies. I have just received more papers and a letter from May, no parcel yet, alas.

Well, I will close till tomorrow when we shall be on the march again. God help us if it is as hot as this. All love to all,

From Bert

XXIX

Friday, Sept. 28th 1917

Dear Mater,

I have a bit of bad news today as my course has been cancelled, so that renders me liable to a little trip over the bags when we go up again. However, it's a horrible war in any case, so we shall have to pray for a good Blighty and not the complete dismissal. They seem to be amusing each other up Wipers way,[1] and there are nasty rumours that we are due there soon, but no one knows for certain.

We are having a good time in this little village as the weather is like perpetual summer, and each perfect sunny day is succeeded by a lovely moonlit night. Yesterday eve was simply gorgeous and I walked out into the orchard back of the billets and found it flooded in limpid moonbeams, and all the grass spangled with dew, and the heavens above in a glory of silvery light. It was simply perfect. I wish it had been the light flooding in the Cleveland Hills and the plain to the sea that I was viewing, but there you are. I have to pack my troubles and a spare shirt in my old kit-bag and SMILE!

I haven't had word from you for a day or two. I wonder if May has got her job at last. We are doing a fair amount of training here, and have to get up too early to suit me. I have No. 4 platoon, and they are a good lot of boys, both on and off parade. Most of them have just come to us from the Kite Balloon section of the RAFC. They are pleased. They now begin to realise they have joined the army. It's a damned shame the way the infantry are treated and paid less than any other branch, although they do all the work and have all the danger, and get nothing for it but glory.

I have just read Bottomley's first article in *John Bull* about his trip to France. What frightful lies and tosh it all is, and how it makes one's blood boil to think of that fat Godforsaken scoundrel coming out here for a week-end and then going back home to serve up that filth to the rotters in Blighty.

Well, all love to all. Will write tomorrow,

Bert

XXX

Saturday, Sept. 29th 1917

The parcel was very bon – send another.

Dear Mater,

I received your first parcel today and beg to return many thanks for same. The butter was a bit bent, and mixed up with the jar supposed to contain it, but these accidents will happen, even in the best Regiments. The toffee was welcome and soon mopped up. I haven't sampled the scones yet, but take it they will be up to the good old standard. How could you spare so much lump sugar? You were running grave risks with the food controller, sending such a monstrous quantity. Father was right about the apples, as we simply bathed in them back in rest here, but, of course, it's a different matter in the line. I shall keep the cocoa and milk for an iron ration when we get in the line once more. The letters were very welcome, too, and the whole parcel was a great treat after we had come from our six hours' pretty slogging work. By the way, I got one of our sergeants to send you a Boche bayonet home, as he was going on leave. I hope you get it safely as it is a handsome looking object, with the edge specially racked and ridged for tough old guts that won't yield to ordinary persuasion.

The weather is still very glorious both night and day and the land looks so lovely in the moon at night, that it seems a pity to go to bed. However, we get plenty to do to make us sleep once we are there, and it's a great pull to get out in the morning.

I note your injunctions about avoiding the lead and steel and will do my best to comply. I'm sorry if my letter put the wind up you, but it's just as well to face things out and to own up what will happen. However, I shall stay alive as long as I decently can.

We have just finished roaring with laughter at Bottomley's second article in the *Sunday Pictorial*. It's a damn shame that such stuff should be allowed print.

All love to all,
From Bert

XXXI

Sunday, Sept. 30th 1917

Dear Mater,

I haven't had much time for writing today as I have been chasing round the countryside with a squad of sick people who had to march half across France to be examined. It was a lovely gorgeous day once again and I rather enjoyed the march. The countryside is very pretty and there are few signs of autumn about as yet, except that at night and in the early morning it is pretty cold. The nights are wonderful, though.

I had a letter from father today which I shall answer at leisure. Meanwhile tell him to shove that fiver in Barclays and not make such a noise about it. What does he think we are facing the foe for, begad?

There are lots of rumours about us going into some kind of stunt, but I hope I shall be left out, as I guess I had my fill of horrors on the Somme. However, Kismet is a good horse, so it's taking my money this time.

I had some newspapers today, and they were welcome as always. I will let you know as soon as we move from here. I wish that course hadn't been cancelled, but that can't be helped now. I hope I shall touch for another, anyhow. Our Company Commander, who has been away for a week, has returned today, and we have run out of whisky already. A home from home, isn't it? I haven't had a letter from you for a day or two, but am looking forward to one. Have you got me that Ingersoll? I want a watch badly. I should like that sweater, too. Yes, if you can't beg one, you might certainly have a shot at making one. I only want it to put my feet and legs in. It will be damn useful, and I can wear it on my body when occasion demands. I should think one of the local patriots might let you have one without much grumbling. I wish I hadn't lost my old one. Well, I'm pretty tired and want to get to bed now, so will say good night, and after one more look at the gorgeous moon will turn in. We have just been for a lovely walk along the old French road.

All love to all,
From Bert

XXXII

Monday, October 1st 1917

Dear Mater,

I don't know how I find time to knock off a line as we are rushed off our feet with parades just now. I had a letter from May at lunchtime and was very glad to have the news. You seem to have had another gorgeous day at Riftswood – wish I were there, as I can imagine it would be just gorgeous with the first touches of autumn amongst the foliage. I am glad to have news of old Phil, and amused to hear he has taken an objection to the dog next door.

The weather still holds here, but winter must be very close upon us now, and will come suddenly when the weather does break. I can't say if we will get into a stunt or not before that happens.

Shall I send a cheque for May's coat payable to Foster for £10? Let me know in your next.

After I had finished my letter yesterday our Company Commander rolled in as tight as a lord and had to be helped gently to roost. What a life! Last night was a full moon, gorgeous as ever, just like a fairyland with strange shapes, weird trees, and uncouth shadows to heighten the effect. We have been traipsing over ploughed fields and crops and wire fences since 8 o'clock this morning, and found it more arduous than amusing. One has to do something for the 7/6 a day on this side of the Channel, I can tell you. However, old Fritz is reported to be pretty fed up with life at present so I suppose we must be glad of that small mercy.

Have just been reading a *Westminster Gazette* and a *Sheffield Telegraph* Li sent. Good old Sheffield! I still have a *Gazette* left to look through and remind me of the dirty old streets at home. Wish to blazes I were there, but life's a hard thing these days and has to be faced out, especially for homely ducklings like me.

All love to all at home,
Bert

XXXIII

Wednesday, October 3rd 1917

Dear Mater,

The weather seems to have broken a bit at last, and it was raining all last night and it's very dull today. We have been fooling about in the parade ground all morning. Have just come in to lunch.

I suppose you will be fed up with yesterday's news, but it can't be helped. We move off tomorrow, so perhaps there won't be a letter through for a day or two, or even longer. However, don't worry because I'm not going to, and that's the only way to carry on these days. I expect you can guess what part of the world we are taking train for. All the boys are there just now.

We had a bit of joking last night. One of our subs dressed himself up as a French gendarme, and went round all the company messes complaining about the lights on in the billets, and claiming fines. He acted awfully well, and took everyone in completely, and made about a hundred francs out of it. It was as good as a pantomime to see him take in our Captain who was as drunk as a lord as usual. The Mess was crowded with officers and most of us were in the know, so we had a jolly good laugh out of it, I can tell you.

I'm afraid I haven't time to write a separate note to father, as we are busy packing and preparing, and we have to be up at four o'clock in the morning. Hope he has put that fiver in, all the same. He must send out a couple of bottles of whisky for our Sergeant-Major, if we come out of this stunt. He is my old platoon Sergeant, and about as old a soldier as you could get.

Hope the dog is alright and that you send her to the vet's when it's time. Have just had a couple of your oat scones which are very bon. Have you enough sugar to make rice biscuits? I shall be sorry to leave this funny old farm with its flowers and orchards for heaven knows what.

All love to all,

Bert

XXXIV

Sunday, 7th Oct. 1917

Dear Mater,

It's raining mercilessly outside, it's beastly cold, my feet are wet, my nose is blue, the fire won't light and nobody loves us. We are in a funny old French farm, fourteen officers in one moderate room: coats tunics, equipment, gas-bags, books, papers, caps, whisky, enamel tots, bottles, sticks, all jumbled together like a rubbish heap. The others are out in the bleak fields practising the attack in a foot of mud, and about six of us who are unlucky or lucky enough to be left out of the stunt are sitting round the farm table trying to catch cold. Servants are trying to fix up the groggy stove which doesn't seem to have been lit since Noah landed from the Ark.

I haven't been able to get any letters off home for several days, but you need not worry because as long as I am left out of the stunt I shall be safe enough. There is a sign or two of the war being over this winter, as everyone seems to be fed up with the show, and the Germans are a beaten army in the West here, and they know it and show it. We have hopes that another three months will see things finished. Winter has settled down at last and we find it very cold after the glorious September we have had down Southwards.

I had a letter from Mrs. Coates yesterday. She wants to know if May is interested in Suffrage at all as she can find some work for her, if she is willing. Shall I ask her to?

I saw the Guards marching past us a day or two back and they looked magnificent. I'm afraid they put the Staffords to shame, but, of course, they are the pick of England as far as physique goes. We felt like mannequins watching hosts of Goliath go by.

We have got a fire going at last, but the rain is still coming down in avalanches and the wind is howling. There was a gorgeous sunset last night, fiery, but very cold. This is a bleak, flat land, and I will tell you more about it in my next. It is all grim and war-ridden – not a bit of comfort or softness anywhere.

All love to all from Bert

XXXV

Wed. Oct. 10th, 1917

Dear Mater,

As I write the date I reflect that another week will see my 25th 'bifday'. Three good years gone West since this war turned up to interrupt aspirations. It's about time the whole show was napoo, don't you think? I was in St. Omer yesterday, and had quite a good bit of fun. I tried to make love to a pretty flapper in the Hotel de France, but she was très sérieuse, and much too old for the size of her ankles. She called me a brigand, so I gave her up as hopeless and went and had some dinner. I have been putting on flesh, and am very pursy and scant of breath – can't get any decent exercise, only worry and jiggering about. It's a miserable day again, rain, rain, rain and beastly cold too. I had a rotten night on the hard, hard ground, with everything damp and shivery. I shall have to hunt round for some straw today, to soften things down a bit.

We set out to walk the ten miles back last night but after we had done a couple we picked up an A.S.C. convoy and journeyed merrily on with a fair amount of bumping but no bones broke. It was a lovely star-lit night, but rather icy, and we enjoyed the rumbling ramble across country.

This part of France is much more like our own land than the more Southerly parts. The Flemish are not unlike our own Yorkshire folk, and they are clean and busy, and hospitable.

The farms and villages are built much stronger, and furnished fairly decently. In the Albert district the farms are only mud and a percentage of whitewash, and you can shove your stick through the walls. The people too are slipshod and dirty and usurious. Up here, however, it is more like home. The villages are just like any Durham mining village, and the last billet I had was owned by an old gardener chap, very like Grandpa Laurence. The women too are fair and sharp-featured.

All love to all from Bert

XXXVI

Friday Oct. 12th, 1917

Dear Mater,

It is still about as cold as it can be, but we have got our tent fixed up more comfortably now with a couple of beds and some canvas and boxes. In fact, I am actually writing this at a table, sitting on an ammunition box. I only want about half a dozen more blankets and I shall be quite comfy. My tummy is troubling still, and it is no joke to have to get up in the middle of a cold night, raining and windy, and dodge in my pyjamas for the nearest hedge.

I see they have been having a bit of trouble in the German navy, but don't suppose it amounted to anything. We have been watching the cavalry pass through here all the morning. I don't know if they will get into action or not. We haven't had any definite news through lately, and I suppose the weather must have held things up a bit. Good luck to the jammy Staffords.

I expect Haig[1] is up here besides myself and one or two other nibs. We haven't had any post, of course, for some time now, but we haven't had any leisure for reading either, so that did not matter much. I can't say when we will get any mail, but have hopes for tomorrow, I could do with a good solid sleep on a decent bed what 'opes!

I don't know why we made such a fuss about this Belgium place. It seems to me to be about the last place made, while God was practising for Hell.

Well, I hear various shouts anent 'falling in', and getting ready, so I suppose it is time I finished this off, and got my pack on, and my tin hat.

The roads are in a gorgeous state of consolidated squelch, so we shall have some march amidst the shot and shell – wish I were back with my mammie – what 'opes! By the time this gets to the post I expect it will be pretty well illegible.

All love to all from Bert

XXXVII

Saturday Oct. 13th, 1917

Dear Mater,

Same address and same weather. We meant to go to St. Omer this afternoon to get cleaned up and buy some clothes, but I think the weather will be too thick for that. We haven't had any news of the battalion yet, but they must be having an awful time in the shell-holes this horrible weather. According to *The Times* this morning peace is further off than ever. Why we should want to take Alsace-Lorraine from old Fritz I don't know, as I am jolly sure he would make better use of it than any froggies are likely to. However, it's a great war, and I want a bath very badly, as I am covered with chats[1] from some straw we used for bedding. Send me some more lump sugar if you have any to spare. Are there any Tommy Cookers to be had? Or you might let me have that old methylated stove I used to have at Cambridge. It's under the stairs, if I remember. I am looking forward to that sweater for my feet. We are more comfy now than the first few nights, as we have managed to loot beds, and washing material and so forth.

The rain seems to have set in worse than ever, so I am afraid St. Omer is off for today. We shall have to make it Sunday instead, and I shall write letters all today, and get a bath at the Tommies' baths – perhaps go to an estaminet for tea.

All love to all from Bert

XXXVIII

Monday Oct. 15th, 1917

Dear Mater,

I have just had the cheery news that the battalion have come out of the line with two officers, after doing well in the attack, so I dare say I shall be moving soon. However, anything sent to this address catches me up in a day or so, and you need not miss a letter on that account, By the way, the butter arrived in good fettle this time, but the toffee was throwing its weight about a bit to the detriment of the rest of the packet. The biscuits were full of pluck but a bit broken. However, they were very bon notwithstanding.

There is no more news of the battalion this morning, nor do I know how the war is going on today as I have not had a paper. That poem of Sassoon[1] is very much to the point. I have just sent Ogden[2] a little contribution of my own. I don't know whether he wants any or not, but I had to get it off my chest.

I have been trying to fix up to buy a Primus stove off one of our lads, but he wants about 25/- for it. I have offered him 15/-, and I don't see that it is worth all that really. However, it might come in jolly useful, for shaving-water and so forth, and casual cups of cocoa. I suppose the war will last into next summer at least now.

'Cookhouse door' has just blown, so I must be getting away to lunch. There is always a rush at the mess and I was shut out yesterday and had to take second sitting. Our own servants could cater for us better than the mess do. I have got Jerry down here with me, and he is waiting anxiously for his cigarettes.

I did nothing all day yesterday except sit over our fire and read Rider Haggard's *Lysbeth*[3] and write letters. My tent-fellow, a nice kid called Murphy, whose brother had just been killed, and who is only 19, has not got up yet 12.45 because I didn't have to get up this morning, and drag him out as I usually do.

All love from Bert

XXXIX

[start of Incomplete letter]

Tuesday Oct. 16th, 1917

Dear Mater,

I am 25 today and have got to wish myself many happy returns as no one else seems inclined to do so. Perhaps the post will bring me some after lunch. It is still cold, and a blowy, bleak sort of day, with promise of rain. I have to go over to the neighbouring station to bring some reinforcements to the camp after lunch. It is about four miles away and I shall go on an A.S.C. lorry. We have a gorgeous fire going in the tent, strictly against regulations, but it warms and dries everything splendidly, and smokes us out like the very d—. The servants have made it up in an old petrol-can, riddled with holes made with a bayonet, and they are cooking themselves oatmeal on it all day long to supplement their rations. They found the oatmeal left behind by another division and they make a weird dish out of it in their mess-tins. I haven't risked any yet, but it smells fairly nice, and they seem to mop it up pretty quick. I have just finished a long letter to Doris, and am still living in the fond memories it awoke. We had a jolly good time together we two, and I'm sorry I'm such a selfish brute, or we might have settled down happily enough. However, I've been spoilt sure enough ever since I was a naked nothing, and I don't think anything but fame and freedom will suit my temperament. I must have my own way, and I must be in the picture.

XL

Tuesday Oct. 16th, 1917

Dear Pater,

The parcel with the new pad and envelopes has arrived just as I finished the first one, so I am using the first page or two to drop you a line. I am waiting for the A.S.C. car to go to the nearest station to fetch reinforcements. It is 4 miles away but I don't expect I shall be back till late tonight. I hope they don't bomb the railway while I'm there; they are rather busy just now. It is my birthday today, and I had a huge mail – about a dozen letters and a parcel. Thank Mother very much for the sweater which is A 1, and the salts, dates etc. The toffee was a bit squashed but is quite eatable. We have polished off the dates, which were not too dirty, already. I had three lots of papers and will read them in bed tonight. They bring a fine touch of home out here. I think the boy I wanted the pads for is killed, but I am not sure. I hope not, however, I am using it myself now, so he can have the next, if still alive. Tell Mother I will reply to her Wednesday's letter tomorrow. I had another nice letter from Doris today. I believe she is engaged again. She is on War Work and at it pretty hard. It is about time May got going, isn't it? She is getting no value at all out of her life at present, and that is not a nice charge to have up against you, is it? I think you had better think of her debt to the world a little, and not so much of her creature comforts. Make a sports-man of her, whatever you do, and not a mere tuck-box slacker. I'm rather fond of the tuck-box myself, as all spoiled kids are, but I know how to put it aside when there's work to be done.

Your remarks about Bertrand Russell[1] may be to the point, but I shouldn't take so much notice of cheap newspapers if I were you. He's really a very decent fellow at heart, though a frightful ass, I must admit, and he thinks he is doing his best for mankind by trying to stop the slaughter. He may be wrong, but he is a far better educated and more widely travelled man than yourself, and he may understand things that you miss.

I dare say we shall worry through the war yet in spite of the wash-out, rascally crew left at home, who float about modestly alluding to their bit, and how they did it. I have more respect for the pacifists than for the ordinary crowd of humbugs and job-snatchers over there.

By the way, I am 25 today – years are flying a bit, aren't they? I hope you have shoved a couple of fivers in the bank for me by now, as I have been away two months. It's very hard to keep count of money over here on account of the different coinage and valuations. I never know exactly what I am paying for anything and how much I am leaving myself in the bank.

Cheeroh for the present, from Bert

XLI

Friday Oct. 19th, 1917

Dear Mater,

I arrived back at battalion yesterday to find the remnants camped in the mud, where I forthwith joined them, and haven't been warm since. They did splendidly in their recent attack, and have added laurels to their name, and been thanked by Sir Douglas[1] himself. They were about the only battalion to take their full objective on that day, and went further than the Guards themselves. We are now in the Guards Corps, and they want to keep us – an honour that has its drawbacks in the way of stunts and so on. Of course, we had to pay a price for our success, and 350 of our lads were put out of action, and all the officers except one, but *very few killed*, nearly all 'blighties', which is the most satisfactory part of the business. The man who took my place at the last minute was killed, poor chap. His name was Gale, and I used to know him well up on Rugeley Camp in 1915. All our lads say the attack was almost a walk-over, and the old Hun is well beaten, in spirit at least. We may have a long way to go yet, though, and the rantings of such hot-air experts as Bottomley and the rest make the lads out here, who have to endure and keep silent, go blue in the face, more often with mirth than vexation, it's true. Our little Colonel was badly laid out. He was up in the very front leading his men himself. He was the pluckiest chap for a senior officer I ever met, and terribly blood-thirsty. Up to the Somme he earned my respect, and I got on with him very well this time out. He may lose his leg, but they hope to save it for him.

My O.C. Company, the whisky fiend, was slightly wounded in the arm, and is in Blighty. I fully expected him to be killed, but the Lord looks after children and drunken men.

I don't know what our next move will be, but we shall probably have to fill up again before we can 'stunt' again. At least, I hope so, as I am not particularly keen on these 'blighties'. The Somme business killed my pig for excitement.

We are well in the mud here, and I pitched my valise last night in concentrated slush. However, the sweater just saved my life, and kept me splendidly warm. I expect we shall have wet feet for the rest of the winter now. We are doing fairly well in mess just now, as parcels keep turning up for the 'departed', and, of course, we don't bother to send them back to Blighty again. Besides, as so many have gone we have an overplus of rations till things get settled again.

The watery sun is doing its best to get up a smile, and the band is making a noise just near. Well, I wish it were all over for the winter, and I could come home and take you to the Pictures and then get on with some bookwriting. All love to all at home,

Bert

XLII

Monday Oct. 22nd, 1917

Dear Mater,

I have not had time to write for a day or two, but we are quite safe and sound now, and many miles from the war. We had a long bus ride yesterday, and we came right back almost to the coast. You never saw so many buses strung together in your life. The traffic out here is a wonderful sight, and the roads are execrable. You can see what a mess the few buses running to Stokesley make of the roads at home, so you may guess what strings of them two miles long will do. It was rather cold riding, as the officers were in front with the drivers, but it was a lovely Autumn day, and we had a lot of good fun out of it. I was on a 24 bus, which runs from Victoria Station to Hampstead, and I always used to use that service to get from the Club up to the New Theatre.

The latest news is that I am going on a course for a month down on the coast the day after tomorrow. That should keep me alright till the end of November, and I should get my leave about Xmas, as so many officers have left us and that has brought my turn nearer. I am sorry to go as we are in a fine little village here, and there are plenty of girls, and shops and estaminets.

There is a pretty mademoiselle in my billet, and we have some giddy times when the cheap champagne gets flowing – a little divertissement, as they call it. I did not get up till lunch-time today, as we are enjoying a rest, for we were travelling all day yesterday – Sunday. It is splendid weather again, mild and sunny, though a bit lukewarm as it were. However, I have a bed and sheets, so don't mind the cold, especially as I can get dried as soon as I get in. My old tunic is always at the tailor's nowadays, and it is patched all, over. Yesterday my servant burned a huge hole in the breast pocket, but we have it mended as good as new again.

I have a very fine billet, and the madame has done my washing in quick style and very clean too. When I was at the Depot I sent my washing out, and they kept it a week and then when I sent in a hurry they had lost it. However, I sent my servant back to loot the place, and he found it stowed away in a cupboard, in its original dirty state. He got it back alright, and one or two spare hankies and shirts as makeweight.

Your first letter to the Depot arrived here today, and one from May too. I don't think there is much to answer in them. You don't say whether I should send the cheque for the coat or not. Can it wait till I get some leave? Has May started the V.A.D. business at the new hospital yet? There are thousands of W.A.A.C. girls out here now and we were talking to three or four of them last time I was at St. Omer. I am glad the bayonet has arrived as the sergeant was rather worried about its non-arrival. It will make a good mantel ornament, and ought to cheer them up a bit at Red X.

We are in a pretty little village with a canal not far away, and there are plenty of hills, and trees and woods on every side. The sun has just set and the old moon has been curved up in its last quarter for an hour or so now, while the evening mists begin to creep over the meadows and up amongst the tree-trunks. I will close till tomorrow. Meanwhile, all love,

From Bert

XLI

14 Corps School,
A.P.O. S. 68,
Tues. 23rd Oct., 1917

Dear Mater,

The weather has turned again today, and it has been rain, rain, rain, the whole morning. It is a great pity as I believe we were due to have another rigorous 'push' this very day, and there has certainly been a terrible bombardment for the past week. Sir Douglas has the most terrible bad luck with the weather. However, I think he has the Boche beaten alright, so the end is bound to come sooner or later.

I have just been taking a cup of excellent coffee with mademoiselle down below. She is a neat little girl with big black eyes, and we get on very well together. I think I shall have to treat her to some champagne before I go away, and see if it makes her eyes sparkle. I don't want to leave here a bit, and would much prefer to go on a course when the battalion are in the line. However, that's just the army way. If ever, and that's not often, you slip by chance into a good billet, you may be certain you are for a move very quickly. This is a ripping little village and the people are awfully decent – they have not had much experience of soldiers before, as it has not been a billeting area long.

I don't suppose I shall have time to write tomorrow, but you won't mind missing a letter now you know we are far from the line. I can't say how long the battalion will stay here. The war is not going to finish for years yet, and America will have to take a full share before it is over. Old Fritz has not properly started to realise his defeat and it will take another couple of years to knock it into him.

There is no news much except that the push was supposed to start today. I'm afraid Winter is well upon us now, and, as you say, I shall need some winter undies. Is father attending to my bank account? I had to pay £1 for two days' messing yesterday – a bit thick. We don't have the games we used to have last time out though, when ' Snowie' used to present us with bills that swallowed a month's in one. They are not the boys of the old brigade nowadays.

All love. From Bert

XLIV

14th Corps Infantry School,
Thurs. Oct 25th, 1917

Dear Mater,

I have arrived after much travelling by various vehicles and devious routes. The place we are at was only about 20 kilometres from our little village, but we have travelled nearly a hundred, and have spent a night in a rest camp en route. We set out at 8 o'clock yesterday morning and arrived 9 o'clock this morning, so you can gauge the little idiosyncrasies of travelling in France. All this in order to get back to the place we left a week ago, and as I have reported, we have done nothing in the meanwhile. At any rate, we are apparently set down for a whole month's course at this school, though of course, you never know what is going to turn up to spoil things. I have a neat little billet with a retired butcher and his wife – no children, no mademoiselle. They are very clean, and there is a bon bed, and big garden, all vegetables, behind. The village is a good-sized place and very well-built and arranged, with plenty of shops, but not a single presentable girl anywhere. The School is a good place too, with a decent clean mess, and plenty to eat in the way of solid rations at any rate. We have a full programme of work and don't get much time to ourselves, but the instructors are very good and we ought to pick up some sound information on how to run an army if there weren't any trenches. The commandant is a very queer stick, but he's pretty sound at the bottom, though he lets his humorous faculties have full play in his lectures. We are to have a riding school and plenty of concerts and football, so we ought to be well fixed on the whole. Anyhow you will be pleased to know I shall be out of the danger zone till nearly the end of November. The war shows no sign of shutting down, and I'm afraid it is a two years' job yet at least.

I had five N.C.O's with me yesterday, and while we were waiting for the train they all went away and got blind tight. Someone had been giving them cognac, strictly against regulations – some d—spies, I expect. At any rate, I had a terrible time looking after them, and getting them and myself and my kit to the school here – it's some business, this army!

Well, I must hurry along to a lecture now. Meanwhile, all love to all at home.

From Bert

XLV

14th Corps Infantry School
Friday Oct. 26th, 1917

Dear Mater,

It's a miserable day, has been raining ever since last night, so we have come off parade an hour earlier to get dried up a little. We have plenty of work to do here and we have to do it smartly. This corps is the crack corps of the Army, and it's a great distinction for a division to keep its place in it. We have been doing 'Riding School' this afternoon, and as the field was soon torn up, we poor amateurs were jolted and bumped about till we felt like a bit of coal in a ship's bunker. I am pretty well out of condition with smoking too much, and eating too often, so the exercise found me out.

I have spent the last hour smearing myself with sulphur ointment, and my undies with blue unguent, as I am simply full of 'life', and the little devils have made my life miserable for the past ten days – ever since I slept on that wet straw. The one bath I had in that time didn't do much good, and I had no clean things to put on, so I have had to grin and bear them. They are a regular torture at night, I can tell – for anyone who has never been in the habit of them, that is – and I lie in bed and scratch and scratch and think of poor old Phil and sympathise with her and her kindred from the depths of my heart. I'll never let a dog go unwashed again after this little lot, I can assure you. I will have a good hard soak in the hottest water I can get tomorrow, and try a change of shirts, and hope for the best. My arms and body are absolutely covered with rash.

There is no news, except that the French appear to be doing very well in their latest attack, though I suppose this rain will hold them up again.

We are amongst the super-impressive Guards here, and have to look to our p's and q's. Some of the officers are magnificent men, much over six feet tall and broad and handsome like Marie Corelli's Apollos[1]. It does the heart good just to watch them, the acme of that curious product, the English Gentleman, I suppose. It's like being in Cambridge again, where we poor working-men, five-footer kind of people, used to feel like pygmies from the Dark Continent. It's horrible to think of the hundreds of those big bonnie boys who have been shot down wholesale and retail.

We have a half-day off tomorrow, I believe, and I shall take the opportunity to have another hot bath, as I have not yet rid myself of those lurking myriads.

I see all our casualties are in *The Times* today, and there is one more killed than we thought – died of wounds.

We are doing a fair amount of parade-ground drill, like they do it at Wellington Barracks, where I have watched them many a winter morning, under a long Guards sergeant, who jerks himself about as if he were all sockets and springs, and had been bought in a lot. He has a voice like shunting a goods-train. Everything is very strict, and we have to do pukka salutes, and turn up on parade to the minute. The Colonel is rather eccentric. He is long and twisted, and he walks up to subalterns and pulls the peak of their caps, or tweaks their ears, and says, "You're a funny little fellow, aren't you?" The officers here don't know how to take him at all – lacking imagination and a classical education.

All love from Bert

XLVI

14th Corps Infantry School
Sunday Oct. 28th, 1917

Dear Mater,

It is a gorgeous Autumn day with a nip of cold and a haze in the air, and the sun flaring away low in the heavens. Last night was paradisaical and I expected to be bombed, as we were on Friday night, but for this occasion we enjoyed the sleep of the just. There was a huge old moon and racing clouds, and the streets were as light and bright as though made with crystal. There was electricity in the nip of the night air, and one simply had to chase about and shout and make movement and noise enough to ease the bursting, buoyant life cooped within.

I have just had a hot bath after Church Parade, and am writing this before lunch. I had a bath yesterday afternoon too, but those awful strangers have established themselves in my undies and it will take some time to be rid of them. However, I have eased off the itch a great deal, and sleep better o'nights.

I am writing this in the ante-room of the mess, which has been the village school-room, and is now transformed into a sterner kind of school. We have a fire going and are as warm as toast, stuffy in fact, with all the baccy smoke and general frowst. Most of the ' students' are playing bridge, one or two reading the *Bystander* and so on, and one or two standing about doing nothing. The rest are letter-writing, including myself, at a desk-table which may possibly have come form Waring and Gillows, as it is quite an elegant piece of furniture.

We had one of the best services I have ever attended in the army, with a decent piano very well played, and quite a sensible little sermon from the old padre. We sang 'Fight the good fight', of course. That always crops up in the service in the army.

The scones arrived whole and in fresh condition this time, and not a mere glomeration of meal crumbs. They are very good, and so were the rice biscuits. The sugar and cocoa will come in useful too. I was glad to get the underpants, and I have got them on now, and the two pair of sox are jolly warm and thick, and will be very useful. The pills arrived in good condition, and are quite useable so far. I hope they won't share the fate of the others.

There is no news much, and except for visits from the Gothas,[1] we are well enough placed here, with plenty of comforts and conveniences and so forth. I wish it could last for the strife's duration.

We had a very curious lecture from a major on Friday on the 'Human Animal in Battle'. He treated the subject in an awful, cold-blooded, calculating fashion, and spoke just like the Bernhardts and the other old Fritzes. I see Horatio prophesies Xmas dinner in peace, but I shouldn't believe him if I were you – two years more to go at least. I see they are talking about cutting down the army at home, a kind of companion idea to shooting it down out here. Wish they had cut it down, by one particular officer last year.

All love to all,
From Bert

XLVII

14th Corps Infantry School,
Tuesday 30th Oct., 1917

Dear Mater,

It was a glorious night last night, and we had the usual boom, boom, boom, so I am rather glad to say that it is a wretched miserable day, and does not look like clearing up tonight. However, 'them sintiments' [sic] don't show much thought for the fellows up in the shell-holes, and I don't want to purchase a night's rest at the expense of their enhanced misery. Still, I am just about fed to the teeth with raid, raid, raid, every night, just as you are sinking into well-earned repose. This is a jolly good locality to keep away from, and that's the best that can be said for it.

We are fully launched on the course now, and it is very interesting work, though there's a frightful lot of it. However, as along as they leave me in snug quarters like this with a bed and sheets and no call to be up at unearthly hours in the night, I don't grumble at a full day's programme.

There is little news. The Italians seem to have done about as badly as they could,[1] – and we seem to be doomed in our allies – hardly a winner amongst them. Let's hope our brother, the Yank, will improve upon former selections.

The battalion are somewhere up the line, and they only had two days in that little town, so I have been lucky to get on this course after all. Unless something unusual happens I shall be here four weeks. I hear some of the W.A.A.C. were killed in recent raids on St. Omer, but you can never depend on these rumours. There are lots of spies about in this district, so we have to be very careful what we say in billets and estaminets and letters too. We had a lecture from a man on bayonet fighting, and he told us he had been talking to a V.C. sergeant in the K.R.R. whom, from his description, I recognised as our Stockton lad. He described his capturing the pill-box, which was much simpler than the papers make out, though a very brave deed none the less. We are going to have a lecture tonight on 'The Human Animal in the War', which promises to be interesting, especially if our George Robey[2] C.O. is going to give it.

I wonder if May has got her job yet – pity she can't drive a car – I see the R.F.C. want a few thousand more girl drivers.

I have just had your letter of the 21st, and, for heaven's sake, don't send any *shirts* as yet. I have quite enough shirts to go on with. Besides, I got two 'buckshee' shirts back with my laundry the other day. 'Buckshee' means anything over and above and extra to what one ought to have by right and regulation. I have had three parcels from you now, and I am pretty certain the others, including the fleece lining, will appear in good time.

I like your philosophising about matrimony, but I'm afraid the Fame stunt is in my blood. I shall never settle down in peace anywhere. I always have an object behind everything I do, whether it's working my brains out, or pig-slacking it, or coming to the war, and though the latter little event has certainly thrown me out for some years, I shall take up my prunes and poetry again as steadily as ever, if I get through the 'holocaust'. However, as you say, what is FAME? Some people seek it in the bellies of the howling guns; some in the portly porphyry pulpit, and some in the columns of the current 'dailies'.

I note Father's plaint about the price of foodstuffs, but he doesn't say anything about additions to my bank account – I suppose it can't be expected with FOOD at 10/6 a bottle.

There is a fine old moon again this evening, but it's hard to get enthusiastic about the weather when you know it is going to herald Zepps and Gothas and all the rest of the blooming gang. There certainly is a war in this part of France, or rather Flanders, and I wish we were happily on our way Southwards once more. However, I am alright so far.

All love to all, from Bert

XLVIII

14th Corps Infantry School,
Sunday, Nov. 4th 1917

Dear Mater,

The weather has changed a bit, and it has been dark and foggy the last night or two, thank the weather Gods! On fine nights we can hear the planes passing here on their way to England, and they return about an hour and a half afterwards, a bit lighter probably. Sometimes they don't pass but stay over us, and then there's trouble.

I have been out riding this afternoon and feel pretty tired. I shall be a horseman in about another ten years' time, but meanwhile it do make 'ee stiff, it do.

We are pretty busy here, but enjoy it nevertheless. It is our day off tomorrow – Saturday night now – and I hope there will be a mail for me. I mean to have a good 'barf' in the morning, as I am still quite 'lively'. I get my washing done very well here, which is a great boon.

I have just been reading *John Bull*, who still predicts an early finish, but don't believe him. I wish we were going off to Italy to stop the eager Hun, but that's not the luck of the 17th div.

I am still waiting to hear if May is swaggering about with a Red Cross on her manly bosom yet. How is the coat getting on?

Our General was in the *Mirror* 30th October – wounded, gassed as a matter of fact – name Bond.

It was very muddy riding this afternoon, but the country here is very pretty, and there are hills and woods, quite different from up in Flanders. I nearly got knocked off by a motor-bus, but a magnificent display of horsemanship (I don't think!) managed to pull clear. Winter is coming on fast, but I have the fleece now and my yellow 'mac', and my great-coat, so should be alright. I can manage quite well till I get some leave, which ought not to be much beyond Xmas. I think I shall have to apply for a journalist job when I get back to the Batt. – must place my miraculous talents to the best use – to say nothing of keeping away from the front line.

The couple in my billet are the most miserable old sinners on earth, but they are awfully clean and tidy. They sit all day over an empty stove, sipping black coffee, and coughing like onion sauce. They sleep just above me, so if the bombs do drop, they will act as sand-bags and give me a chance, though the whole house wouldn't stop a flock of sheep. I think a bomb in the back garden would collapse it like a cheese-cracker.

All love to all from Bert

XLIX

14th Corps Infantry School,
Tues. Nov. 6th, 1917

Dear Mater,

We got over Nov. 5th safely enough without any fireworks from the Alleyman, though we rather expected some kind of celebration. It was a pitch dark night, however, and we slept in peace and did not wake up in pieces. Today it is drizzling and foggy, and our field manoeuvres are cancelled in favour of lectures.

There is no news here much. I believe the Boche is still being beaten, but it's a bit slow. Meanwhile we hear a rumour of Revolution and Red War in Ireland, though we have had no confirmation yet. I wish our division were going to Italy, but I don't think there's much chance of that.

I am rather disturbed to hear that you have been overdoing the wash-tub, but I put faith in your stout constitution to pull you through – if it has not been undermined with those night-caps. I notice Father turns up with his ancient maxim, "Go easy" – seems to spend his bally existence on that tack, but it's not the way to make Lloyd Georges or Douggie Haigs. They believe in riding *hard,* thank heaven, and not that stolid Dutchman go-easy stunt. After all, you might as well make something manly of your life, and not slide along like a rusty barge on a choked canal all the days of your life. Leave that to meaner spirits, eh?

I was surprised to hear you had had snow already. I think the world has turned topsy-turvy, and the whole outfit is going to chuck up the sponge and fall into the sun. We have warmer weather here now, muggy and drizzly and wet-feety, but not at all chilly. So the pear-crop has gone to futility again. It wants a man at them and then you might be able to get some eatable fruit. Any ordinary Fritz would have them bearing full and well in a couple of years. The trees are alright. It is only care and tending and common savvy that is required. Advise a careful study of the Parable of the Talents.

I have a bit of cold, and am trying to nurse it into pneumonia, but I don't think I shall have any luck, as I have been in much better health since I started the course, and have had plenty of exercise and regular hours sleep and so forth. I am a bit podgy and keep bustin' my buttons, but that's neither here nor there. Better than poetry and prunes, I expect you will say, and in some ways I agree, but I'm afraid the fame canker is in my brain, and I am sure to get back to the desk, and 'plain livin' and 'distorted thinkin' at the first opportunity.

All love to all, from Bert

L

Friday Nov. 8th

Dear Mater,

The weather has been lovely today, a fine Autumn day with just a touch of cold . We have been out on the countryside making maps, and the briskness and freshness of the afternoon made it very enjoyable. We got lifts on motor-lorries to and from our village and had a tour of tramping over stubble and marshy fields, and a general roam round. The trees have almost finished shedding, but the hedges are still very beautiful, and the bright yellow leaves and the vivid scarlet berries make a pretty picture. The fields are sodden, and a few old magpies are all the feathered folk that are left to cheer us. There are whole flocks of magpies in this district, and with their long barred tails and snowy tummies are as common as peewits at home. Villages are dotted about the countryside as frequent as farms at home, and every hamlet has a big church and a tall steeple, so that you can see a dozen or so spires in quite a small area. Windmills too are stuck up on every ridge, and you can see their long sails swinging round in the breeze wherever you look. The farms are well-built and carefully tended, much different from the ramshackle, haphazard affairs we found further down in France. The French girls are awfully clever at dressing themselves, and when you see them walking out after Mass on Sundays in all their finery, and neat costumes and pretty hats, you can't imagine they are the same girls you have seen doing their housework every morning in dirty old smocks and thick ugly clogs. It amuses me to hear the fuss English girls make about "going on the land". Why, all the women work like fury here, and in every field you see old women, who look about 108, bent and tough as trees, and young girls of 15 and 16, with their flappy hats, huge boots, and thick stockings, gathering in the beet crops, or spreading the manure like so many young horses. They don't seem to go in for fancy costumes or *Daily Mirror* photographs like the dear girls at home, but I bet they are ten times as useful.

They tell me we are going straight up the line when we leave here in a fortnight's time, but, of course, you never can be sure.

I am down to play football on Saturday, and shall enjoy it if the weather is as pleasant as today. I would give a tenner or so to have the chance to break my arm, as I did in the days of yore, but you can bet I shall have no luck. However, it won't be for want of playing a robust game, and somebody will get some bruises.

I am going over to the nearest railway-station – five miles away – to see a girl just like Jenny Peacock. She is in an officers' estaminet and quite one of the attractions of France.

She is fair and peachy, and awfully like the Redcar beauty without any of her meretricious aids to handsomeness.

They are bombing over Dunkirk way as I write this, and I hope they don't push over here as it is no great way off. Has May started off yet? Your accounts of Phil are very funny, and I wish I were there to watch her. I wonder if she has gone to the Vet yet? Well, good-night and love to all,

From Bert

LI

Sunday 10th Nov. 1917

Dear Mater,

I am writing this in an estaminet with some paper borrowed from a mad-emoiselle très charmante, but I can't write very fast because she will insist on sitting in the next chair and overlooking operations, so there is rather too much distraction. The weather has been pretty bad since my last, and the roads and paths are worse than ever.

I went over to see the belle of the district again yesterday, and tramped back at some unearthly hour of the night. The roads are absolutely inde-scribable, with great ruts about two feet deep, and sliddery [sic] and dan-gerous. I have seen a good many of the big waggons upset in the ditch, and it is a terrible job to get them out again. I should think they must be jolly good drivers to keep them on the road at all.

We have a good band at the School now, so we get a little good music, and there are concerts about three nights a week. All the best men are here, I think, so we manage to amuse ourselves among ourselves. There is any amount of bridge played in the mess, but I haven't taken it up yet – can't afford to lose, so I suppose I can't afford to play.

I shall have to refit myself when I get some leave, as my tunic is just about falling to bits, but it will do for winter, or till I can get home. I got a new pair of boots for nothing and they are jolly good and dry, though not very pretty. The old lady in my billet washes my things for me beautifully, though I don't know where she gets the water from, as they never seem to have any conveniences of that kind – never have a hot water cistern, or a decent open hearth. You would laugh at the stoves here, all closed up, with great long pipes running through the roof. They put the stove in the middle of the room generally. Their Sunday dinner smells simply awful, like an old cabbage-patch, and they never seem to have any meat, always lettuce and carrots and little turnips. I don't know what savouries they use, but the smell is enough to spoil your appetite for a week.

All love to all,
Bert

LII

Friday Nov. 16th, 1917

Dear Mater,

I was playing football on Wednesday, and I am still stiff and tired from that, as we had a very hard game, and I am very much out of condition. However, I enjoyed it immensely and hope to get some more. I discovered a shop where they have boxes of dates, but they are 1/6 a lot, which is rather exorbitant even in war-time. However, they are very good and fresh, and we expect to be done down. When I get back to the battalion I intend to put in an application to go to the 'Propaganda' department, which would be a nice cushy job, and suited to my journalistic acquirements, but what a 'ope!! I'm glad my concern as to your health was taken to heart, and am sure you will be more reasonable about the 'mentalities' in future. You will get the new disease, 'ache-backitis', which all the dear ladies who have to resign their domestics and footmen are suffering from now. The latest lead-swinging device at the front is 'barragitis'. I think I shall catch it at the earliest opportunity.

We have just had an address from a Bishop chaplain chap, which did *not* impress us, as it was mainly incredible stuff about God Almighty, and his problematical offspring, and a lot more inexplicable stuff. I think the Churches ought to keep out of this business, or better still, shut up shop at home and come out here as fighting-men, and not as hot air experts. Anyhow, I know if Church Parade were not compulsory they would not get many of the boys to attend them. That fact alone is enough to condemn the whole silly system. The darn clerical mob at Cambridge always used to feed me to the rear molars, and they were nothing but humbug, humbug and again humbug. They are just the same out here, and as they are arch-humbugs themselves, so they are open to any old humbug that anyone likes to feed them with.

My cough is getting better, I think, and my live-stock have practically disappeared, so I feel a little happier about myself nowadays.

I got to know a young sergeant-major in the French cavalry who lives at Paris, and he has invited me to see him there when possible. His wife is premier mannequin at Paquin's.

The weather has been pretty fair this week, and I have done a good deal of tramping about darn ploughed fields and so forth on manoeuvres. However, we have plenty of fun and rather enjoy it. We have a fine band at the School and get plenty of music.

We miss the ladies though, as there is nothing presentable within five miles. I am going into the town tomorrow, and hope to have some 'divertissement', as the French say. My French is greatly improved nowadays.

Well, au revoir for the present and all love to all from Bert.

LIII

Tuesday Nov. 20th, 1917

Dear Mater,

I was very upset about poor old Charlie, but in a way it has given me more courage to face death if it has to come. After all, it is simply a case of joining the great majority, and following the path of all the very best of our generation. Besides, when all our friends and comrades are killed off, and scattered to the winds, very little remains in life worth the continuance. Poor old Charlie, he was very keen to get out here again, and refused a post in the orderly room at home, which was offered him. As you say, it is so sudden and disastrous that one can't properly realise it.

I was very pleased to hear that May had got going at last, and hope to see her as a V.A.D. when I get some leave, which will be Lord knows when. It ought to be a good education for her, and she will enjoy the regular hours and settled work too. Does she live at the hospital, or at home? I can't understand what objections Father could have to her doing a bit after three or four years lazing, but will put them down to the usual prolific source.

Tell Nurse Tomlinson that I am not in the habit of being "friendly" with my servant, but if she means to ask has he been received into my good graces once again, I can't say he has. He is too young to make a good batman, and I shall get him changed when I get back to the Batt. He has to be told everything, and even then, as often as not, he doesn't do it. He has no idea of shining leather, and makes buttons about as bright as a wet day in Middlesbrough. No, sah, he sure 'ave to go.

I'm afraid your idea of poetry is a trifle conventional, and personally I don't think that kind of thing can be used for the purposes of mere artistic dexterity, at least not till long after the event has been softened and assuaged by the passing years.

The parcel was very welcome, and the watch seems to be fairly good, and has not stopped yet, though I don't think I would trust it very far. I will wear the body-belt if need be, but the weather is very mild so far. The scones arrived in good order, but the butter was a bit lofty. Thanks very much indeed for the whole outfit.

I like your objections to Italy, because "the enemy is in great strength there". There are one or two Germans on this side too, and beaucoup guns, and quite a few side-shows. However, they haven't sent us, so we are fixed here for winter at any rate. I go up the line on Saturday, and hope you have started to address me at the battalion once again. I don't fancy lying out in the shell-holes, but don't mind as long as there are no 'stunts' on. We can hear the guns roaring like Hades here.

There is no news much from here, and I haven't a bit of an idea what is happening up the line, except that we hear much bombardment and general hullabaloo. However, I shall know soon enough, so don't worry. I was in St. Omer last Sunday and had a very decent time. We were driven by a staff car which went like mad on the greasy roads, and we had a fine breezy run and thoroughly enjoyed it. I had a chat with one of the W.A.A.C. girls and it was good to talk to an English girl again, although rather against orders, I believe, though the orders on these matters get so mixed and contradicted that one never knows when one is right or wrong. I had a look round to see if there was anything worth buying Li for a wedding gift, but couldn't find anything suitable. All the best shops are stocked with English goods at treble prices, and the few French articles are pretty trashy and not worth sending over. Would you like some hand-made lace, as this is a lace district, and if so, what article would you like, collars or table-cloths or what-not?

I expect I shall be playing football again tomorrow – I am just recovering from my stiffness from that last dose, but I enjoyed the game.

There is a new moon tonight, worse luck, so I suppose we will be wakened by the rotten old boom, boom. I expect they will be after London. I don't think aeroplanes can reach the North, thank the Lord – wish I were there with you, to enjoy the lovely moons over the hills and the cold sunsets. In my last letter to Charlie I asked him when we would have another trip into the dales together. It's difficult to think that he has gone unto the hills for ever, and will never come again to rest in the vale of Tees.

But I don't think anything material counts much nowadays, and the only thing is to go on living decently and cleanly, and hoping for a clear passage when the time comes. I don't see any sign of the finish of the war, and am thoroughly sick of both English and Boche. They are both fighting for the same bone, and the rest of the world can go to Hell for them.

Well, I will write again soon. Meanwhile, all love to all and to Nurse Tomlinson,

From Bert

LIV

Thursday Nov. 22nd, 1917

Dear Mater,

There is no news much. The School disperses on Saturday, but we don't know whether we are going up into the line or where or anything at all as to where the battalion are at present. I will let you know as soon as possible. I had a letter from Father today, but notice that D.L. & Co. were not going to give a bonus, though whether it referred to shareholders only or to the works staff as well could not make out from the *Star's* report.

I hope my banking account has been improved, in spite of the delay in bonus. I have been away three months now, and it should have seen several accretions. I shall need a bit if I get any leave. Food is a norrible price out here. I have just bought some wee little macaroons that you wouldn't have given ½d. each for in the old days. They were 1½d. each, exactly three times as much and a quarter the size.

Eggs are a prohibitive price and we get one for breakfast about three times a week, whilst fresh milk is thin and scarce. Good butter is about 4/– a pound.

We had a good news-sheet this morning, and we have done a good stunt down near Cambrai[1] apparently – a great surprise to everyone. I hope it continues as well as it started. The cavalry have already been in it apparently.

The School staff entertained all the kiddies of the village to tea yesterday and gave them bon-bons and presents and whatnot. There were three hundred children – it's a terrible prolific village, and they seem to grow kiddies like tomatoes or Belgian hares – and it was a great sight to see them all buzzing about, and chattering in Flemish and French. What a noise! When they had all been supplied with toys and tuck they got up to depart, and all sang the Marseillaise in fine style. Some of them were slipping out to dump their gifts at home and then coming back for more – just like the Tommies with the rum ration. All the old people in the village seem to think about is that it must have cost an awful lot, and that Monsieur le Colonel must have beaucoup money! They are like a lot of old Hebrews for money in this district, and they hoard and save the clothes off their backs.

We had a very fine concert last night with the band of the 1st Black Watch.

There is very good news from the South again. We seem to have got five miles ahead, and the cavalry are operating. The latest is we have taken Cambrai.

I am going into the town this afternoon again, as we have a half day off before the course breaks up. There's nothing much to do when we get there except dodge air-raids, and buy things you don't want.

The weather keeps very mild, praise the Lord, and it is a lovely day today, with quite a warm sun. The roads and training grounds, of course, are in a very vile condition. I hope the weather holds for our offensive in the South, as we have had very poor luck with the weather hitherto, and that has been one of the main reasons of the slowness of our advance, that and the desire to minimise casualties.

I wonder how May is settling down to the hospital. I shall have to get a blighty and come up to be nursed. What a nope!

I did quite well in the written exam here, and came out second top, but I'm afraid if they have hopes of making me a soldier they are going to be disappointed, as I'm darned if I can get interested in military matters, too much of the freelance about me, I'm afraid.

Well, will close now with all love to all,

From Bert

LV

Monday, 26th November 1917

Dear Mater,

I'm very sorry I have not been able to write you before this, but I have been kept busy since I left the School last Saturday, and the conditions prevailing made letter-writing impossible. We are not very comfortably fixed even now, but we have a table and a fire, so that is the beginning of a home. I received two letters from you while I was in the line yesterday. One was addressed to me at the battalion, written last Wed., the 21st. The other had been wandering all round France, and had been addressed to the Divisional Depot Battn. and written exactly a month before – October 17th. It wished me many happy returns of my birthday. With it I received a card from poor old Charlie written from Salisbury Plain just before he came out. I shall keep it as a very precious souvenir. It is a photo of the Lady Chapel in Salisbury Cathedral . He says, "Am on draft for France – thank God – and should leave early next week. Will write soon as I get an address." He never got his address, poor old chap, and he will never write me again.

I had a letter from Father yesterday, and was glad to hear that May is settling down at the hospital. How does the fur coat go down with a V.A.D. apron? – reminds me of Bath, and the little girl who used to stay with my friends there.

It's durn foolishness to go up into the line amongst all the noise and trouble and nasty death. I don't want to see any more. I think the Somme about fed my pig. Nowadays I have 'beaucoup wind up'.

We have been living in tin huts for the last fortnight, and though they are about as chilly as charity they are better than tents for this weather. They say there is no smoke without fire, but we manage to get pretty near it. At any rate, we get the hut absolutely bang full of fumes and smell and thickness, and our eyes stream with tears of joy, but I'm hanged if we see so much as an odd flame for our trouble. When we do get a nice red coke fire going it is usually bed-time, and it has to go out again. Oo-er, isn't it cold getting up in the mornings? I took our company to the Baths this morning – weird affairs and had one myself. I did a little big game hunting in my vest, and had a fine bag. The bath was well-meant but a bit cold.

I note your designs on my bachelor state, but refuse to be party to these underhand transactions, and refuse to betray the brotherhood of bachelors.

I have bought myself a new pair of big black knee-boots. They are a size too big, but I wear three pairs of sox and keep fairly warm. It was terribly cold for three days, but has gone mild again. I used to wash in water with great chunks of ice in it, ugh!

My tummy is not so well again, as the life is too irregular. It was getting fairly well at the School. Well, I will close tout de suite with all love to all,
     From Bert

LVI

Saturday, Dec. I st 1917

Dear Mater,

We are on the move today but I have a minute or so before lunch. It is terribly cold but we have not had snow yet, so I suppose it is a little warmer than up on the Northeast coast. There are rumours that we are to go out for a rest very soon, but as yet it is rumour and no more.

I am pleased to hear that May is settling down to a little toil, though not before time. Father's complacent remark about us all doing our bit is a screaming joke, all things considered. We have been at war three and a half years now! It looks as if we will still be at it after another three and a half too. We had a game at football yesterday with the shells bursting round about at a pretty safe distance, but it was certainly a funny experience.

On Thursday we went over to have a tour round a ruined town, whose name is now famous all over Europe.[1] It was a sight of desolation – hardly one stone left upon another, and the famous Hall[2] nothing more than a tall mound of riven stones and slate and cement. There were two English ladies there as we came away, though it was being shelled spasmodically at the time. Old Fritz is rather active up this way with his metal and his nasty noises. In fact, I don't like the war in this region, and shall be glad when we move Southwards, if ever.

We have been inspected by our Brigadier this morning, and I think we put up a pretty good show. They will be putting us into fresh stunts, for we are getting a name as a fighting division. It's rather a double-edged kind of honour, of course.

This district is the human limit in the way of inconvenience and rush and worry. I wonder if the world will ever settle down to peace and quiet again.

We are burning up our hut to keep ourselves warm – strictly against orders.

With all love to you all.

From Bert

LVII

[part of undated letter]

We are a little way from the line for a few days now, and then we do another tour for a week or so, and then I believe we will be having a fairly long rest, but you never can tell. I joined them in the line last Saturday, and it is pretty awful. By the way, the boy that went instead of me did *not* come out of it, as you hope in your letter. Moreover it seems that my old sergeant Bricknell was killed after he had got a very nice Blighty. He has not been traced to any of the hospitals, and his wife has heard nothing, so I'm afraid the dear old chap has gone away, after over two years out here, and at least half a dozen marvellous escapes. He had been in everything, and should really have been allowed out of that show, but, as he said when I saw him last, that wasn't his luck. He was like a father to me in the old days, and we had queer times on the Somme together. I have slept huddled up on top of him many a night, amongst the mud and slush. I used to give him my share of the mess whisky and he used to make me tea on his 'Tommy Cooker'. We were real pals, and I am very sick at his passing. If ever a man had done his share, and deserved a good billet and a rest, he did.

As you say, there is not much feather bed about this business, and at present we are twelve in a little hut. We sleep on the floor and mess in the same hut, so you get your face trodden on, and find people shaving in your tea-cup, and lose your boots one at a time, and find your shirt under the table, and enjoy yourself in thousands of ways – especially when you are lying awake waiting to be bombed.

I had Father's letter of the 19th just before I came away, and note his exhortation to take care of myself, but there are other and heavier monitors quite close by, to warn me of that. Besides, you can't take much care against a barrage of six-inch shells. Perhaps I had better tu quoque, and tell him to take care of himself and his good name.

I am rather porky once more, but quite cheerful about it, and my stomach is coming round slowly. It was getting quite settled in the peace and settled hours at the School, but I don't suppose the shell-holes will do it any good. I don't think I can manage the war-kit photograph, but will look round corners and see what can be done. A Captain who has just come out, and who saw me last at Forest Hall in January, asked me if I had a brother in the Staffords! He didn't recognise me in my war-flesh! I'm a bit of a chameleon, but will return to normal when the war lapses, and I get settled work and plenty of golf.

I am surprised to hear your account of the ration famine, and the police-men on guard. I ought to be back at Cannock again, eh? What price bacon?

Your accounts of Phil are very amusing. I'm afraid she is being spoiled, and turning into a slipper-worrier. Would like to see her once again.

I had a letter from Mrs. Hansen, and she hopes to see me Prime Minister some day. I hope the Boche does not frustrate her hopes. She writes me very nice long letters, and she is really very charming.

All love to all at home,
From Bert

LVIII

[part of undated letter]

I am looking forward to hearing some of the experiences of Nurse Tomlinson, and expect to find her enormously improved, and a bit more tidy and thoughtful than of yore.

I received your last parcel safely and must thank you very much indeed. The cards came in very handy for the mess, though I don't play myself – can't afford it. The biscuits were très agréable, but the sugar shortage was very evident. It strikes me we are better off out here for supplies than you are at home nowadays. We seem to have plenty of sugar, and we often get fresh country butter, though the army issue is margarine, of course. Eggs are 2 for 8½d. We get plenty of good jellies and jam, cheese and bread and so on. We generally have about five courses for dinner, and three for lunch. We have soup, fish (salmon or herrings), meat and vegetables, fruit and custard, and sardines on toast to finish with. One of our mess had a plum-pudding sent today – the first to arrive, so we are starting early. By the way, I have taken over the post of Mess President today – some occupation. I am losing money on it, as they won't pay up their mess bills.

I was in the village last night, and had a good old jabber in French for a couple of hours with the madame in the laceshop. She had some very pretty little affairs in lace – handmade, and I was tempted to buy some, but there would be difficulty in getting it home, so shall wait till I get leave.

I have heard a lot of nasty things said about the Belgians, but, for myself, I like them better than the French, and find them very straightforward and plain spoken. They are much more industrious and sanitary than the French, and much more like the English. They hate the Boche, as they have had more dealings with him than we have. Like everybody else they are tired of the war, and as they get bombed and bombarded every night, you can't be surprised at that. Some of them are rather too keen after business and are too much like Jews in that respect, but, of course, there are always goats and sheep.

We will have a pretty long railway journey tomorrow, I expect, but it is in the right direction. I hope I shall 'touch' for a posh job somewhere before we go back again. I am in for one as instructor on GAS what 'opes!

LIX

Wed. Dec. 12th, 1917

Dear Mater,

I had a letter from you and one from May yesterday. I was glad to notice from May's letter that she seems to have a sane appreciation of her own age and her duties in the world, and think the work must be doing her a world of good. I note she received the cheque, and will be glad to come home to see her in the coat, and also in her swagger uniform.

I have put in an application for employment on the journalistic staff of GHQ, but I don't suppose anything will come of it. I don't think I will ever be of much use in the trenches again, as my nerves seem to have gone very queer these days.

I like the way May writes about people who have been killed: "Isn't it awful?" Well, just a bit, if she can't say anything more adequate than that. I should think she might leave out the lamentation touch and simply state bald fact.

Your letter is full of woe, but I discount a bit of it for the winter nights and the loneliness, though I know you don't have an easy time with the 'whisky fiend'. Pity he can't summon up a little self-control.

We are on the edge of a big forest, and the country round about is very pretty, though the roads are in a terrible condition., We are only a mile from the little village where we stayed for six weeks in the summer when I was out before. I went over to see my old billet this afternoon, and Madame recognised me straightaway. She's going to give me some handmade lace for May. Her daughter makes reams and reams of it, and it is sold at Paris. All the boys who were in that mess with me are dead now, all except Wood. We used to have some riotous times and turned the old farm inside out. But Madame was very glad to see me, and was desolated to hear about poor Snowie and the rest.

I receive the papers regularly and am glad of the news, though it is largely death and desolation. I have had no time to write for days, as we have been on the move the whole time, and even now we have notice to quit. However, we may stay here over Christmas and we should have a good time if we do, as there is lots of livestock on the farm, turkeys, geese, ducks and so forth, and plenty of honey, fresh butter and coffee. We are miles and miles from anywhere, right out in the country, worse than Ingleby. However, we can always make a noise amongst ourselves and should be quite jolly in our mess, with plenty of songs and jokes going round. There are no Mademoiselles, but we are no worse off for that, as women are more often than not a blamed waste of time – yourself excepted, my dear. I note that you have sent another parcel, and will look out for it. We get plenty of parcels and cakes and things in the mess, as there is one boy who has about three a day, sent by his lady-loves.

The country here is very pretty with great open sweeps of landscape and long ridges with shallow valleys. The forest, of course, is leafless now, but it is very pretty nevertheless. We were out felling saplings for fuel this afternoon, and there was a grand red sunset far away behind the forest, and then the bright stars began to shoot out and the peace and quiet of the night came down and wrapped everything in cosy, friendly darkness. We had a holiday today after a long march yesterday, and we shall be hard at it to-morrow. I shall write as often as possible and will let you know as soon as I get anywhere in the danger zone again. But meanwhile you may rest tranquil.

Well, good night and bye-bye for the present, Mater. Love to all at home. How's the dog? Hasn't she gone to the vet's yet?

From Bert

LX

Friday, Dec. 14th 1917

Dear Mater,

They have spoiled our vision of six weeks' rest again, and we are en route for you may guess where. I received your parcel just before I came away, and have only now found time to open it and read the letter therein. We are waiting for the train in a little village, and I have just had a shave and wash and feel fairly fit. I slept on the floor in my clothes last night and did not get much sleep out of it. There were orderlies and generals and staff-captains and all manner of weird folk coming and going all night long, and I never knew when I was going to have my face trodden on. However, it is all in the war, and when you do a move at a minute's notice you can't expect to rest in the lap of luxury. I suppose we will have another happy evening on the train tonight, O joy, O rapture!

The watch keeps pretty good time, and shows no sign of slacking off as yet. By the way, if you are so badly off for sugar, butter etc. you need not send me scones and so on, as we get plenty out here, and I am quite an enormous size as it is. The shortbread was a good idea and it will go down well with the boys in the mess.

I was glad to read Lansdowne's[1] letter, and hope it will do something to slacken the corpse-creating business which is in such a fine swing at present. It's a pity if England can't state definitely what she is out for. It looks rather shady, at any rate.

I have been watching regiments entraining all day long, as I came along with Brigade H.Q. by automobile – much better than walking. I have seen them come up in their hundreds, poor blighters, after a twelve-mile march, and they are played bravely into their trains by their band, and off they go! The Staffords are not due here for hours yet. We may be going into a warm show or we may not. It rather depends on the Boche really, but we are hoping for the best anyway.

All our plans for the Xmas goose are upset, and I had a good chance of a post as Brigade Gas Officer, but that seems to have gone west too, as we came away in such a hurry. However, I shall do my best to push it.

I'm afraid my leave is postponed indefinitely now, as all leave is stopped, but it may crop up again towards the end of the war. Well, I had better have another look at these trains, so will say bye-bye with all love to all.

From Bert

Don't be anxious if you get no news.

LXI

Sunday, Dec. 16th 1917

Dear Mater,

Just a line to tell you that we are fairly near the trouble once again. I had one of the most norrible [sic] journeys the night before last in a carriage with no windows in it. There was a freezing cold wind and six people in the carriage and we were there for 14 hours with never a drop to drink or eat, so you can guess we rather enjoyed the picnic. To add to the hilarity we had wind well up in the attic regions as we knew we were going to a very nasty district, and did not know whether we might not be going into the line. It is rather beastly cold here and we are in tin huts once more and sleeping on the floor. The Battalion had a footer match this afternoon in a snow-storm, and we managed to draw with the Sherwoods. I have had no news of you for a day or two. One more officer has gone on leave, so I am next but one for leave, though if I get my brigade job (what a nope!) I shall not get my leave, of course. However, I would rather have my job.

By the way, I have discovered my old British Warm with the fur lining. The officer in whose charge I left it has returned to the Battalion, and on Church Parade this morning I found the blighter was coolly wearing my old B.W. He never offered to mention it to me, and when I accused him of it, he actually denied it and said he got it at Teague's in Jermyn St. However, it had your old fur lining in it and I knew it too well to mistake. I don't know whether to have him up or not, but as he has promised to return it, and seems to be rather frightened about it, I may let him go. Rather a horrible thing for a temp[orar]y gentleman to do!

There is no news much. We may move at any moment – rather depends on the old Boche. There does not seem much chance of the Xmas peace coming to anything. I was surprised to hear that Bottomley's meeting was such a success, as I should have thought people had more sense by now, than encourage such an outsider as that. He has been proved a liar and a bumptious rogue often enough to put him into any gaol. His visit to France goes one better and proves him a very gullible fool too.

We are in the midst of a most desolate district, with ruined villages, and battered woods, and old trench lines as far as the eye can see. However, it is not so muddy and miserable as Belgium. I don't know what the trenches are like up this way and I am not bursting eager to find out. The usual bombing business is now on umpteen times nightly. I am about fed up with this war, but somebody seems to enjoy it. The Russians have thought better of it, and one wonders when more enlightened folk will do likewise.

We managed to borrow a gramophone in the last place we stayed and we had a little music – the first I have heard here except for regimental bands. It was very enjoyable and we kept it running overtime. I wonder how May is getting along with her music – still as rag-timey as ever. I often think of that new song she had, 'The Bells of St. Mary's', but I can't quite remember it properly – wish I were home to hear it again. I would give a penny or two for my discharge, eh, what?

Well, all love to all at home,
    From Bert

LXII

Wed. 19th Dec. 1917

Dear Mater,
It is horribly cold here and I don't feel very much like writing as my feet are frozen through, and we have absolutely no conveniences. We have two or three inches of snow and icicles and a regular arctic kind of landscape. There

are great chunks of ice floating in my pail when I wash in the morning, and my toothbrush bristles are frozen stiff, and my sponge like a chunk of stone. We are on the move again tomorrow, and I fancy we shall get Xmas in the line. I hope it is quiet, that's all

We hear rumours that it is fairly safe, but can't say till we arrive. I have taken up 'Bridge' for something to do, and find it quite an absorbing pursuit especially as it is no use attempting to write letters under these conditions. I wish I could be with you for Xmas, but I am still one off leave, and will not get it till the end of January probably. I may have a 'blighty' before that with luck – what a nope!

I had better wish you the compliments of the season in this one, as I don't suppose I shall be able to get another off in time to arrive for Christmas. I don't suppose we shall be particularly happy, but if people will have wars, what can you do? There is a great deal of outcry against Russia,[1] but I think she had a good deal of common sense, what do you say? Well, we have had a plum pudding and some mince pies already.

I haven't time to write Xmas greetings to all the people I should like, but perhaps I shall be able to make up at New Year. I was a bit better placed last year, eh? Almost makes me wish I had stayed in the War Office. Never mind, I am amongst all the boys and best people here, and the rest can go to blazes their own way.

Well, all love, mater, and a merry Xmas to all at home, including the dog,
    From Bert

LXIII

Christmas Eve, 1917

Dear Mater,
I just have a minute for a short note. We are all safe so far, but darn shivering cold and uncomfy. I sent a field p.c. yesterday. We are well in the war and having an amusing time with old Fritz. We are wondering if he will come to 'fraternise' tomorrow.

All love to all at home, and all the season's greetings,
    From Bert

LXIV

3rd General,
Thurs. Jan. 10th 1918

Dear Mater,
Still in bed and just waiting for the doctor to put in his daily appearance. The weather is the last word, and the Channel looks grey and threatening, washing round the cliffs opposite. I don't know what my fate will be when I leave here, possibly go to the Base and from there back to the Battalion. If so, I

shall probably get my leave pretty soon. There are millions of VADs here, but they all complain they are overworked, and they don't seem to have much time to spare. The war seems to be going to last for ever, though Lloyd George's last speech was certainly much milder. Doctor says my lungs are getting better.

All love to all at home,
From Bert

LXV

3rd General,
Friday, Jan. 11th 1918

Dear Mater,

I received your letter yesterday and must say you seem to have vocal 'wind up'. I am really quite alright though I had a terrible chest for about a fortnight. However, I got over the worst of it in the trenches, and it was only because I started to vomit that I had to come down the line. I don't know what they are going to do with me when I leave here. I'm rather a duffer in the winter and can't stand cold. We have a lovely view of the Channel from our window. It's rather tantalising, though I'm not so very keen on Blighty.

All love to all,
From Bert

Notes to Letters

I

1. C.K. Ogden, 1889-1957. Founder of the *Cambridge Magazine*, and inventor of Basic English.
2. On 3 April British troops attacked the mine crater at St. Eloi (which had been held by the Germans since March 30), captured it and established the line beyond it. This success was officially reported on April 10.

II

1. On 16 December 1914 the port of Hartlepool was shelled by three German warships: the *Seydlitz*, *Moltke* and *Blücher*.

III

1. Later, on 11 July, during the Battle of the Somme, Maj.Gen. T.D. Pilcher, commander of the 17th (Northern) Division, was to be relieved of his command by his corps commander, Lieut.-Gen. H.S. Horne, for not driving his men hard enough. Pilcher had been reluctant to throw men forward into wasteful assaults that were doomed to fail with unnecessarily heavy losses.

IV

1. On 24 April serious disturbances broke out in Dublin, with the rebels seizing the

post office and other key buildings. On 26 April 11 rioters were killed in street fighting. The remaining rebels surrendered on May 1.

2. Herbert Asquith, Liberal Prime Minister. At this time he was head of the coalition government, and was becoming increasingly unpopular for his handling both of the war and of the Irish question. He was eventually forced to resign in December 1916, and was replaced by Lloyd George.

3. Tommies' slang for anti-aircraft gun.

V

1. In the Battle of Jutland on 31 May, 14 British and 11 German ships were sunk. On 5 June H.M.S. *Hampshire* sank with Lord Kitchener on board, after hitting a mine.

2. Almost certainly Armentières.

VI

1. Voluntary Aid Detachments. These had been formed in 1909. At the outbreak of the war there were some 75,000 volunteers, mostly women and girls. They were to play a key role supporting trained nurses in hospitals and on hospital ships. Many of them came from refined and sheltered middle-class backgrounds. They were required to carry out menial tasks, and the shocking wounds they confronted gave them first-hand knowledge of the effects of the weapons of war on men's bodies, an experience given to few civilians.

XII

1. On 6 and 7 September British troops made some significant progress on the Lens front.

2. A night raid on 3 September resulted in 107 naval personnel killed and 86 wounded.

XVIII

1. Horatio Bottomley, 1860-1933. Founded *John Bull* in 1906. Liberal MP for South Hackney, 1906-12; Independent MP for South Hackney, 1918-22. Declared bankrupt more than once; imprisoned, 1922-27. This fraudulent character was remarkably influential in the popular press and as a public speaker. He was reviled by the serving men.

XXI

1. Tommies' slang, meaning 'finished', 'all gone' (from French 'il n'y en a plus').

XXIII

1. A major British offensive was launched on 20 September east of Ypres on an eight-mile front.

XXIV

1. In the Menin Road area on 22 September strong German counter-attacks were successfully resisted.

2. Officer's kit-bag.

XXIX

1. On 26 September British forces renewed their offensive east of Ypres.

XXXVI

1. Field Marshal Douglas Haig, 1861-1928.

XXXVII

1. Tommies' slang for lice.

XXXVIII

1. Siegfried Sassoon, 1886-1967. His first war poems were published under the title of *The Old Huntsman,* on 8 May 1917. It is not possible to identify with any certainty the poem referred to here. Some of Sassoon's poems appeared in various issues of the *Cambridge Magazine,* for example, 'The Redeemer' in April 1916, 'The Kiss' in May 1916, 'The Hero' in November 1916, 'Base Details' in April 1917, 'In an Underground Dressing Station' in June 1917, 'To Any Dead Officer' in July 1917, and 'Does it Matter?' and 'How to Die' in the issue of 5 October 1917. In addition 'Stretcher Case' appeared in the *Westminster Gazette* in September 1916. Sassoon, a courageous officer and holder of the MC, became gradually disillusioned with the prosecution of the War, and, in July 1917 issued a statement protesting against the politicians and on behalf of the suffering soldiery.
2. See Letter I, note 1.
3. Sir Henry Rider Haggard, 1856-1925. His better known novels are *King Solomon's Mines* and *She.*

XL

1. Bertrand Russell, 1872- 1970. In 1915 he joined the No-Conscription Fellowship and was removed from his lectureship at Trinity College, Cambridge. He maintained his pacifist stance throughout the War, encouraging Sassoon to publish his statement of protest, and, in 1918 was imprisoned briefly for an article regarded as seditious.

XLI

1. See Letter XXXVII, note 1.

XLV

1. Novelist, pseudonym of Mary Mackay, 1855-1924. Her books were highly popular with the pre-war middle classes.

XLVI

1. German bomber aircraft which replaced the slow and vulnerable Zeppelins. On 13 June 1917 they carried out their first daylight bombing raid, killing 162 civilians in London.

XLVII

1. On 24 October, at the Battle of Caporetto, Austro-German troops broke through the Italian advanced lines, taking thousands of prisoners. On 25 October the Italians were in retreat over a twenty miles front, with again many thousands being taken prisoner. On 29 October Udine fell.
2. George Robey, 1869-1954. Music-hall comedian, popularly known as 'The Prime Minister of Mirth'. He starred in a successful war-time revue, *The Bing Boys are Here.*

LIV

1. The First Battle of Cambrai started on 20 November. British forces smashed through the Hindenburg Line on a 10 miles front between Arras and St. Quentin, and advanced four to five miles. Further progress and consolidation took place on 21 and 22 November, with many prisoners taken.

LVI

1. Ypres.
2. The Cloth Hall.

LX

1. Lord Lansdowne, 1845-1927. Member of first coalition administration in 1914, and member of the inner committee responsible for the conduct of the war. In November 1916 he had produced a private memorandum for the Cabinet on the possibility of an 'accommodation' with Germany. In a letter to the *Daily Telegraph* of 29 November 1917 he proposed initiating peace negotiations with the Germans. He was attacked for these views, which were seen as disloyal and harming the Allied cause, by both the government and the press.

LXII

1 . On 15 December the Russo-German armistice was signed at Brest-Litovsk, with an agreement that all hostilities were to cease for one month from 17 December.

Part IV
THE BURNING BOCHE
A Play

Introduction

In spite of its suggestion of a German soldier's gruesome death, Tomlinson's title for his play is nothing more than a piece of facetious punning: the 'burning bush', a feature of the College grounds, is used symbolically at the end of Act I, as will be discussed below.

Apart from Tomlinson's letters to his parents (written in pencil), the only other material in manuscript, as opposed to typescript form, are the sheets written in pen and ink for his play, 'The Burning Boche'. The paper is of poor quality, unlined, and the sheets appear to have been torn from some kind of army service notebook. Given that all Tomlinson's post-war writing is typed, as was the material he composed while working in London during the war for the War Office, it seems reasonable to assume that the play was put together while recuperating from his wounds, either in France or in England in hospital, a place where he would not have had regular access to a typewriter. There are some crossings-out and insertions which look contemporaneous with the original composition, but Tomlinson appears to have abandoned the play subsequently, and not to have thought it worthwhile resurrecting for the purpose of revision or typing out.

The play is written in three Acts. Act I takes place in the rooms of John Saxon, a student at St. Giles's College, Cambridge, in May week 1914. The setting is a thinly disguised Emmanuel College: the name of the College is a reference to Peter Giles who was Master of Emmanuel from 1911 to 1935; there is the Fellows' Pond which figures significantly in Act I; a fleeting appearance is made by a curate, Mr. Mildmay, who shares the same surname as the College's founder, Sir Walter Mildmay, Chancellor of the Exchequer to Elizabeth I. Act II is set in the trenches, somewhere in France, two years later, in 1916. In Act III, three months later, the characters reassemble in the town house of John Saxon's mother in South Audley Street, London.

The three Acts are of unequal length. Act I is as long as Acts II and III put together, and is in serious need of some judicious pruning.

Tomlinson's cast list reads:

Masculine Element

John Saxon	Undergraduate and soldier
Cecil Fewless	Another one
Ronnie Frankman (Cecil's cousin)	Another
Collier	Still another
Miggs	Saxon's Gyp
Banks	Fifth underporter
Doctor	Anyone will do
Gardeners	No one in particular

Feminine Gender

Mrs. Saxon	Saxon's Mater
Renée	Her daughter
Mrs. Frankman	Frankman's Mater

The names chosen by Tomlinson raise certain expectations by virtue of the qualities they suggest: 'Saxon' and 'Frankman' – traditional English manliness, strength and reliability; 'Cecil Fewless' – weakness and foppishness (he is, in fact, a poet, with pacifist tendencies).

ACT I

Act I reveals quite clearly that in this Cambridge College the class-structure of pre-War England is firmly in place, and Tomlinson has convincingly captured the behaviour and language of these privileged young bloods. Miggs and Banks begin clearing up after the previous night's binge and horseplay (a bath full of water has been placed on the Hall chimney). The only one who is not suffering from a hangover is Fewless:

Miggs: They're gentlemen on this staircase. All drunk, except Mr. Fewless.
Banks: The poet chap?
Miggs: Mr. Frankman's cousin. Cecil the smug, the cousin calls him. Talks like Hamlet's ghost with a swelled head. He looked like one last night. One tumbler of [*drinks and winks*], sent him to the pond to be sick.
Banks: What did the others do?
Miggs: They were sick, open and unashamed, in their room, like gentlemen.

Miggs describes his attempt to enter Saxon's room and rouse him in mock military terms that anticipate Act II:

Miggs: I bombed that dug-out an hour back and got bombed. I'm all for Asquith now, wait-and-seeing.

Saxon's mother and sister and Frankman's mother are due to arrive at any minute for the College garden-party. Collier enters with a parrot he has just bought in Sidney Street. He announces a new club he is forming 'The Benedictines ':

Collier: There's only two rules. Drinking Bennies, and getting married. Do the one and don't do the other, see? Subscripsh three quid a term.

Saxon surfaces with another military reference:

Saxon: Ugh! My head's like a straw-bag with a bayonet in it.

He realises that after the previous night's activities his watch and chain and a purse full of sovereigns are at the bottom of the pond. Renée arrives before the two older women, and from the playful banter she has with Fewless and Frankman in turn, we see that she is a rather flighty, irresponsible young woman, who is stringing them both along in a tantalisingly indecisive manner. Meanwhile from the windows those left inside can witness the attempts to retrieve the lost belongings from the pond. Frankman contemptuously tells Renée of Fewless' pacifist stance in a debate at the Union. They watch Fewless withdrawing in apprehension from the bank of the pond lest he fall in. Renée says to Frankman:

Renée: You're better plain and blunt. I only like Cecil the more when you are so English and intolerant of him. . . . He's a bit effeminate, though. The servants don't obey him like they do you.

Saxon falls into the pond but Fewless' apprehension gets the better of him and he can do nothing to help. A gardener comes to the rescue and Saxon is carried up to his room to recover.

Fewless: I funked it. I suppose I lost my nerve.

The Act ends with Fewless returning to the pond to retrieve the missing valuables with a pole. Renée then tells Fewless and Frankman that the sight of the guelder-rose bush (the 'burning bush) growing by the pond will serve as a sign for her and that she will tell them which of the two she has chosen:

Fewless: Renée, Renée, I got them! What does the bush say now?
Renée: It says you'll both wait till it's burning again.
Fewless: The Burning Bush. . . .
Renée: Yes, when its leaves flame again like love. . . . Autumn. . . .
Frankman: August, you said . . . August 1914.
Renée: Yes, August 1914.
Fewless: I'll wait till Domesday.
Renée: Oh, not so long as that, only till. . . .
Frankman & Fewless together: August 1914!

CURTAIN

In Act II most of the male characters are still together, serving in an infantry company in the trenches, and their class and status as seen in Act I are reflected in their Army rank: Saxon is a Captain; Frankman and Fewless are Lieutenants; Miggs and Jackson, the fifth under-porter at St. Giles's College, are privates.

This Act is in many ways the most successful and most convincing of the three. The paraphernalia of trench life are fully detailed. The banter, the songs and the black humour of the other ranks are accurately rendered.

A conversation between Miggs and Jackson reveals to us the ways in which the character and morale of their officers have been affected by the experience of front-line trench life:

Miggs: . . . Clean beats me what's come over Frankman. So confident and masterful he used to be, and now. . . . Well, he's never outside the Mess dug-out.
Sentry: He's got the wind up worse than a dead sheep. Never stops drinking all day long.
Miggs: A war like this is a great testing-house. The true steel comes out purer, and the rotten buckles like butter.
Sentry: . . . And Captain Saxon, he'll be true steel, eh?
Miggs: You bet.

Sentry: And Mr Fewless, he doesn't buckle more than a bit anyhow?

Miggs: No, he's stood the fire pretty well. He never was more than half a man at College, and the servants fair despised him, but the war's done him a lot of good.

Towards the end of the Act the 'stunt', that is, a raid, takes place, with the ensuing confusion vividly realised.

This Act is given below complete:

ACT II

A section of trench, with communication trench running off. Narrow trolley-rails run across stage foreground. To one side is a dump, with stakes, corrugated iron, sand-bags, picks, shafts etc. At the head of C. T. stands a sentry, heavily wrapped up, standing in a sentry 'dug-out '. Two recumbent figures in depths. A brazier coke fire lights up his alcove. Light night. He beats his arms together, trying to keep warm.

Sentry [*singing*]:   Then up stood the sergeant bomber
                  And he swore as a sergeant can
                  "Oh, they've loaded us up with their lumber
                  And twenty bombs extra per man;
                  This night while the riflemen slumber
                  The bombers will bomb, goddamn!"

There'll be excitement at the sap-head tonight, Miggs. They're going to bomb out Fritz from the crater.

Miggs [*recumbent and sleepy*]: Gag it!

Sentry: Mr. Fewless has just been along to warn me. Captain Saxon's on the stunt himself.

[Noise of approaching trolley, and suppressed voices]

Miggs [*stirring*]: Who the 'ell's making that noise? Is there no rest in this rotten war?

Sentry: 'Alt, oo are yer?

*[**Voice off:** Father Christmas with a barrel of beer]*

Miggs: It's the R.E.'s; noisy swine!

Sentry: Pass, Father Christmas, but 'alt the beer.

[Enter R.E. corporal, and two men pushing trolley, loaded with timber.]

Miggs: Evening, corporal. How's things at the vicarage?

Corporal: This B Company?

Miggs: No, D. Pass right along, till you come to a man's leg with a fieldboot sticking out of the sand-bags. It's pointing right at the door of B Company mess.

Corporal: Righto, constable. They are going for the forward sap tonight, aren't they?

Miggs: 'The bombers will bomb.'

Corporal: Well, we're off. Must get back out of it before the strafe. Push on, boys.

[Exeunt with trolley. As they pass off, the corporal trips in the rails and falls headlong, but picks himself up, and carries on without comment]

Sentry: Ah, stealing the soldiers' rum!

Miggs: R.E.'s, so they say, double ration, double pay!

*[**Corporal, off:** 'King's own foot, so we think, half the work and twice the drink.' Trolley rattles off down the track]*

Miggs: It's a wonder the corporal hasn't been along to change the guard. Must be about my spell now.

Sentry: I'm dead sick of it. Two hours is a dreary long stretch at a rake-hell corner like this.

Miggs: Anything been by?

Sentry: Only bombs. Must'a been six carrying parties to and fro this two hours. Too tired to blasphede, most of 'em.

Miggs: Blaspheme, my lad.

Sentry: I said blasphede, and I mean blasphede. It's in the prayer-book. If you didn't dodge Church-parade so much, you'd know it for yourself.

Miggs: Feed? Feed? Blasphede?

Sentry: You make me hungry.

Miggs: Rations up yet?

Sentry: Not yet. Captain Saxon's just been along to see. The bombers want their rum.

Miggs: Some of 'em will want morphia before the stunt's over.

Sentry: The bombers will bomb, And they must have their rum, And what will fat Fritzy do then, ole thing. He'll throw up his hands, And cry, 'Mercy, my friends, I've got a gold watch and a ring, ole thing.'

Miggs: Then you wake up, with a draught where your brains ought to be. You trust Fritz. He'll smell Hell tonight all the same.

Sentry: Shush. Here comes old stripes, changing sentries. It must be nine o'clock.

*[**Voice off:** 'Miggs, oy, Miggs. Drat the lad. He'll sleep himself into dropsy yet. Oy, Miggs.']*

Miggs: Here I am, sergeant. Couldn't get any sleep for the rats running over me.

*[**Voice:** 'Well, you won't have any for the next two hours. It's your spell on. Are you fixed alright?']*

Miggs: Yes, sergeant. All present and correct.

*[**Voice:** 'Carry on, then.' They change over]*

Sentry: Keep the charcoal going. You'll likely want to make a taste of tea when you come off.

Miggs: They'll be slinging old iron over by then, my lad, and tea napoo.

Sentry: Well, wake me up when you hear it whistling. I'm for the sheets.

[Turns into the sentry dug-out]

Miggs: Mind you don't lie on old Whiskers.

Sentry: Who's that, a performing rat?

Miggs: Yes, the old grandpa. Tame and civil as a Yankee, he is. Comes and licks your hand, and goes to sleep on your tunic as pleased as punch.

Sentry: I'll be good to him. I've got my bayonet handy. Night night.

[Short pause, during which Miggs stamps up and down, leaving his rifle leaning against the sandbags. Muffled booming of distant bombardment. Intermittent flashes light up the stage]

Miggs *[into the dug-out]*: Queer war, isn't it, mate?

Sentry: Eh?

Miggs *[raising his voice]*: I say it's a queer war.

Sentry: Ruddy chump!

Miggs: It seems a mortal long time sin' you were fifth underporter at the old place, and me gyp to Mr. Saxon, Captain as is now.

Sentry: Cut it out.

Miggs: Surprising, it is. And now it's Lieutenant Frankman, and Lieutenant Fewless, and Private Miggs, and Private Jackson.

Sentry: Reduced from corporal.

Miggs: For drunkenness. After all, things aren't so very much changed.

Sentry: Oh, indeed! And what about Mr. Frankman and Mr. Fewless. Aren't they just changed some?

[Enter Fewless, unobserved]

Miggs: They are, sure! Clean beats me what's come over Frankman. So confident and masterful he used to be, and now. . . . Well, he's never outside the Mess dug-out.

Sentry: He's got the wind up worse than a dead sheep. Never stops drinking all day long.

Miggs: A war like this is a great testing-house. The true steel comes out purer, and the rotten buckles like butter.

Sentry: Lad, that sounds fine! And Captain Saxon, he'll be true steel, eh?

Miggs: You bet.

Sentry: And Mr. Fewless, he doesn't buckle more than a bit anyhow?

[Fewless steps quietly forward, and purloins the leaning rifle, and steps off unseen]

Miggs: No, he's stood the fire pretty well. He never was more than half a man at College, and the servants fair despised him, but the war's done him a lot of good.

Sentry: Has such a nasty way with him too, if anything's a bit out. And curse! My old woman's a saint to him!

Miggs: And yet he has such taking ways too.

Sentry: Yes. He was after taking me to the C.O. for a dirty rifle, last time out.

Miggs: What did you get?

Sentry: Fourteen days, and five minutes home-truths.

Miggs: Shush, here he comes. [*loudly*] ''Alt, oo are yer? [*undertone*] Where the 'ell's my gun? [*aloud*] ''Alt, or I shoot. Oo goes there?

[Fewless, off: 'Officer on duty. Report your post, sentry.' Enter Fewless, sergeant on duty, and orderly. Miggs snatches up a pick-shaft]

Miggs: Post correct, sir!

Fewless: Good God, man, where's your rifle? Do you see this, sergeant?

Sergeant: What have you done with your rifle, Miggs?

Miggs: It was there against that frame a minute ago, sergeant, and now it's not.

Fewless: The worst crime a soldier can commit. Have him up, sergeant.

Miggs: Sir, give me a minute to search round.

Fewless: Shot at dawn is too good for you. They'll shoot you in the dark, my lad.

Miggs: Sir, give me a chance. I know it's somewhere about.

Fewless: Somewhere about! That's good. Better tell that to the first German that comes along. Better have him under arrest, sergeant.

Sergeant: He deserves it, sir.

Miggs: Give me a chance, sir. Somebody's been playing a trick. We all have a slip occasionally, sir. Remember the Fellows' Pond, sir, two years back?

Fewless: That'll do. Get him his rifle, orderly. You'll do a double stretch of sentry tonight.

Miggs: Thank you very much, sir. You caught me properly, sir.

Fewless: And don't forget the lesson either. Close the cut-off on that tongue of yours.

Miggs: Constitutional reticence, sir. A life-long sufferer.

Fewless: The lesson's wasted, I see.

Miggs: You have my respect for it, sir, if I may say so, sir.

Fewless: That's something. No sign of the ration party yet?

Miggs: Not even the smell of the rum-bottles, sir.

Fewless: Perhaps they've opened 'em half-way up. Devil take them. The bombers must have their rum within twenty minutes.

[Sound of voices off]

Miggs: 'Alt, oo are yer?

[Voice: 'It s Captain Saxon, wants Mr. Fewless.']

Fewless: Righto, I'll come.

[Enter Saxon, and orderly]

Saxon: There you are, Fewless. No sign of these rations, yet?

Fewless: Nothing astir at all. It's two hours since the corporal went off with the fatigue.

Saxon: Everything's ready for the stunt. The sergeant has the bombers waiting at the foot of the sap. The three red lights will go up from H.Q. in less than half-an-hour. The lads mustn't go without their rum. Damn it, we'll lose the war yet. God bless that blighted quartermaster!

Fewless: I say, Saxon, do let me take 'em over instead of you. Why should you have all the sport? Besides, suppose you are scuppered? The company will go to nothing without you. Let me go, old man, will you, John?

Saxon: No, your job's here. You can go for the medals next time. The C.O. has just phoned a message through that you are to take charge of this communication trench while the stunt is on. You are on no account to leave this stretch of trench.

Fewless: Very good, captain.

Saxon: I believe he expects them to put up a barrage just here. So you won't miss all the excitement.

Fewless: Still, I'd rather have a smack at Fritz.

Saxon: Of course you would, old man. Still, they may send over a counter-attack. Besides, they have that flying-pig of theirs registered dead on to the head of that C.T. So look out for yourself.

Miggs [*involuntarily*]: Holy Moses!

Saxon: What's that?

Miggs: I was only coughing, sir.

Saxon: I suppose I woke you up with my talking.

Miggs: Oh, sir!

Saxon: Let's get back to the mess, Fewless. We'll give the rations another ten minutes before we go up to the front.

Fewless: Hurry them as soon as you hear them, sentry.

Miggs: Very good, sir.

[Exeunt Fewless and Saxon]

Miggs: "They have that flying-pig of theirs registered on the head of this C.T." The very spot! I *have* touched for it. I wish I was a bomber.

[*singing*] His watch seemed too long to this sentry
As he dreamed of his dug-out and rest,
But God in his book made an entry
That private is due to go West.

'Fool, this night thy soul shall be required of you!'

[Enter Frankman, a little unsober]

Frankman: Who the devil are you getting at?

Miggs: I was only ruminating, sir.

Frankman: Why the devil didn't you challenge me?

Miggs: I was just going to, sir, when I recognised you.

Frankman: You've no right to recognise. Always challenge in future. Do you hear?

Miggs: Yes, sir.

Frankman: Why the devil don't you report your post?

Miggs: You don't give me time, sir.

Frankman: Do it now.

Miggs: Post all correc', sir.

Frankman: Always report your post in future. Where is the ration party?

Miggs: Not a smell of them yet, sir.

Frankman: Damn them. I'll get back to the mess and report the strafe will be starting soon. [*Exit*]

Miggs: Yes, and aren't you glad to be out of it? Don't I wish Miss Renée could see you now! And, oh, don't I wish I was a bomber!

[Sound of trolley approaching, and voices]

Miggs: 'Alt, oo are yer?

[Voice: 'Ration fatigue ']

Miggs: What ration fatigue? Ours?

[Voice: 'Yes ']

Miggs: Pass along, then, and hurry some. Likely the Captain's been asking for you this hour back.

[Enter party with trolley, piled with boxes and sand-bags, and rum-bottles]

Corporal in charge: Nice sentry you are! What ration party? Ours? Damn fool. Do you think if we were Germans we'd say no, we've just come from Hamburg. Haven't you got horse-sense even?

Miggs: I recognised you, corporal, half a mile away, by the smell of that rum-bottle you've been tampering with.

Corporal: Has the strafe started yet?

Miggs: No, but it will when the Captain sees you. Raging, he is.

Corporal: Transport lost two horses coming by the wood, and turned up at the railway an hour late.

Miggs: Have you got the rum?

Corporal: Do you think I'd come without it?

Miggs: My orders was to hurry you on special, as soon as you came in sight.

Corporal: You flamin' oojar! Why didn't you say so, hours ago? Carry on there with that trolley.

Miggs: The three red lights'll be up in five minutes.

[Exit ration party with trolley. The men slip and stumble about the rails]

Miggs: "They have that flying-pig of theirs registered on the head of the C.T." It'll be flying pigs and dying Miggs before the night's out. 'Alt, oo are yer?

[Enter Frankman]

Frankman: Alright, sentry. Can't you recognise your own officers? What the devil do you want to challenge like that for?

Miggs: Why, sir, you just told me.

Frankman: Don't answer me back. Has that ration party come yet.

Miggs: Yes, sir. Just gone by to the mess.

Frankman: Thank the Lord. They brought the Mess whisky, I suppose?

Miggs: Couldn't say, sir.

Frankman: I'll shoot the swine if they haven't. I could drink a distillery.

[Exit singing 'Have you seen the muffin-man of Armentières? ']

Miggs: No. But I've seen some muffin officers in my time. 'Alt, oo are yer?

[Enter Saxon, Fewless, bombers, and orderlies with two rum-jars]

Fewless: Officer on duty.

Miggs: Post correc', sir.

Fewless: This is the top of Shaftesbury Avenue, Captain Saxon.

Saxon: Righto. We part here, then.

Fewless: You won't let me come at the eleventh hour?

Saxon: Nothing doing, Cecil. Your post's here, and you mustn't leave it. Remember the C.O. depends on you specially to get my reports through. It would amount to desertion to let you come up. He'd be fed.

Fewless: What's Frankman doing?

Saxon: Um, least said soonest mended. If there's any bombardment, or a counter-attack, keep your platoon well together. Don't let them panic, for God's sake.

Fewless: I'll shoot them first.

Saxon: For the last time, on no account are you to leave this trench.

Fewless: Very good, captain.

Saxon: Double the guard on the Avenue head here.

Fewless: Very good.

Saxon: The three red lights will go up in another few minutes. [*The stage is lit by the blue light of a flare*] Rot their rotten flares. I believe they know we're up to something tonight. They're sending lights up by the score.

Fewless: Fritz always knows too much. You know word has come from the battalion on our right to keep a sharp look-out. They believe something is brewing the other side of the waste.

Saxon: And we're certain something is brewing this side. Good-bye, old man. I must get this rum up to the front and doled out. Then God help the Boche at the sap-head.

Fewless: Good-bye and good luck, John. Wish I were with you.

Saxon: I wish you were. If any accident should happen, look after my kit. [*giving him letters*] Take these and post them on. There's one to Renée. I've told her how splendid you've been out here, and that I hope you two will fix it up together.

Fewless: You brick. Good-bye, John.

Saxon: Good-bye. Forward in front there. Don't fail to forward my report. Keep a sharp watch.

[*Exeunt Saxon, bombers etc. up C. T.*]

Fewless: Don't you wish you were a bomber tonight, Miggs?

Miggs: That I do, sir. I promised my girl I'd take her a medal home. Besides, didn't the captain say they had their flying-pig registered on the top of Shaftesbury Avenue here?

Fewless: They have, dead on.

Miggs: Well, an early death saves a bushel of bother. [*Stage lit up by flares*] My, they are sending the fireworks up tonight. It's a bad sign, sir.

Fewless: Don't croak. Wake up Jackson and tell him he's got to take a spell with you tonight. I'll get the corporal to send up a double relief. Double sentries all round, and keep a careful watch.

[*As Miggs wakes up his comrade, a murmur of bombarding is heard, and the stage is lit by gun flashes*]

Miggs: Busy up Wipers way tonight, sir.

Fewless: They'll be busy here soon. It's past time for the signal. [*A searchlight sweeps across the stage*] What the devil's that?

Miggs: That's that old search-light of theirs, sir. They've had it out nearly every night. Back in the supports it is, on a trolley-rail. Bullets won't touch it either. Noah's Arc-light the men call it.

[The search-light sweeps across again, pauses an instant, then off. The booming is heard again from the distance.]

Fewless: What's happening at H.Q.? It's long past time for the lights. Come here and strike a match. I can't quite make out my watch. Shield the light now.

[A red rocket lights up the stage]

Miggs: There they go, sir. They're off.

[Two more rockets go up]

Fewless: Now for the joy-ride!

[From the front comes a murmur of firing growing rapidly to a violent uproar. The rattle of machine-guns, the crack of rapid rifle fire, mingles with the sharp detonation of bombs, and an inferno of cheering and shrieks. Flares go up in rapid succession, flooding the stage with ghostly light. The searchlight sweeps across spasmodically. Fewless paces nervously about.]

Miggs: Worse than Walsall market on a Saturday night.

Fewless: Shut up, and keep a sharp look-out.

[An explosion occurs close by]

Miggs: The flying-pig!

Fewless: Yes, they've started to counter. Now for some fun. It's no good sending a report yet.

[Two more explosions, quite close. Someone comes down Shaftesbury Avenue calling aloud. At the same time Frankman stumbles on to the stage along the trolley-line with his orderlies.]

Miggs *[ferociously]*: 'Alt, oo are yer? 'Alt, or I fire. 'Alt, blast yer.

[Voice: I want Mr. Fewless. I'm a bomber, battalion bomber with a report.]

Fewless: Let him through. It's Handysides.

[Enter bomber, with bomb-bag, knobkerry etc. He has lost his hat, and his hands are yellow with iodine.]

Bomber: Where is Mr. Fewless? Quick.

Fewless: Here I am. Quick, what's the news? Hello, Frankman. Aren't you supposed to be with the platoon?

Frankman: Came here for company. Carry on, bomber.

Bomber: They've done us down, sir. It's all over and failed. Only four of us got back, and we've left Captain Saxon under their sap. Bullets through both legs, sir, couldn't move him. They spotted us as soon as we were over the parapet, and gave us it proper. Captain said, get back to Mr. Fewless, one of you, and tell him to post my letters.

Fewless: He's not dying?

Bomber: No, sir, but badly hurt.

Fewless: Then I'm going for him.

Frankman: You're not going to leave me with the whole company on my hands.

Fewless: I'm going to fetch John.

[Three explosions, in rapid succession, just off]

Frankman: Listen to that. You can't leave us. You mustn't. The Boche is going to counter-attack. My God, Fewless, don't leave me alone. *[More explosions close. The babel in front swells up afresh.]* Fewless, you're going to certain death, don't leave me, Cecil, old man.

Fewless: Damn you, and damn orders. I'm going for John. Here Miggs, take these letters. You hear what the Captain said about them. Do it. Handysides, come back with me. And you, and you, and you. [To orderlies] That's enough. Forward up the trench.

[Exeunt Fewless, Handysides and orderlies]

Frankman [*running to trench-head*]: Fewless, stop, stop, don't be a fool. My God, they are sure to counter. What a swine he is to leave a chap in the lurch.

Miggs: They're dropping pretty close now, sir.

Frankman: Too close for me.

Miggs: A bit short, though. That flying-pig ought to use a Zeppelin. Might do some damage. Hello, someone coming up the track. 'Alt, oo are yer? 'Alt, damn yer, or I'll fire.

[Voice: 'Colonel Cameron. Is Mr. Fewless there?']

Frankman: No, this is Mr Frankman.

[Enter Colonel, Adjutant and orderlies. Frankman salutes smartly]

Colonel: Where is Fewless? He hasn't sent a single report through. Left us eating our heads off on absolute ignorance. Damn fool. Where is he?

Frankman: Couldn't say, sir. I've just come here from my platoon. I shouldn't hang about here sir. They're dropping trench mortars very close.

Colonel: I suppose that accounts for Fewless disappearing. I'll have him court-martialled for it, the dirty little blackguard.

Frankman: The stunt has failed, sir. There's just been a bomber back with a report.

[Loud explosion very close]

Colonel: This is a bit too warm. Where's the mess? You can give me the report in full, over a drink.

Frankman: This way, sir.

[Exeunt C.O., Adjt., Frankman and orderlies]

Miggs: Mr. Frankman, you're a very gallant gentleman!

Sentry Jackson: Sh. . . . What's that?

[Close explosion, and sound of a voice calling down the C.T.]

Miggs: 'Alt, oo are yer?

[Voice: ' Stretcher-bearers, stretcher-bearers. Oh God, I'm done!']

Miggs: It's Handysides. Go and fetch him. Leave your rifle.

[Exit Jackson up C.T. Two explosions very close, before he appears dragging Handysides badly wounded. Frequent flares light up the stage, and the

machine-guns are still active. Murmur of distant bombardment swells up again.]

Handysides: I'm done in, this go. Oo, my side! Stretcher-bearers, aren't there any stretcher bearers?

Miggs: They'll be here in a minute, mate. Hold up. What's happened to Mr. Fewless?

Handysides: My flamin' side! They've got Mr. Fewless alright, and the Captain – prisoners. [*Violent explosion, very close*] For the sake of Christ, get stretcher-bearers. Oh, mother! [*Lies groaning sadly*]

Miggs [*shouting*l: Mind this one!

[Very violent explosion in the middle of the stage, and dense smoke. As the fumes clear, Miggs is seen lying silent, Handysides has disappeared, and Jackson is sprawled against the trench-side clutching his side. Enter Frankman, with large party, running, brandishing revolver.]

Frankman: Up this trench, quick. Keep your heads down. Hurry past the bend.

[Exeunt up C.T., Frankman follows. Enter R.A.M.C. party with stretchers. They take up Miggs and Jackson, and exeunt. Some continue up the C.T. As they disappear, a second violent explosion occurs on the stage. As the fumes clear . . .]

CURTAIN

The following section or scene appears to be a variant of the middle section of Act II, since the sheets of manuscript containing it were folded together, and separate from the sheets that comprise Act II. (Editor)

Sentry: 'Alt, oo are yer?

[Voice: 'Officer on duty.' Enter Saxon and Frankman.]

Sentry: Post correct sir.

Saxon: Nothing fresh, I suppose?

Sentry: No, sir. That machine-gun sweeps very low across here, sir, where the parapet's worn, but they're very quiet tonight.

Saxon: I don't like that. He's up to something. No sign of the ration party yet?

Sentry: Not since they went down at stand-to, sir.

Frankman: Curse that quartermaster. There's not a drop of whisky left in the mess, since tea-time.

Saxon: It's the rum I'm thinking of. The bombers must have their tot before the stunt. Warms them up marvellously.

[The stage is lit by a blue glare, and, as it dies down, a machine-gun is heard traversing the parapet. A short fusillade of rifle fire follows.]

Frankman: I don't envy you taking the bombers over tonight. Not much chance of coming back.

Saxon: Not so loud, you fool. Do you want the sentries to hear that kind of talk?

Frankman: Don't care a hang if they do. Where the devil's that ration party with the whisky?

Saxon: Look here, Frankman, I'm just about fed with you. You drink too much, and do too little since we came to France.

Frankman: Better report it to the C.O. My lord, they are sending the flares up. They've spotted something.

[A succession of flares light up and die away on the stage, followed by a fresh outburst of machine-gun and rifle crackle.]

Saxon: I know you're well in with H.Q. You're both fond of the barley wine. Anyhow, I'm not going to have you tight tonight. It's too risky. You'll stand to with your platoon till the stunt's over, and keep out of the mess.

Frankman: Very good, captain. I'd sooner have that job than yours tonight. It's much too light for a bombing stunt.

Saxon: I think so too. But we must get them out of that sap-head.

Frankman: Listen to that.

[Distant murmur of bombardment swells on to stage, preceded by a series of gun-flashes.]

Saxon: Oh, that's far away up at St. Eloi.

Frankman: They're sending two officers' patrols out from the battalion on our right. They think Fritz is too quiet for their peace of mind. They're expecting gas.

Saxon: So I heard. But they always were a windy crowd of blighters. Think it's a gas attack if they smell a dirty ditch!

Frankman: They say they've heard working-parties fixing in the cylinders three nights running.

[Enter orderly]

Orderly: Captain Saxon.

Saxon: Well?

Orderly: Adjutant wants you on the phone, sir.

Saxon: Righto. Don't forget what I told you, Mr. Frankman. *[Exit]*

Frankman: Any news from H.Q., signaller?

Orderly: Battalion on our right expect gas, sir, and have asked Brigade to be reinforced.

Frankman: Anything else?

Orderly: Our bombing is fixed for 9.45 with three red lights for a signal. While Mr. Saxon takes the stunt, sir, Mr. Fewless is left in charge of the company.

Frankman: Rather him than me.

Orderly: It's the Captain's order, not the C.O.'s, sir.

Frankman: No more news?

Orderly: Rations have left the railway-crossing ten minutes ago, sir.

Frankman: They can't be long now then.

[Exeunt Frankman and Orderly]

Conclusion

At the start of Act III Mrs. Saxon is sitting at home, waiting to receive Mrs. Frankman and expecting Renée to return at any moment. She is in half mourning, since her son, John is reported as missing, and possibly a prisoner. Straightaway Tomlinson has some gently malicious fun at the expense of these middle class females and their charitable activities:

Mrs. Frankman: We seldom encounter one another in the daily round nowadays. I am so very busy with our war activities. I take a very serious view of the crisis.

Mrs. Saxon: Me too. I've never finished flag-selling, I'm sure I've sold enough to flag all Fleet Street. And Renée too; why, she's been out since eight o'clock this morning with her tray, and not back yet.

Mrs. Frankman: Remarkable! Don't you think flag-selling is just a little passé, though? I often wonder the police allow it. . . . Now, I myself am particularly addicted to canteens.

Mrs. Saxon: Really!

Mrs. Frankman: Serving, I mean – in soldiers' clubs and munition workers' food-rooms.

Mrs. Saxon: Interesting, I'm sure.

Mrs. Frankman: Occasionally, I sing at concerts.

Mrs. Saxon: Our poor suffering heroes – they deserve all we can do for them.

Mrs. Frankman: Every evening I attend lectures on Vegetable Cookery for Voluntary Aid Nurses.

Mrs. Saxon: How very useful. And meat so risen in price.

Mrs. Frankman: You must come to one of my Vegetable Dinners. Every Friday I invite a few friends.

Mrs. Saxon: Thanks so much, but Friday, we always dine at home. I'm very fond of fish.

[Shortly after this Renée returns, still carrying her flag tray]

Renée: Sold the last two minutes ago for a ten-shilling note.

Mrs. Frankman: Some generous misguided young man!

Renée: Oh, no. It was an old lady in a bath-chair. Most of the young men are much too quick getting to the other side of the street.

Mrs. Frankman: Whose flag-day is it?

Renée: I don't know our latest allies. Who are they, mother?

Mrs. Saxon: Surely it's the Red Cross?

Renée: Is it? What's today? Thursday? I know Friday is Bulgaria's day. Or is it Roumania?

Mrs. Frankman: They say the war will settle the Balkan problem.

Renée: Well, it's printed on the flags. You should have bought one. Then you'd find out.

We learn that Ronnie Frankman is to receive his Military Cross at Buckingham Palace that morning, and that both women expect that he and

Renée will shortly announce their engagement. Mrs. Frankman passes a newspaper to Mrs. Saxon:

Mrs. Saxon [*reading*]: 'With great endurance he held on to an important trench which was being heavily shelled. Afterwards he led a party up into a sap-head to save his company commander, who had been wounded. He risked himself ungrudgingly to make good the defection of a brother officer.' His cousin, I suppose, Cecil Fewless.

Mrs. Frankman: My dear, don't speak of him. The skeleton at the family feast.

Cecil too is missing, and his disappearance is a mystery. A letter arrives for Renée from Camberwell:

Mrs. Saxon: Who can she know in Camberwell? Across the river, I believe.

Mrs. Frankman: The war is a great leveller. I'm sure my own activities are most cosmopolitan.

Renée picks up the letter:

Renée: Well. I wonder what this letter is. Camberwell? Where's Camberwell?

Mrs. Frankman: Across Waterloo Bridge. Where the Zeppelins go, don't you know. Quite respectable.

Renée: Perhaps they want me to sell flags there. I've quite a name for it, you know. Could one sell flags there?

Mrs. Frankman: Hardly. But of course, in war-time. . . .

Renée opens the envelope. Inside is a second letter in an envelope 'covered with mud and chalk'. The first letter is from Miggs who has been recuperating in hospital in Camberwell. He informs Renée that the other letter is from her brother, and that he will be coming to see her that morning. Frankman returns from the Palace. The news that John is safe and well and probably on his way home disconcerts Frankman somewhat. Left alone with Renée, Frankman presses her to accept his proposal of marriage. She hesitantly agrees, and he dashes out to buy a ring. Before letting the maid show Miggs up, Renée makes an admission:

Renée: I'm sure I'm still in love with Cecil.

A telegram arrives from John, announcing that he and Cecil will be with them later that morning. Miggs enters:

Renée: You spoke about a letter from my brother?

Miggs: That's right, Miss. I have it with me. Mr. Fewless gave me it special, only. . . .

Renée: Mr. Fewless?

Miggs: Yes, Miss. Just before he went up to rescue the Captain, only what with. . . .

Renée: He went to rescue my brother?

Miggs: Of course he did, Miss. Very surprised I've been, not to see his name amongst the medals. I never saw a braver thing. And what surprised me more, Miss, was to see his cousin, Mr. Frankman, in the paper this morning.

At that moment Saxon and Fewless enter, 'in old uniforms, and burberries. Very dusty, no belts, and dirty, thick boots'. Renée has a scheme: she makes her brother and Cecil hide just before Ronnie re-enters. The sight of Miggs comes as a bit of a shock to him. When John and Cecil emerge from their hiding-place the game is up for him.

Frankman: Renée, I've been a rotten cad. I'll go back and drink myself to death, or get shot. Goodbye. . . . The worst are good, out there. *[Exit]*

Mrs. Frankman enters, amazed to find that Ronnie has gone, that Cecil has returned, and that Renée has accepted him:

Mrs. Frankman: You rejected my boy Ronnie? You minx! You take after your vain, foolish old mother. . . . I leave you to your poltroon lover!

Mrs. Saxon enters and embraces her son. The final words of the play rest with Miggs, as he and the maid seem to have hit it off together:

Miggs: Only a wounded hero!
Maid: Will I do?
Miggs: Thumbs up. (They embrace)

CURTAIN

Appendices

Appendix A

I did not fall dead at his feet when I met Rupert Brooke. I didn't even put Nunc Dimittis on the gramophone. Sure enough his countenance was as the sun, ruddy and comely withal, but [in] other ways he was not more than ordinarily sacramental. He had a masculine vox humana and a large ration of freestone hair, but no two-edged swords, or seven stars, or other supernal gear. The sum of his obituary sobstuff is colossal enough to give the public myopia and him wings. . . .

He had a sweet smile. He was doing a dissertation on Russian plays to a crazy club at Cambridge – the Heretics,[1] whatsoever they may be, something to eat possibly. His facial outfit should have recalled Apollo, Romeo, . . . but I have no SOUL. I was thankful to be not more than bearably bored. I thought he had almost a squint.

His audience was fine, full, rich and grapy, with assorted Feminines. The room was a medium, nondescript, roomy room just over a fish-shop.[2] His articulation, however, was so transcendental that every syllable was superlatively audible in spite of the turbot. Sleep was not possible. The young ladies hitched their suspenders to every comma in mesmerised coma. They have had their revenge since, in feverish frolics. Perhaps they were doing an autopsy in sonnet form even then.

Those hypnotised virgins didn't seem to get his goat. He ran his artistic talons through his coiffure and smiled absorbedly, as though to say, "I know I am leonine and irresistible, my dears, but not more divine than devilish. I missed being Adonis by three thousand years, so don't you get living deliciously on my account. If you must be enthralled, do be aloof. If you can't be good, do be gentlemen." . . . When he touched on the drama that costs you half-a-crown in the pit these days the Girton harem giggled satanically. I knew I was bunched against the most Skyscraping Thought. . . . The adoration in the rapt eye-balls of those damsels made me damn the hearty feed I'd done at dinner. . . .

When he had finished perpetrating the paper his palpitating audience leaped into the discussion with naked teeth. He dismissed whole choiring quires of queries with the air of a stipendiary magistrate at the Apocalypse.

What he said, went: we all felt that, and so did he. He blew his nose with a white handkerchief every so often – trivial detail, but how human! Any one of those Minervas would have rent her best georgette camisole to have done so much. . . . I smelt that everyone was ignoring me to the very vertices of their ivory, appalling, right-angled shoulders. . . .

So there it is. Rupert's permanent address, Lake Superior, sublimely superior if you like, but superior. Rare character, fine bouquet, full-bodied, great vinosity, generous yet delicate, very superior Cuvée. In other respects he seemed a likeable lad. . . . [He] had such soulful optics that he slipped into a pose as slickly as an actor into a bar, or a comedy chorus into pyjamas. All those hyper-cultivated Eves of Newnham did it. . . .

He lived poetry instead of living life, and he wrote Academic Abstraction. . . . His vapours are pervaded with all the old pedantic Hellenic perfumes – love, landscape, truth, death, duty, and shining things – he merely does a new analysis with prismatic effects and a duplex lens. . . .

[The] cheerful prose of his 'Letters from America' are the most vivid, virile poetry he ever evolved. Read them and rejoice. I could almost recant all the sarcasm I've written recently above. . . .

1. The occasion of this lecture, given to the 'Heretics' in February 1913, is described in some detail in Christopher Hassall's *Rupert Brooke: A Biography,* pp. 376-380. (Ed.)
2. In Petty Cury. (Ed.)

Appendix B

Introduction

After recovering from being wounded on the Somme in July 1916, Tomlinson was employed at the War Office for the best part of the following twelve months. The article below is an example of the kind of propaganda piece he produced for his masters. He worked from Room 406, Adastral House, War Office, Victoria Embankment, Blackfriars. In December 1919 he received a letter of thanks for his work there from Major Cyril Strut of M.1.7.B.(I):

> 'Dear Sir, .
> I have much pleasure in returning you herewith the articles that you have been good enough to write for this Section from time to time.
>   I should like to take this opportunity of thanking you for your assistance which was so freely rendered and has been greatly appreciated by the authorities in charge of the propaganda campaign. It is an undoubted fact that the articles supplied to this Department have had a very considerable share in influencing the opinion of the world towards a proper understanding of the principles that underlie the Allied cause.'

One of the articles written by Tomlinson was 'The Hun in Our Home'.

The Hun in our Home

Last Saturday night I dined with a man who would not attract much notice in a normal street. He and his conversation were equally nondescript. He devoted much time to his meal, and rather less to a tirade on the Hunnishness of the Hun in bombing Venice. He spoke of it as an atrocity, something peculiarly Prussian, an infringement of copyright and a desecration of Art and Shakespeare. On the last two articles he was a little vague. It seemed to smell to Heaven, this word 'atrocity', and in its effluvia no decent-minded human could exist. Yet when my friend and I an hour later were strolling past Trafalgar Square, in all its Tank Week trappings, he did not appear to notice any peculiarly pungent smell. He did not appear to appreciate the tragic presence of an 'atrocity', many times more inhuman than any the Hun could inflict. He accepted the debauching of one of London's most sacred spots and a million grand associations thereto connected, as he accepted meat cards and Mr. Bottomley. His morning pennyworth had not told him that this was an 'atrocity', how, then, was he to know? If I had told him that the Hun who drops a bomb on the very roof of St. Mark's is doing less to foul the universal sanctity of Art and things, than those whirring cinemas, those boorish booths, that bucolic drivelling Fair and puppet-show, on the hearth-stone of the City, he would have thought me a 'white-livered Pacifist', and dined elsewhere in future.

To me, as a not illiterate Englishman, to me, having neither Colonial cuteness nor American hustle, nor a seat in the War Cabinet, nor a Star in the Honours List, nor a very big bit to be 'doing', Trafalgar Square for three years past has been a tragedy. The next step is surely an exhibition of Tanks climbing the steps of St. Paul's, continuous performance guaranteed, and there won't be any War Bonds left to be sold. Why the people who plaster Nelson with paper are so tasteless, and not even virulently vulgar in their colour-schemes, only Nelson knows!

But the Hun in our Home does not confine his Hunnishness to Trafalgar Square. There, true enough, he displays the awfullest acme of his atrocities, but his name is Legion, and his activities as the sands on the sea-shore. Take a walk in what used to be any 'public' park and you surprise him at work. In town he has captured the greenery and the trees of God altogether, uprooted them splendidly, and replaced them with cement, and mortar, and brick, and drains, and chimneys, and rough-cast, very much wholesale. Further out he has up-ploughed their gravelly bowels and produced 'allotments', where people hoard potatoes and take Lord Rhondda seriously. Further out still, and into the country, he has railed in whole square miles and stuck them about with 'Danger' notices, and planted in their midst kite-balloons, and hangars, and hospitals, and aeroplane factories. The birds must go and sing where they may, the flowers bud if they can, the grass grow green and fresh if it dare, we must get on with the war, and the Hun in our Home must be allowed to batten on atrocities here, that we may be saved from suppostitious atrocities from that other Hun over the seas.

Take a stroll through any part of the town and he is all around you. In the schoolyards the unamazed children are marching two-by-two to the voice of their exempt and sickly wan teacher: two-by-two, left, right, left, right, and yet, not many notice the voice of the Prussian. Who would dare to suggest 'cannon-fodder' just because the kiddies' play-hour is used for a bit of wholesome drill? Whether the grown-up 'kiddies' performing in Temple Gardens might be described as an 'atrocity' is doubtful, for there a merger of amusement keeps us to sanity and proportion. Yet the faces of some of the spectators are serious enough.

Nay, walk not abroad at all, but stay in your castle or your office, and the universal Hun still has you by the larynx! He swoops down like an unamusing paper-chase, with forms, and cards, and tickets, and counter-foils, till you simply have to invent 'particulars' to satiate his lust. The ordinary true bill of your existence would never satisfy the Hun of the Printed Form. You devote your winter evenings to the latest parlour pastime of inventing next-of-kin nationality, age last birthday, taste-in-ties, and any 'occupation' that you may spare time for after filling in all his indispensable 'registrations'. Shortly the Government will have to transfer to a country-seat in order to find room for the few absolutely essential offices and officials, departments and departmentals the Hun has insidiously dumped upon them. There will never be room enough in London. The whole land will be taken up with offices and rumours of offices; factories and agriculture will have to flourish on the roofs. It is well we are indisputably mistress of the seas.

How long the Hun in our Home is going to stop, I don't suppose even Nelson on his placarded monument knows. It is certain he will stop at nothing. Probably by the time couples are controlled as to the number and sex of permissable children, and the ration is getting very, very small, some strong men will arise in their might and irretrievably slay the brute.

Appendix C

These who Fly

Who never risks his life must meet death hard,
But when these die the crowded gate of death
Is richer for the passing of their feet;
No braver men than these, no richer flesh,
More insolent of death, are born of men,
They fly in heaven, their courage to the stars
More than half accomplished, they are earth's best
And such their death no friend has need to mourn.

Vapour Trail

Someone takes a brush and paints a line
Straight as a dagger through the empty sky,
Someone pours a flask of smoking wine
Down from the tables of the gods on high,
And a vapour trail from a plane on the climb
Is born in heaven in the evening light,
Joining today to the rest of time
Like a song in the sky to the age of flight;
High in its own eternity,
Hand over hand it climbs up the world,
Climbing as high as the world can be,
Then rolls from the sky like an ensign furled;
Then someone takes a tin of scarlet dye
And spills a sunset on the emptied sky!

Appendix D

The Mineshaft

To feel like one who's sinned and earned the wage,
And hears on earth the tolling of his knell . . .

To feel like one who enters in a cage
Defies the mineshaft, and, as in a spell,
Hears them shout All Clear; hears the bell,
Then seems to dream he's falling; seems an age
Uneasily descending, hears the foreman's yell,
And through a long tube sees the equipage
Of circling constellations come to shine
Bluely up above; hears the cable whine,
The whimpering of the ropeway, and the rage
And friction of the kibble 'gainst the well,
Its grim hydraulic cadences, the fine
High-pitched responses of the line,
And sees the shaft-wall like a donjon cell,
Dripping, oozy; feels his cheeks as well
With drippings scalded, smarting, saline . . .

And sniffs at crimson stenches as they swell
Like lava from the entrails of the mine;
Tar and timber, coal-dust, fungus smell;
Some firm as faith, some lewd and infidel,
And some unindividualised, condign
And sharp but not familiar to define;
Some trembling upwards like a solenelle,
Some subterranean, others fresh as brine . . .

So dreams he's falling, feels the pit confine
And bandage him about; himself supine,
Spreadeagled, powerless to rebel . . .

Then wakes to hear the grimy gaffer tell
The headwayman to hew more parallel,
And thinks those level accents sound divine;
And thinks him how that flimsy cradle fell
And shot on sooty pinions down the line,
Straight as a demon down the flues of Hell,
Or Hell's own image in a Durham mine.

Middlesbrough, Dec. 1921

Furnaces

Tumult of furnaces;
Red and ominous, splashing with flame the wash of the river;
Red and seethed as a jungle dawning, transfused through the mist;
Red as the ebb-swilled flats at sunfall, glazed and a-quiver;
Red, and primordially dour, as the Hell of the Yiddish Christ.

Tumult of furnaces;
Intoned, sacramental, the roaring that climbs from the blasts;
Eery their asthmatic vomiting, baffling the sloth of the night;
While the long geyser flames tongue and leer as the darkness lasts
Staining the low-banked clouds with the bubbling crater's light.

Tumult of furnaces;
An imminent muttering of workers, that fodder and pasture the flames,
Hunched and reticent and straining, like ogre-driven gnomes of the earth;
Yet the menace limps through their glance as they brood on their shames,
And they dream they are fuelling tall autodafés for wealth and high birth.

Tumult of furnaces;
And where our Benares, we fakirs, vagrant through dead-lock and strife?
For the ore-feasted Brahma of Ingots straddles his bulk on the track,
Rusting the plain with his belchings, and stifling the green from life,
While we Juggernaut serfs of his Progress throng for the hooves on our back.

Cambridge, March 1914

Twilight of the Works

The Mother Works, whose milk is melted iron, and white fluid-steel.
What a tableau on the stage of dusk!
Straight, untender lines everywhere; jarring, a fever of accuracy; angles,
scalenes, quadrilaterals, a geometrical hysteria; cones, pyramids, trapezia,
bunched, piled-up, cast this side and that, untidily like papier-mâché
models in an Art-School, a desultory night-class.
An Art-School where both pupils and preceptor, students and dominie, are
advanced, neurotic, unhealthy and unearthly, yet cleverer than a Londonful
of critics; their work outlandish, malformed, trapu, their fruit diseased.
Yet precisely the Works, as they stand to the imagination; the confirmation
of the fruit itself.
Slag-tips, a hundred feet tall, gauntly outflung; grey, like glaciers cooled;
they seem to move – leisurely; stark and gruesome as great ice-bergs,
afloat in mist and sea.

Straight lines of stern utility, of strange undecorative structures; mechanical yet amazingly in tune; offices, power-stations, watertanks, like baleful engines of old baronial wars, sieging-towers, platforms, scaling planks; mean brick buildings, obscene, corrupted, and erupted out of Hell; no soul, just bricks, bricks and mortar, stained, weathered, ravished and possessed, spat-upon, rained-upon, smoked-upon; putridity emblemized in bricks.

Engine-sheds, like great sinks, urinals.

Quaint tubular pitch-containers, like shapeless sausages, black outside as the creosote within; no attempt to whitewash tombs.

Gas-retorts, like altars swilled with paraffin, over-run with flame, altars in Gehenna.

Condenser-Plants! Long black shafts, trunks, cylinders, and tunnellings which seem to have been moulded in the jerky workings of a mine; uncompromising as injection-marks.

Condenser-Plants offend the evening air, and seem to shriek to be repatriated down in Hell, their home.

Alien images of a bygone cult, or futile symbols of a new.

Graven blasphemies; brave in their ugliness, graven in lascivious fresco upon the holy sky.

Long black intestinal crawling miles of condenser-pipe!

Ikons in the isba, on the loveless hearth of that vile New Gomorrah; the furnace-heart which heats that ever-blighted valley of unrest.

Ikons, man-erected to the Gods of Wrath and Steel; Directors of Progress, Chairmen of Civilization.

Ikons, idols of the Great Industrial Epoch, dedicated to Greed; spared by time as yet, though perhaps it were better they had not been spared, but swiftly, incontinently overturned.

Condenser-Plants! Yes, plump black poisonous snakes; fathoms of writhing hideousness; untwisting furlongs of them, across the bleak laconic estuary of Tees.

Their fatly-rusted, riveted square yards of iron plate; their grouped inbreeding bolt-heads, their tressels, all creak and rumble; the whole lank carcase of them gives forth its hymn of hate.

Its psalms of hissing steam.

Doubtless some sort of warm confabulation with their relatives in Hell!

Uproar and uprush of hissing steam, deafening to burst the ears' drums, incomprehensible; stunned, you seem to grow aware, to feel the impact, to hear the very rush and hurtlings of Earth's velocity through Space.

At your feet the mudflats, like vast grey Army blankets, mottled in scattered places with anaemic turf like gangrene.

The "Slems", bare and semi-bald, acres of despoliation.

In your eyes that clarity, that sheen of crystal still; that rich transparency, lingering and hovering, like a well-pleased host above the withdrawn sun.

Stillness benign; stillness foreboding, maybe; prophetical of ages to come when all the turmoil, agitation, money-scrambling, shall be cloaked, extinguished, loosely wrapped in dust.

When those sad mutilated acres shall by miracle be purified, made whole; shall rest, released from all that chain of cumbering Works; lying naked to the elemental sun, green and sweet with common weeds, as once in Caedmon's days.

When the Ajax of Commerce no longer taunts the sky, defying heaven and his own precarious health; but prostrate lies in kindly unaudacious dust.

When all that clamour fades; its discord and its dire oppression, night and day, falls back again to mute brown-soil serenity.

When Silence flows back again, tidal, primitive, to that embittered plain; silence long o'erdue!

Appendix E

Cambridge Poems

Cambridge Memories

Memories of ancient walls of stone,
Of staircases that rang with running feet,
Memories lingering like a muttered prayer
From days long past but sweetest of them all!

Memories of Granta flowing through the dusk,
Of trees in bended beauty on her banks,
Memories of hanging leaves along the 'Backs',
Glory of willow gloom on green water.

Memories of poplars waist-deep in mist,
Of moonlight like ice on sleeping fields,
Memories living in the lapping dusk
Like sorrow tolling from a far tower.

Memories of sunlight on October walls,
Of creeper like sunset over whispering stones,
Of wide-eyed freshmen of the college year
Waking green courts from academic sleep.

From Peterhouse to Trinity, half a mile
Of memories that nowhere else on earth can give,
From Magdalene Bridge to Parker's Piece,
Memories that circumnavigate the world.

Memories of greatness, memories of beauty,
Of tall stones stood in place beneath the moon,
Magnificent memories of praiseworthy places
Where King's College Chapel thrills the entering eye!

We who for a few brief seasons felt
The thrill of starlight weeping through green leaves.
We whose were your buildings then, your creeper-crimson courts,
Your old grey echoes and familiar towers.

We saw your moonlight melting into spires,
We saw your memories moulded into lives,
We heard the whispers of your past
And a glory shared with undefeated time!

King's Chapel

O stone of Paradise and stone-made history,
Inside King's Chapel
Staring up at the roof,
This is no roof at all but a new stone sky,
And with my monkey's eyes
I see perfection other monkeys made
With dramatised dirt!
This roof is no roof at all,
But a place of journeys into nooks and crannies
And the curly labyrinths of the human brain !

Men fondled stone, God provided light
Where Hark the Herald Angels Sing
With mouths of rounded rock!
"I know that my Redeemer liveth" sings this stone!
For here is something to love, honour and obey
More than mouldy liturgies!
Stand, stare with me!
Enjoy the leafy Spring of this shaped stone
And find you nearer heaven!
Down there in the dark will be a long, long time,
A deep, deep tomb,
But here is stone that feels,
And rock-made resurrection!

Grey with a million twilights is this roof,
Vocal with nests of nightingales,
A mute miracle of unsung song!
What loving chisel said to soaring stone
"Fill with tiny dreams and well-thumbed snakes,
Curve like open parasols, but sweet as flesh"?
Who gives soul to stone? Who hangs on high
Diaphanous hundredweights?
I see a roof with solid music made,
Fresh as the frothy fringes of the sea,
Sunlight on pale waters, moonlight through tall trees!

Who reached out lofty hands to carve this roof
Made solid stone to flow like gentle tides?
Willows weeping beauty down the Backs
To touch green brothers in pellucid Cam,
See sweetness less than this,
These silvery caskets cut in old grey stone,
This breathless congregation of sweet curves,
This drooping down of all earth's beauty,

This soaring up of paradisial song!
Looking up at the roof I see further than the furthest sky
And seem to hear music higher than the highest trill
Standing on this sacred floor,
This roof is no roof at all
But a weeping of six hundred years of stone!
This stone is no stone at all
But the spirit of a day
We can not and we shall not understand!
No lying tongue worked beauty in these works
Where faithful ropes of light
Strip gentle stone of all things earth,
Exiling earth from heaven
For being far too lovely!

Cambridge

O Cambridge, Cambridge mine, where now the charm
Of streets and curly lanes which soothed
The Dons of leafier days? Where the peace
That lulled the earlier echoes of your walls?
Where the ivied grace of tutors' Tudor courts
And rooms more full of manners though less men?

Today more gowns, less gardens, more diggers,
Less dug, more tolerance and less texture,
More windscreens, less stained-glass windows,
More parsons, less piety, more shorts, less sport,
Today too many leaves on Granta's trees,
For when too many listen, too few learn!

Flicks, motor cars and madrigals you have today,
But where the Dons of wit, the old Masters
Of the Arts of Leisure, the polished pedants,
The larger light of educated eyes,
The colleges and silky lawns of learned
Well-groomed brains? Where that unapeable university
Which labelled for lifetime the minds
Of all who passed its prehistoric gates?
Has it been gravelled over and forgot?
O Cambridge of great pasts, O serious town,
Of famous names, and those who nameless served,
O wise old town, don't move too fast for heaven,

Speed kills many a soul old age has spared!
Let Granta crawl her course to Byron's Pool,
Gurgling her song of sameness through the years;
Let the Leaning Tree, or else its ghost, unaxed,
Make more unmatchable your matchless 'Backs',
Let Heretics and Unions talk their talk,
And never let your non-industrial towers
Be Londonised with soot, nor college gates
Stand any less in state, though state-controlled!

Age greens your lanes, history names your streets,
Relax not dignity, squirm not with the times,
Split not atoms, infinitives nor hairs,
Be not too smart of soul, too shrewd of brain,
Lest some day in the shade of King's, a feudal fish
Shall eye with wet surprise and fishy sniff
The skyward passing of your rarer earth!

Appendix F

A.E. Tomlinson's Published Work: A Summary

Books
Tomlinson, A.E., *Candour* (London, Elkin Mathews, 1922)

Contributions to Journals, Magazines and Newspapers
Mandragora, Cambridge: Galloway & Porter, 1913. (Two poems)
Mandragora, Cambridge: Galloway & Porter, 1914. (One poem)
Cambridge Magazine, Cambridge, 1 November 1919. (One poem)
The Adelphi, Vol. II, No. 3. London, 1924. (One prose poem)
The Evening Standard, London, 10 November 1927. (One article)
The Evening Standard, London, 10 November 1928. (One article)
East Anglian Magazine, Vol. 22, No. 9, 1963. (One poem)

Privately Published Collections of Poetry
Tomlinson, A.E., *Suffolk in Verse*, No date given.
Tomlinson, A.E., *Lowestoft Men*, No date given.
Tomlinson, A.E., *Waveney Sonnets*, 1950.
Tomlinson, A.E., *Suffolk Sky*, c 1964.
Tomlinson, A.E., *Middlesbrough*, No date given.

Anthologies
The Spring Anthology London, The Mitre Press, 1960. (One poem)
Hibberd, D. & Onions, J., eds. *Poetry of the Great War: An Anthology.*
    London, Macmillan, 1986 (One poem).

Books and Publications consulted

Boorman, Derek. *At the Going Down of the Sun: British First World War Memorials.* 1988.

Borg, Alan. *War Memorials.* London, Leo Cooper, 1991.

Cambridge Magazine, 1912-1923.

Carey, G. V. *War List of the University of Cambridge, 1914-1918.* Cambridge, Cambridge University Press, 1921.

Chainey, Graham. *A Literary History of Cambridge.* Cambridge, The Pevensey Press, 1985.

East Anglian Daily Times, 16 January 1956.

East Anglian Magazine, vol. 22 No.9, July 1963.

Emmanuel College Magazine: Quatercentenary Issue. 1584-1984.

Fowler, Laurence & Helen, eds. *Cambridge Commemorated. An Anthology of University Life.* Cambridge, Cambridge University Press, 1984.

Gliddon, Gerald. *'When the Barrage Lifts': A Topographical History and Commentary on the Battle of the Somme 1916.* Norwich, Gliddon Books, 1987.

Hammerton, Sir J.A. *A Popular History of the Great War.* London, The Fleetway House, c 1935.

Hassall, Christopher. *Rupert Brooke: A Biography.* London, Faber & Faber, 1972.

Hibberd, Dominic, and Onions, John, eds. *Poetry of the Great War: An Anthology.* London, Macmillan, 1986.

Howarth, T. E. B. *Cambridge Between Two Wars.* London, Collins, 1978.

Inglis, K.S. 'The Homecoming: The War Memorial Movement in Cambridge, England'. *Journal of Contemporary History,* Vol.27, 1992. 583-605.

Mandragora, May 1913, May 1914.

Miller, Frederick, *Under German Shell-Fire.* West Hartlepool, 1915.

Murry, John Middleton, ed. *The Adelphi,* Vol. II No. 3, August 1924.

Reeve, F. A. *Cambridge,* London, Batsford, 1976.

Reilly, Catherine W. *English Poetry of the First World War: a Bibliography.* London: Prior, 1978.

The Spring Anthology, London, The Mitre Press, 1960.

Symons, Julian. *Horatio Bottomley.* London, The Cresset Press, 1955.

Tomlinson, A.E. *Candour.* London, Elkin Mathews, 1922.

Tomlinson, A.E. *Waveney Sonnets.*

War Diary of the 8th Battalion South Staffordshire Regiment.

Winter, Jay, *Sites of Memory, Sites of Mourning.* Cambridge, Cambridge University Press, 1995.

Index